BLUE SIGHT STUDIOS, LLC.
PRESENTS

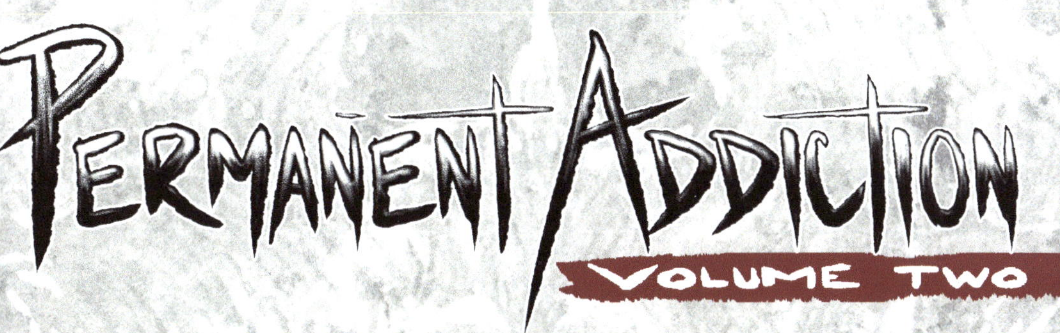

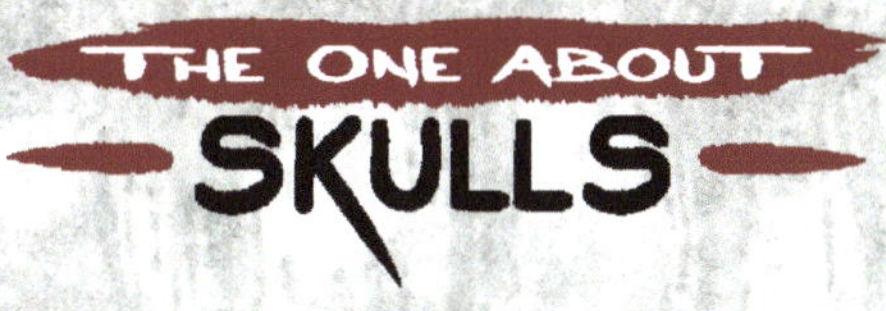

ART
OF

HECTOR J. ORTEGA

PERMANENT ADDICTION VOLUME TWO: THE ONE ABOUT SKULLS

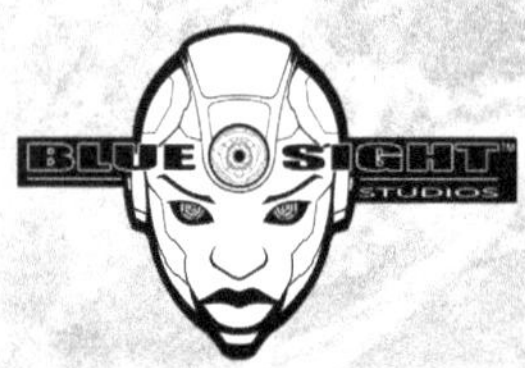

Published by **Blue Sight Studios, LLC.**

First Printing: July 2020
Printed in the United States of America.

First Edition: July 2020

ISBN: 978-0-578-72372-3

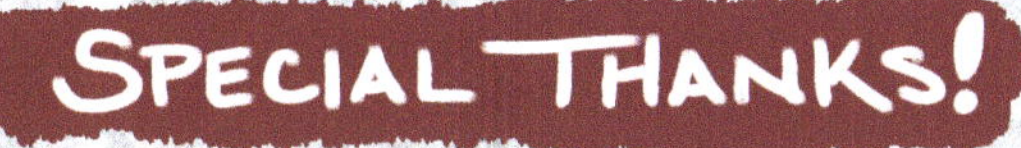

I would like to thank my mom for always believing in me. My son and my daughter for reminding me to keep pushing forward. And for everyone who continues to show me love and support on ths journey to creating greatness. THANK YOU!

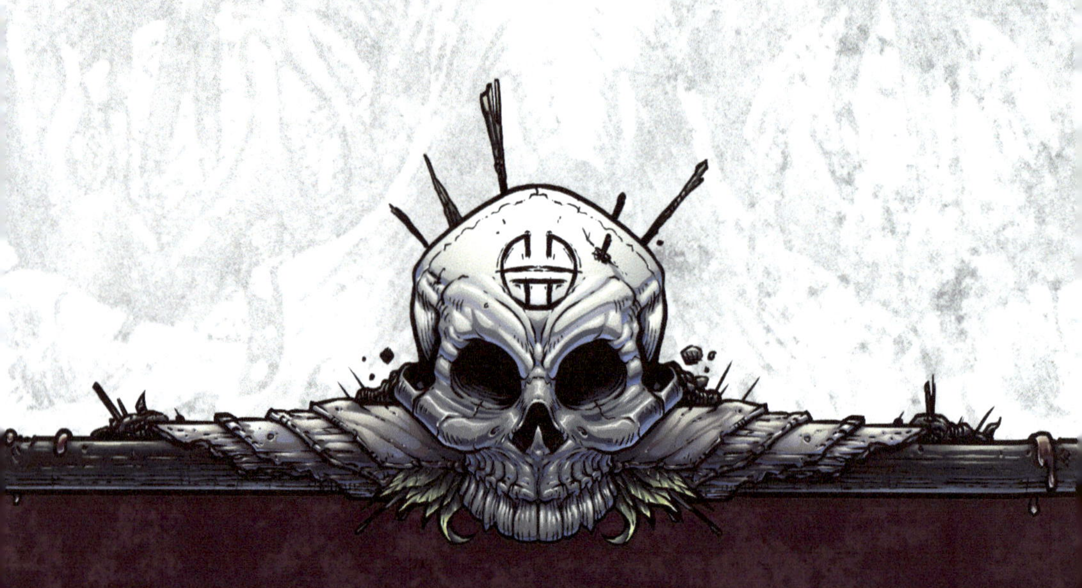

COVER ART

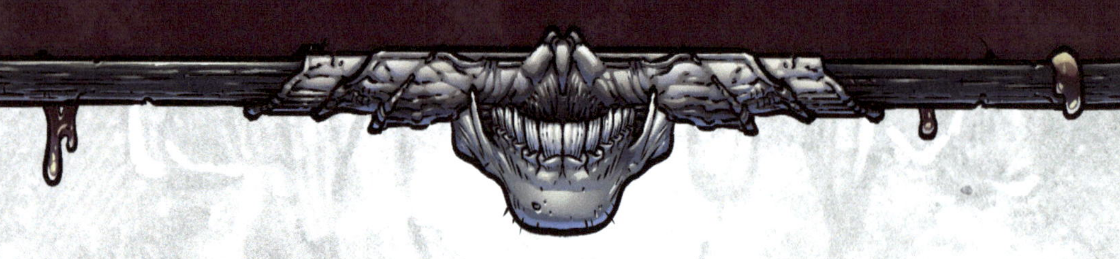

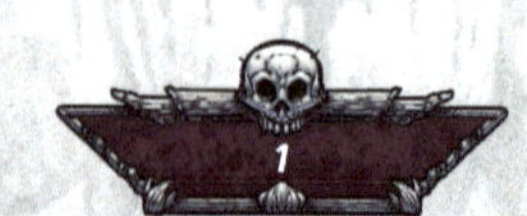

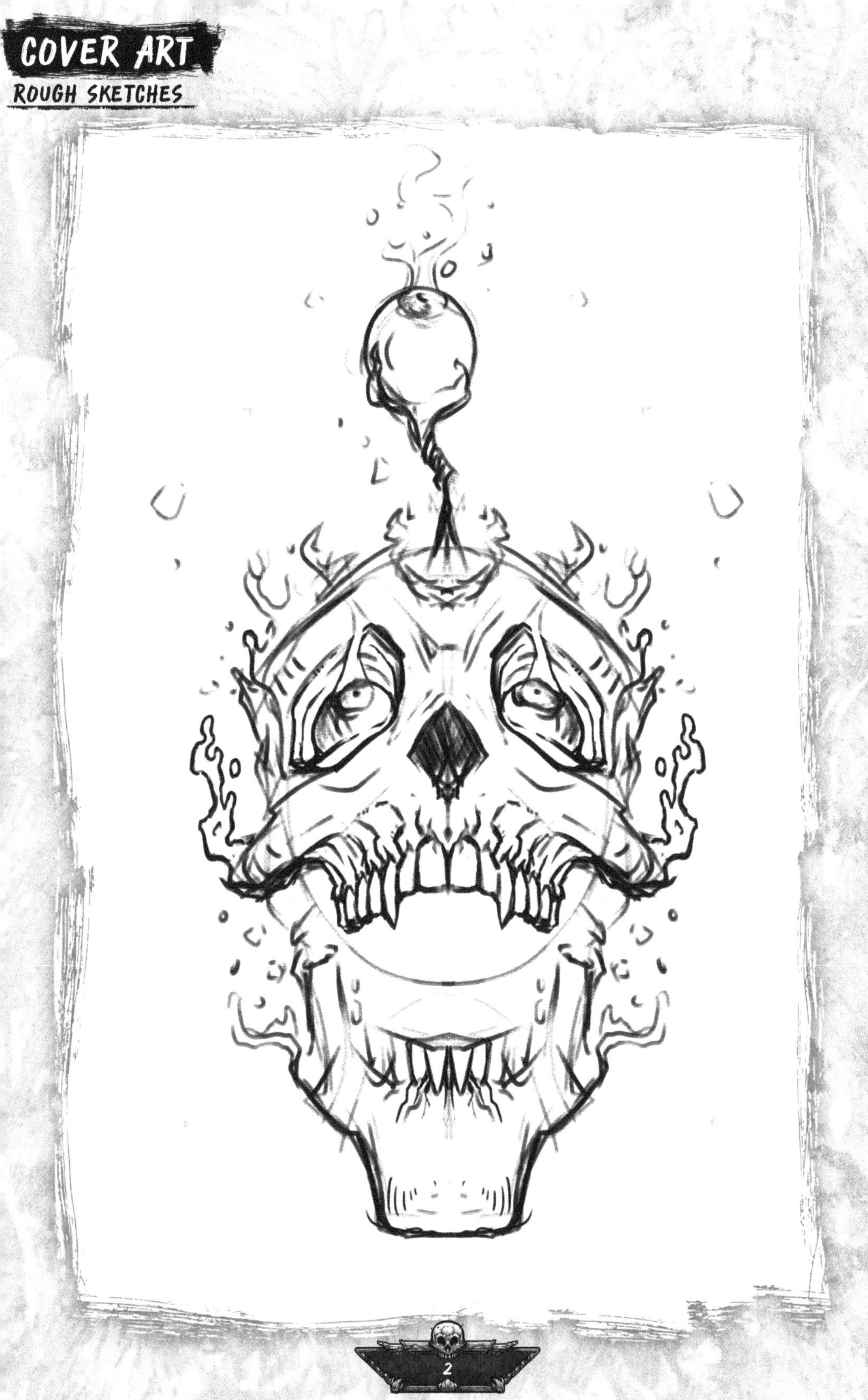
COVER ART
ROUGH SKETCHES

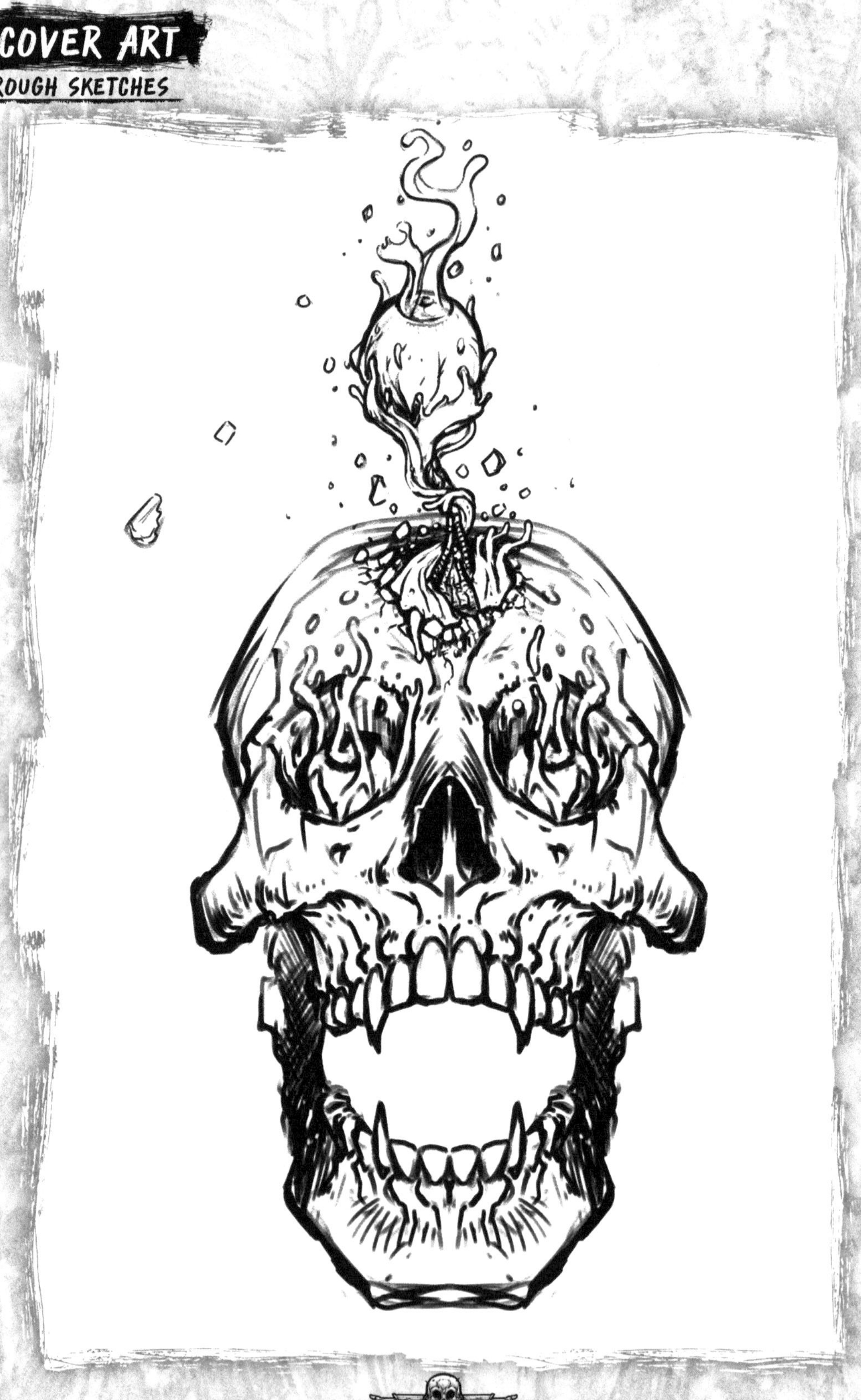

FINAL LINE ART

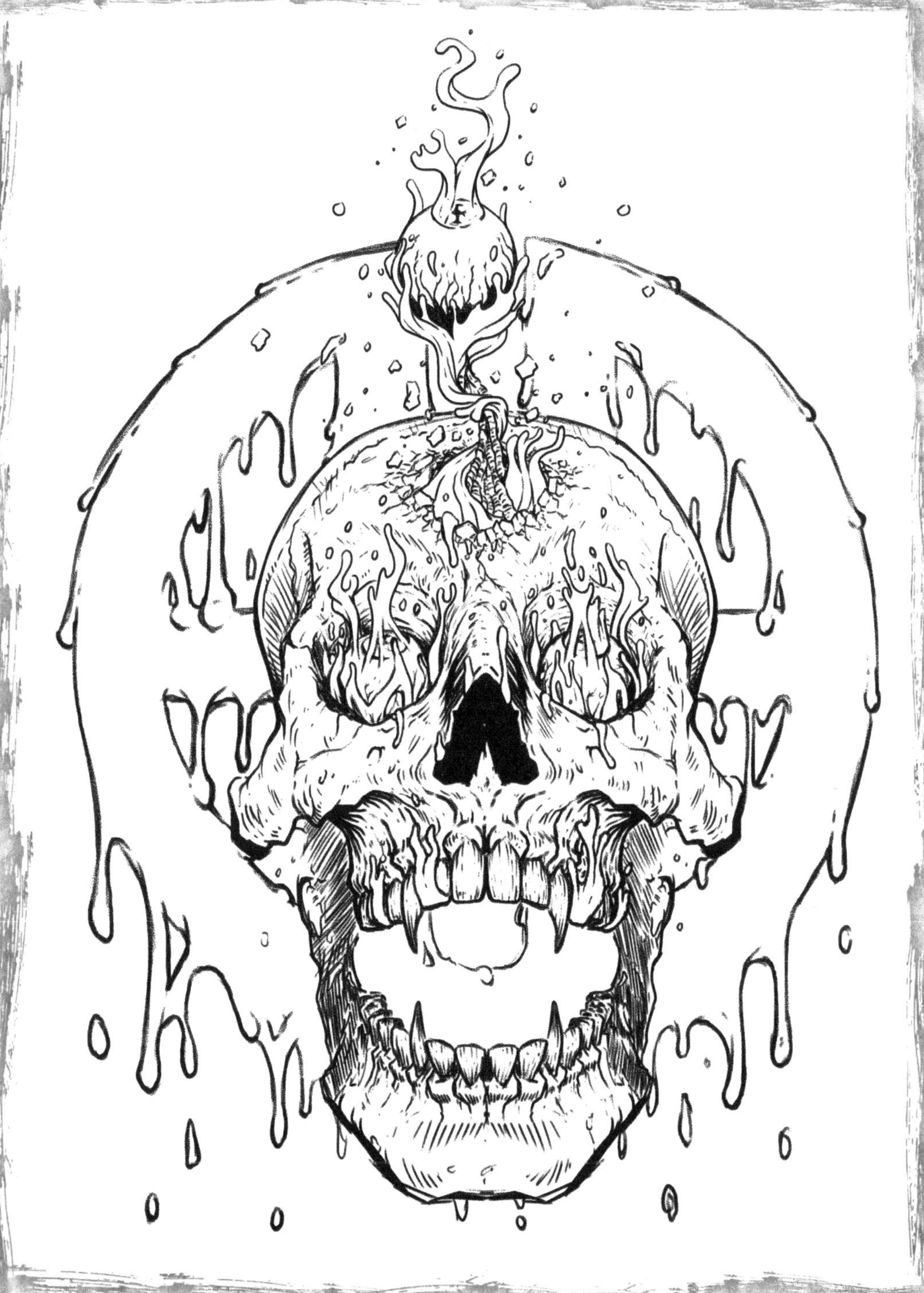

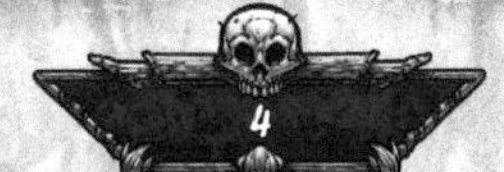

COVER ART

FINAL ILLUSTRATION

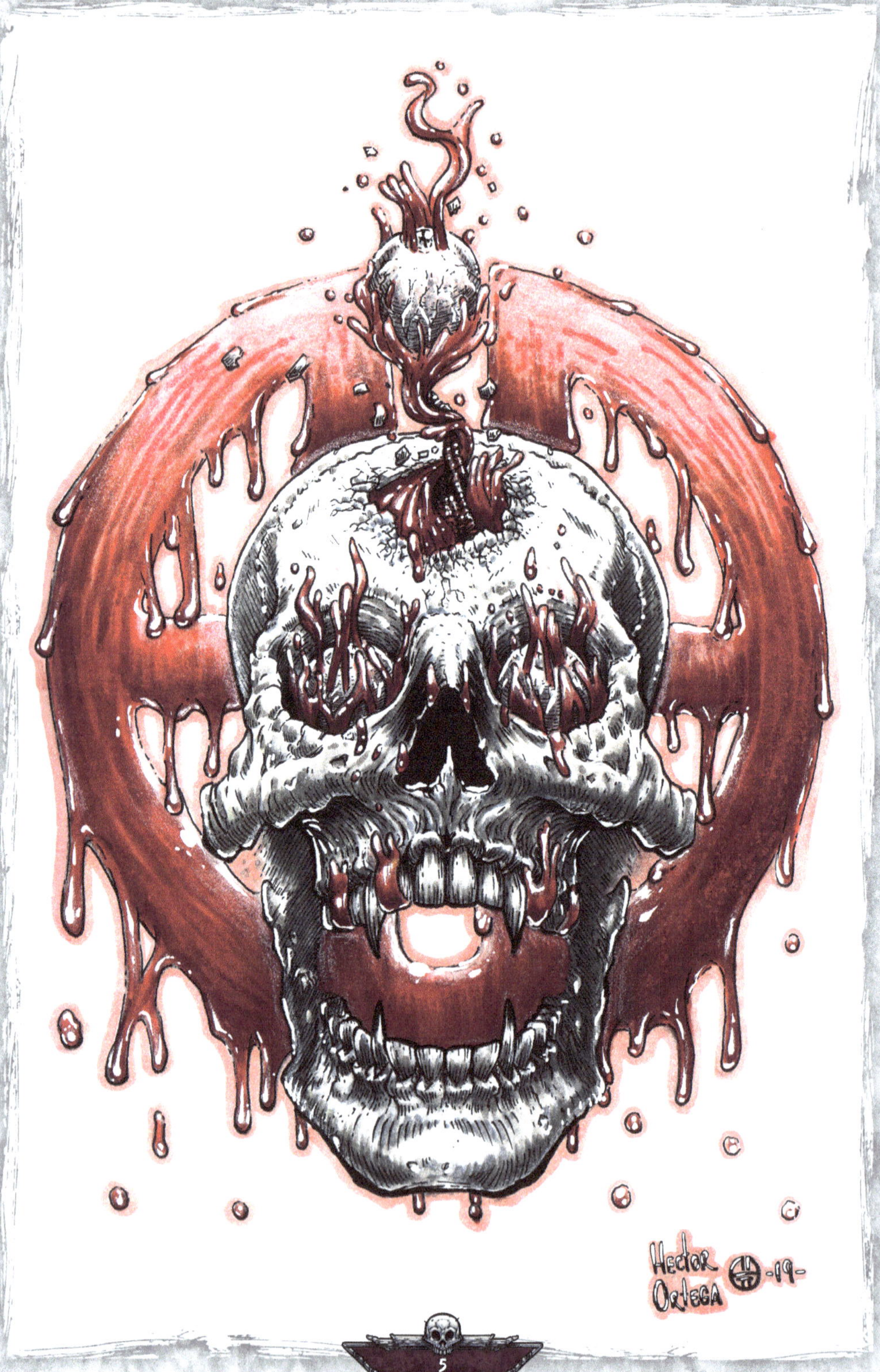

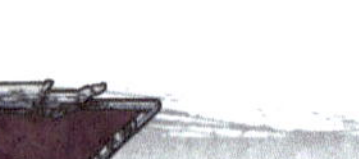

- DAY 1 -
RING

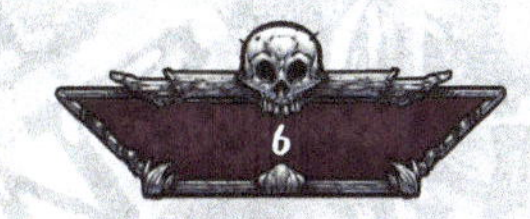

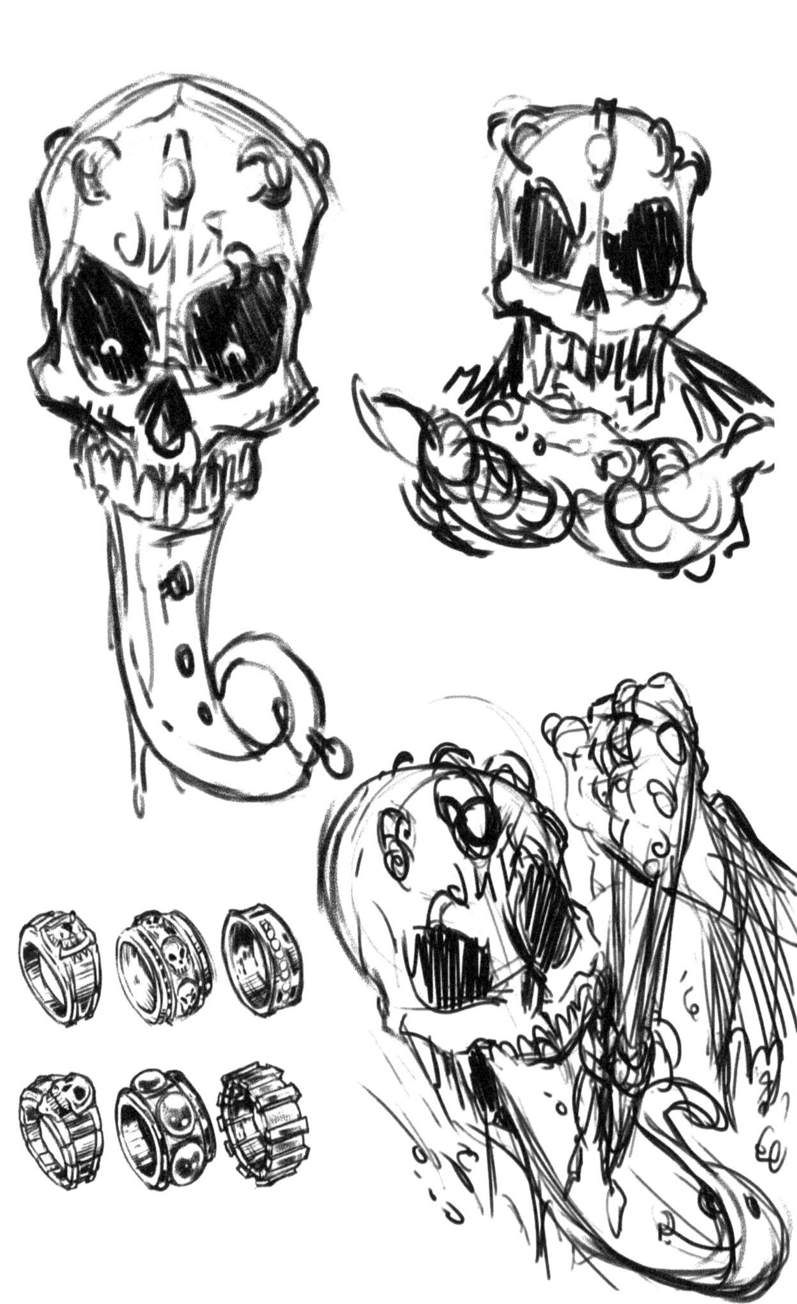

D1-RING

FINAL LINE ART

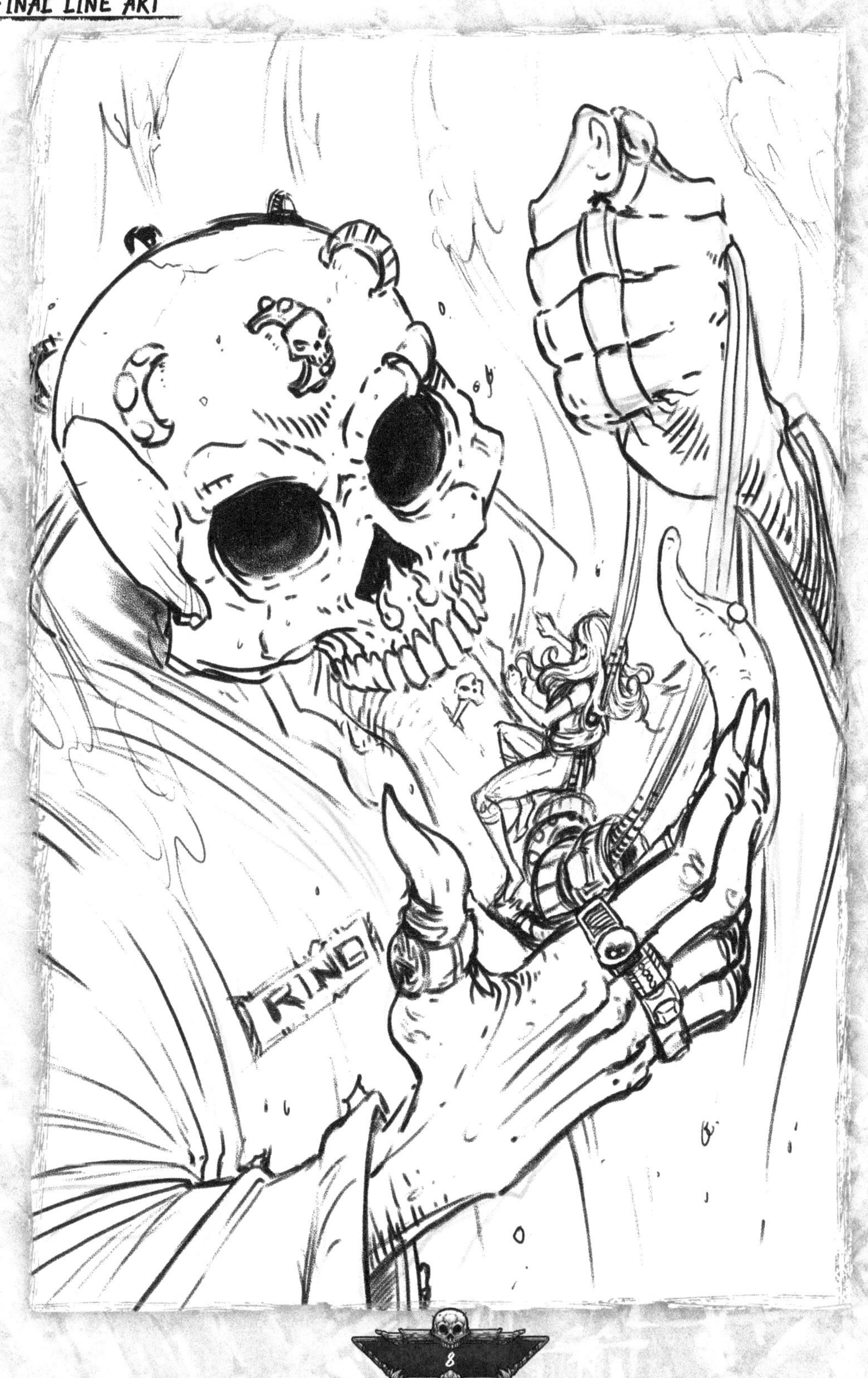

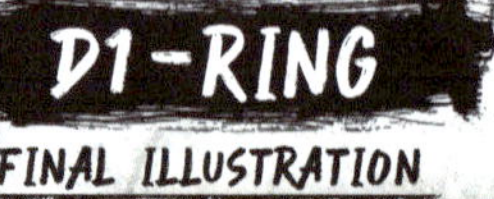

D1-RING

FINAL ILLUSTRATION

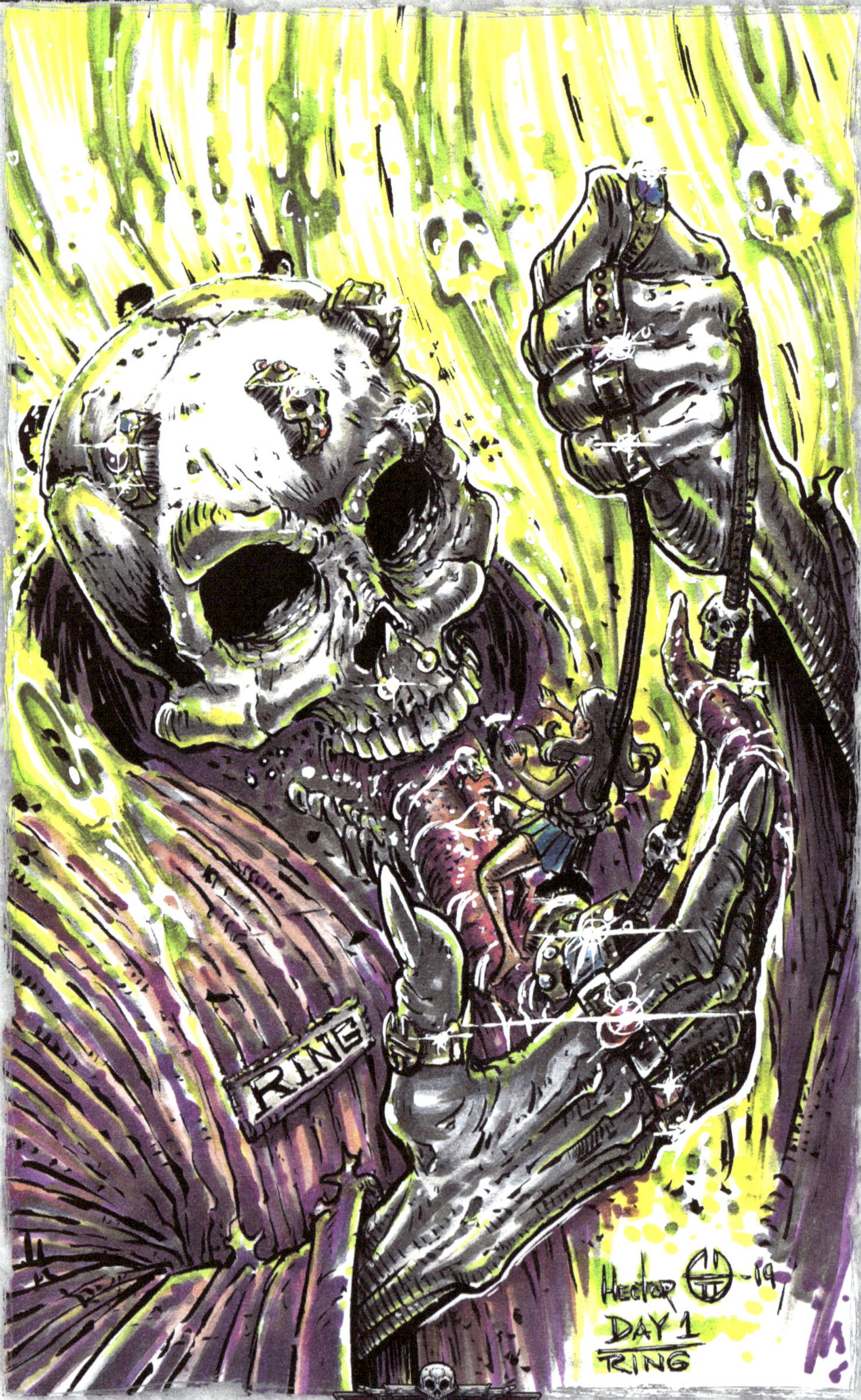

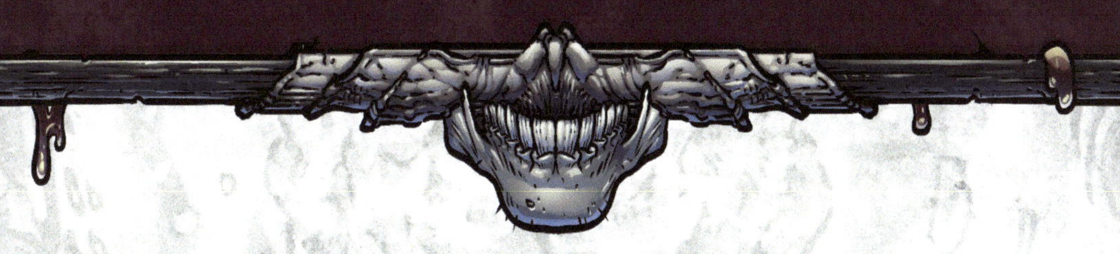

- DAY 2 -
MINDLESS

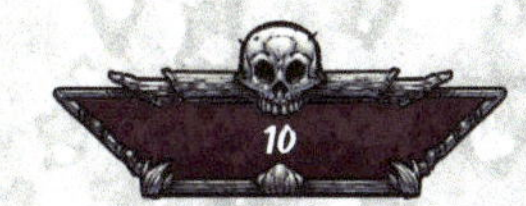

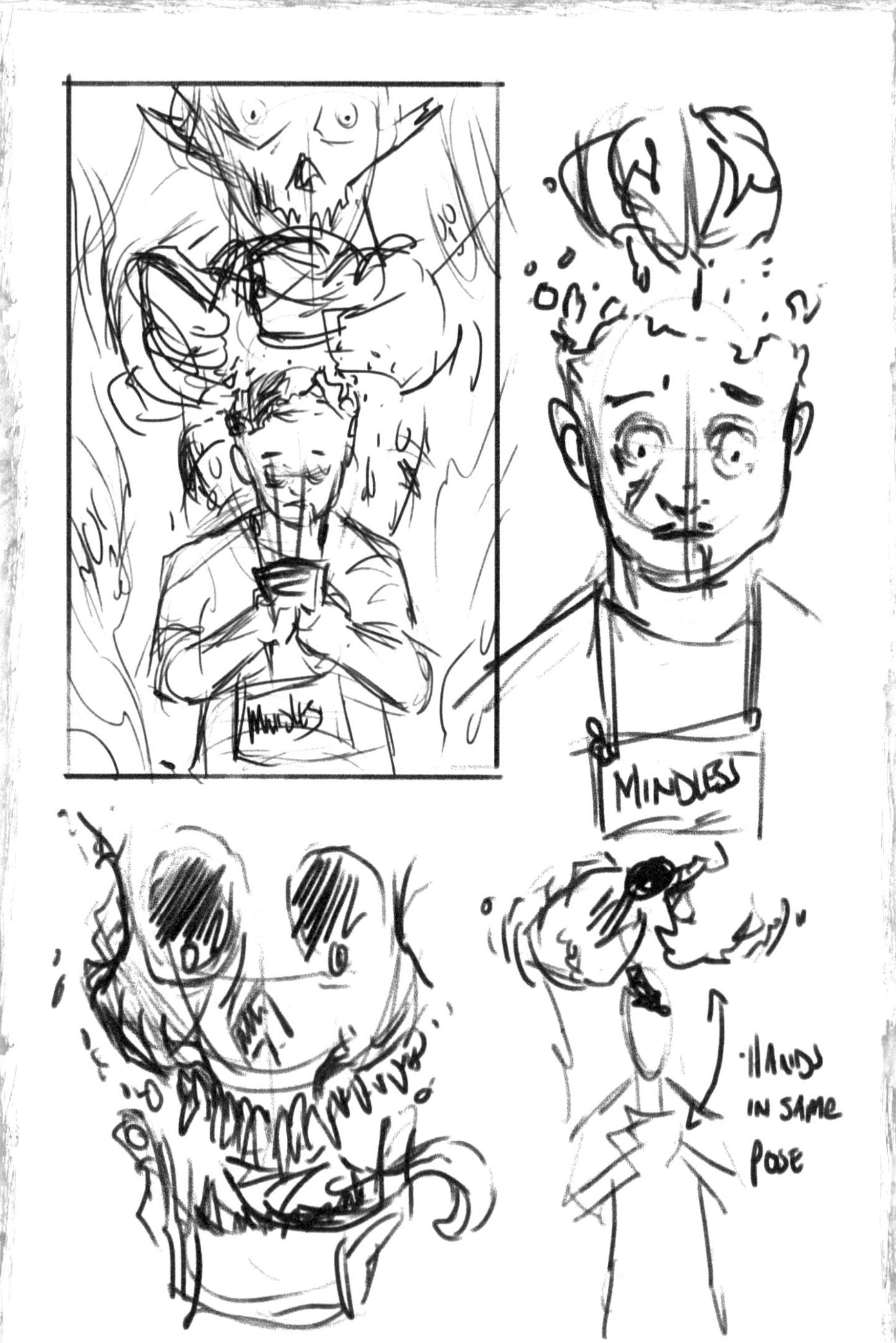

MINDLESS

HANDS IN SAME POSE

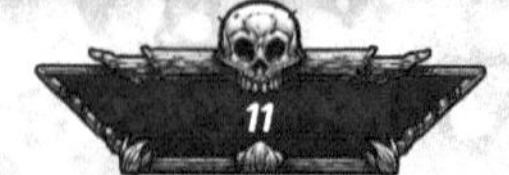

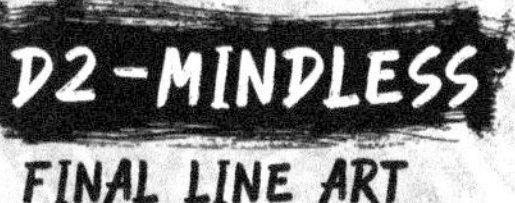

FINAL LINE ART

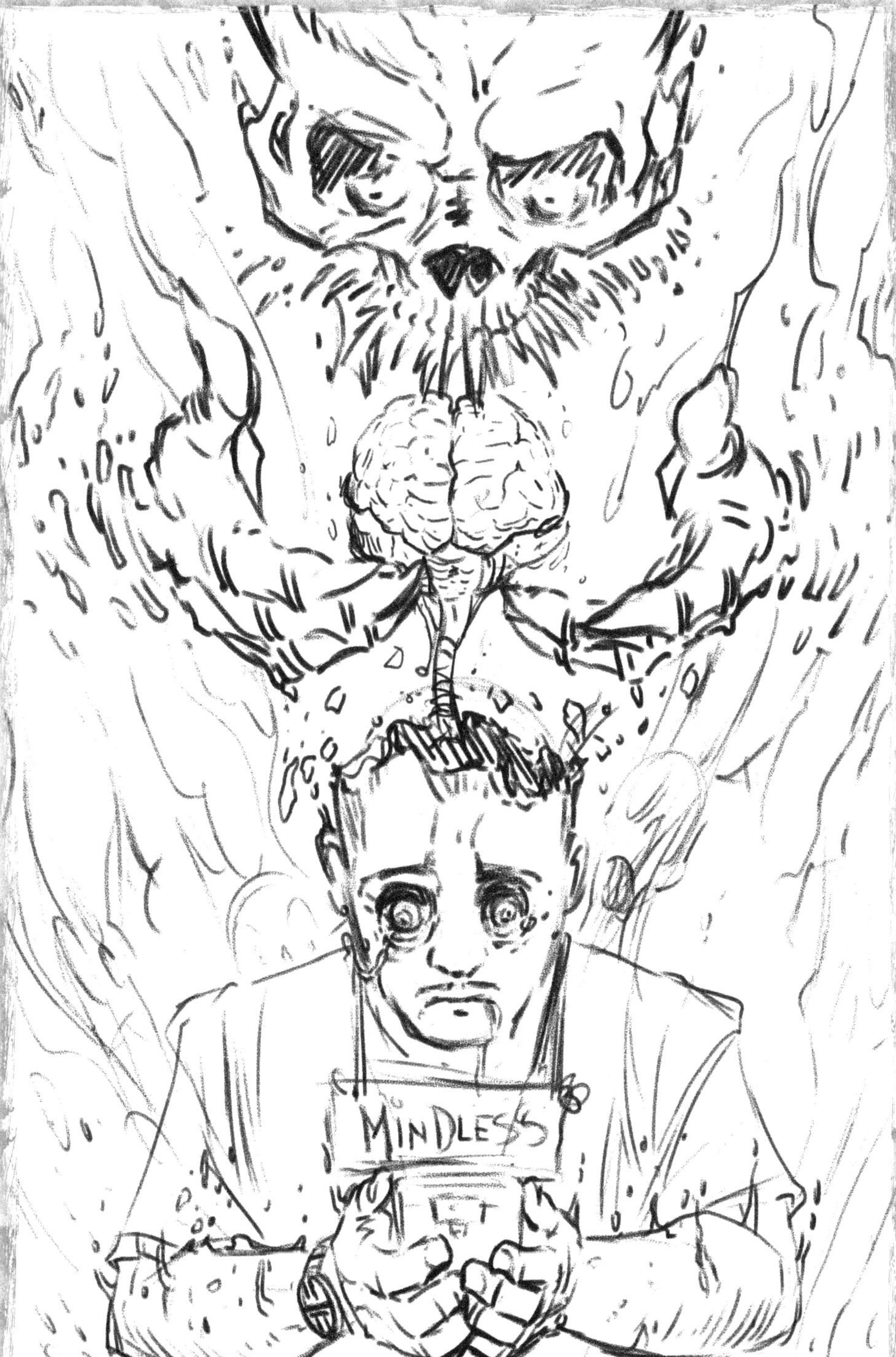

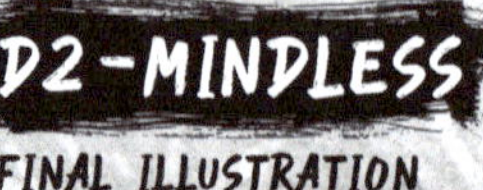

FINAL ILLUSTRATION

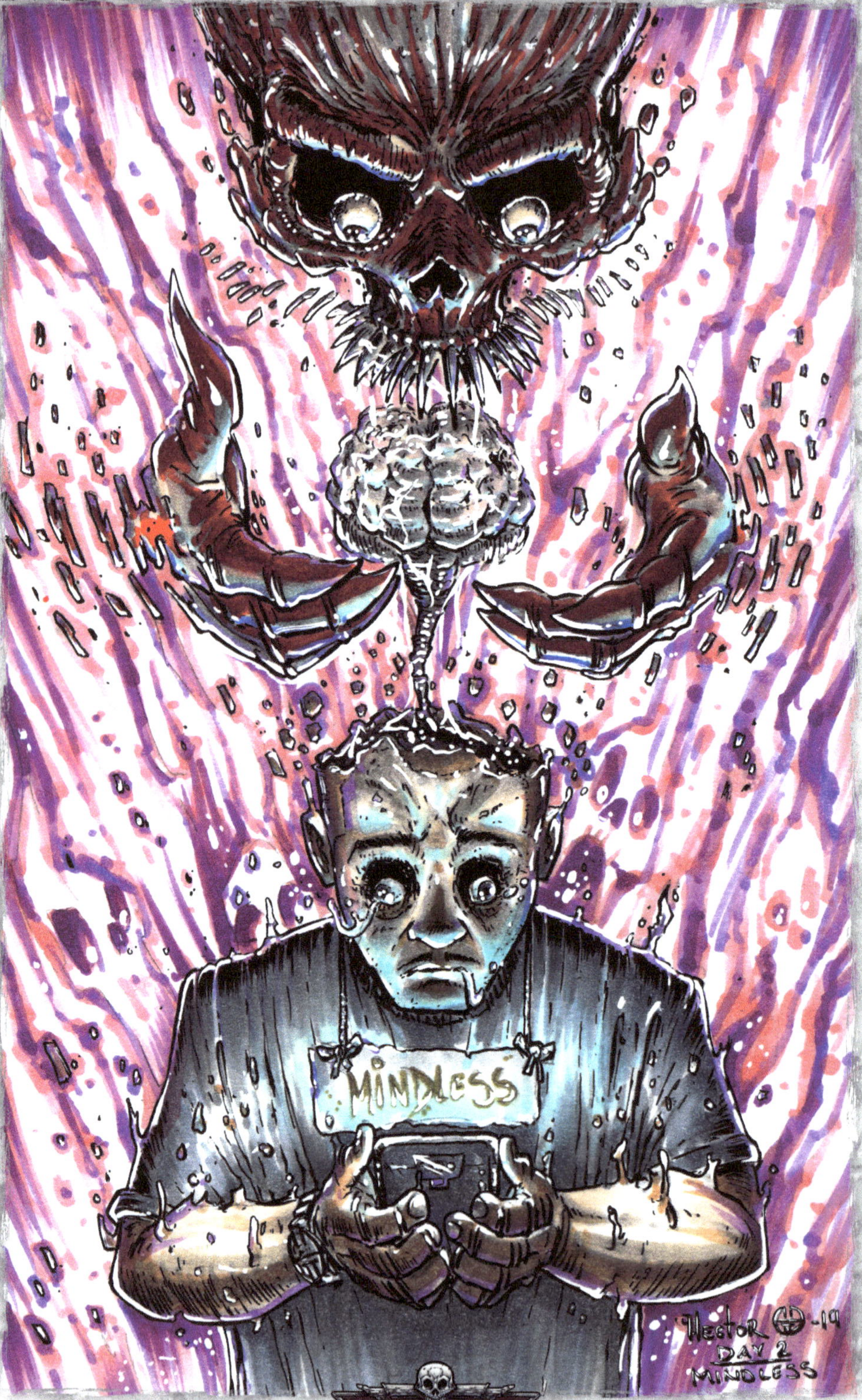

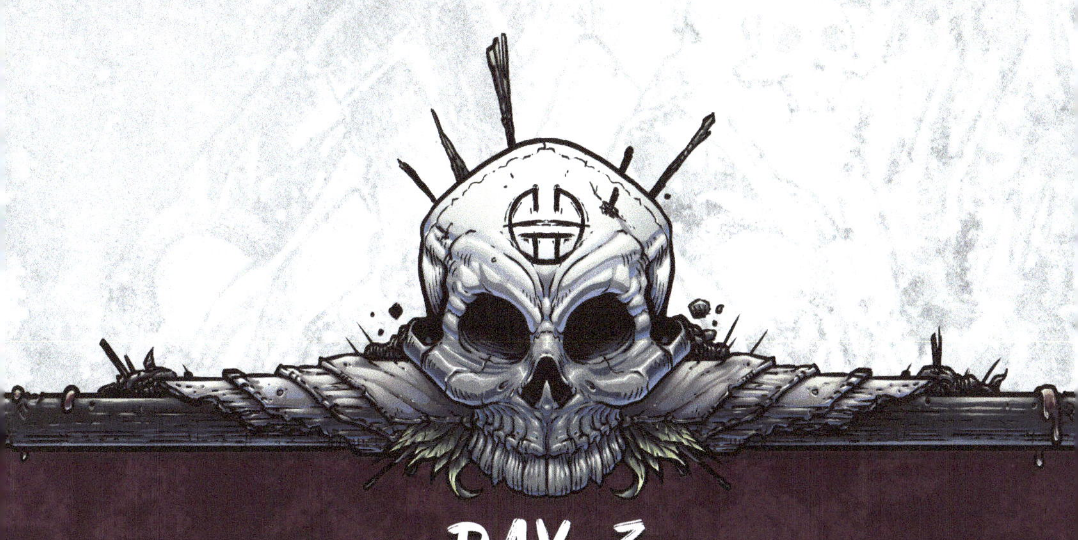

- DAY 3 -
BAIT

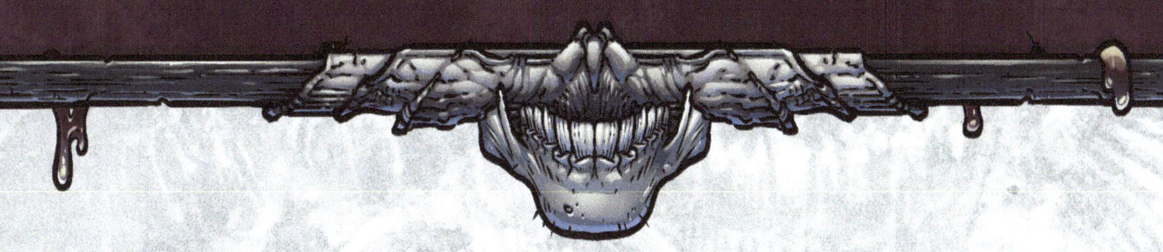

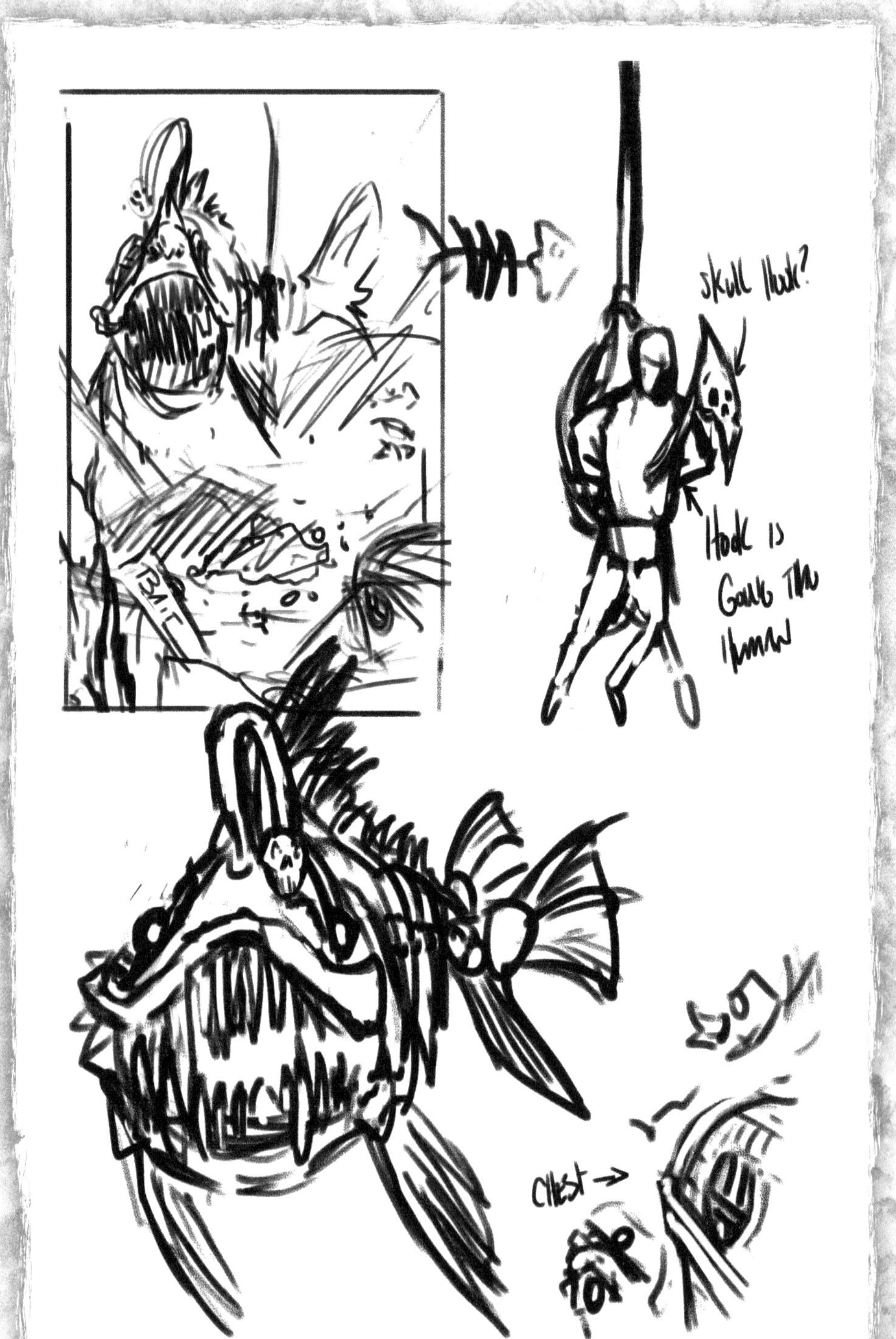

BAIT

Skull Hook?

Hook is Going thru Human

Chest →

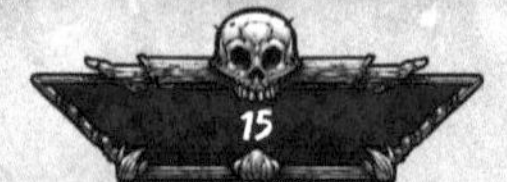

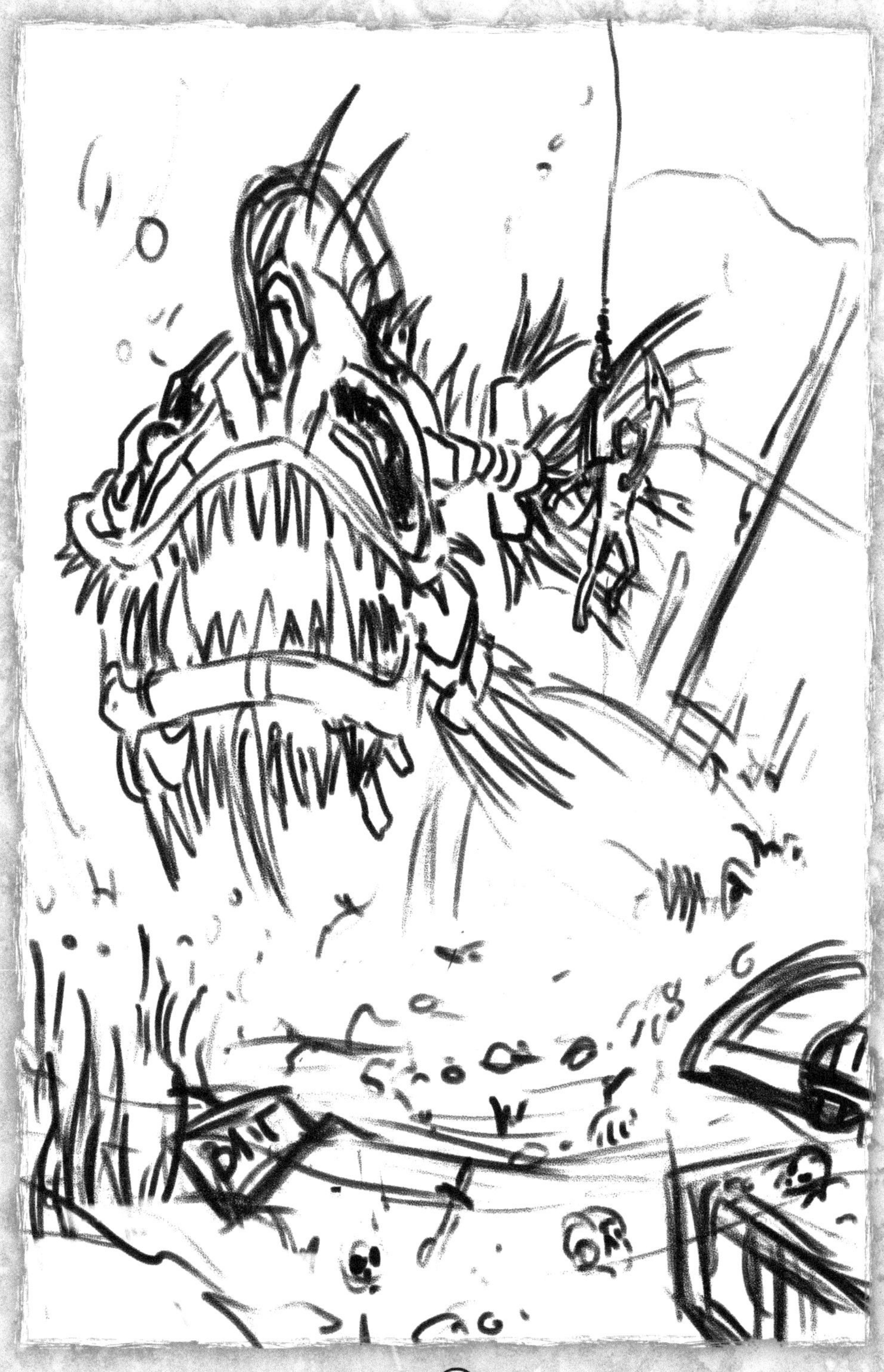

D3 - BAIT

FINAL LINE ART

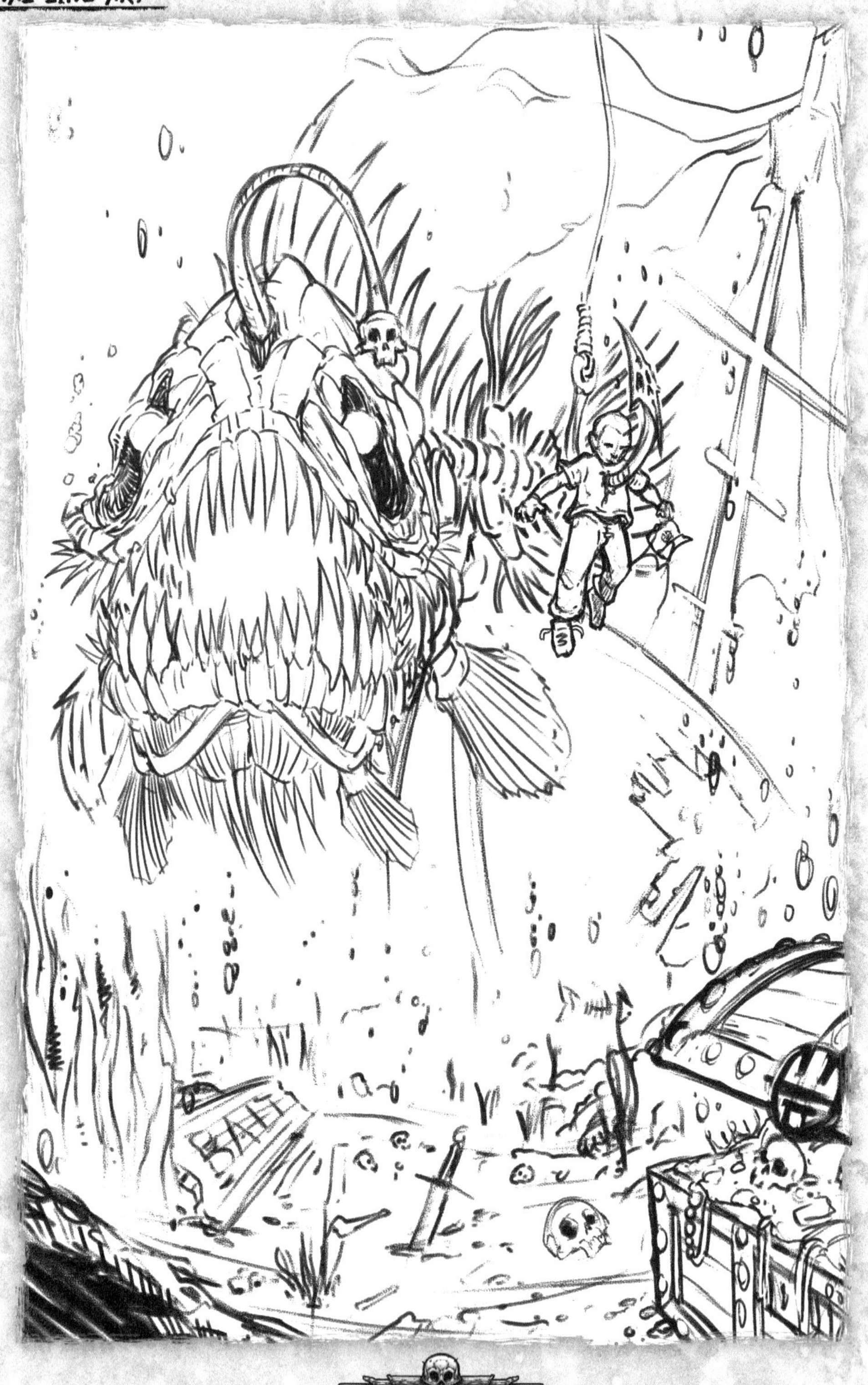

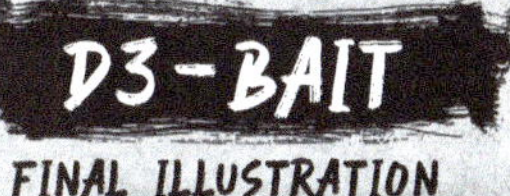

D3-BAIT

FINAL ILLUSTRATION

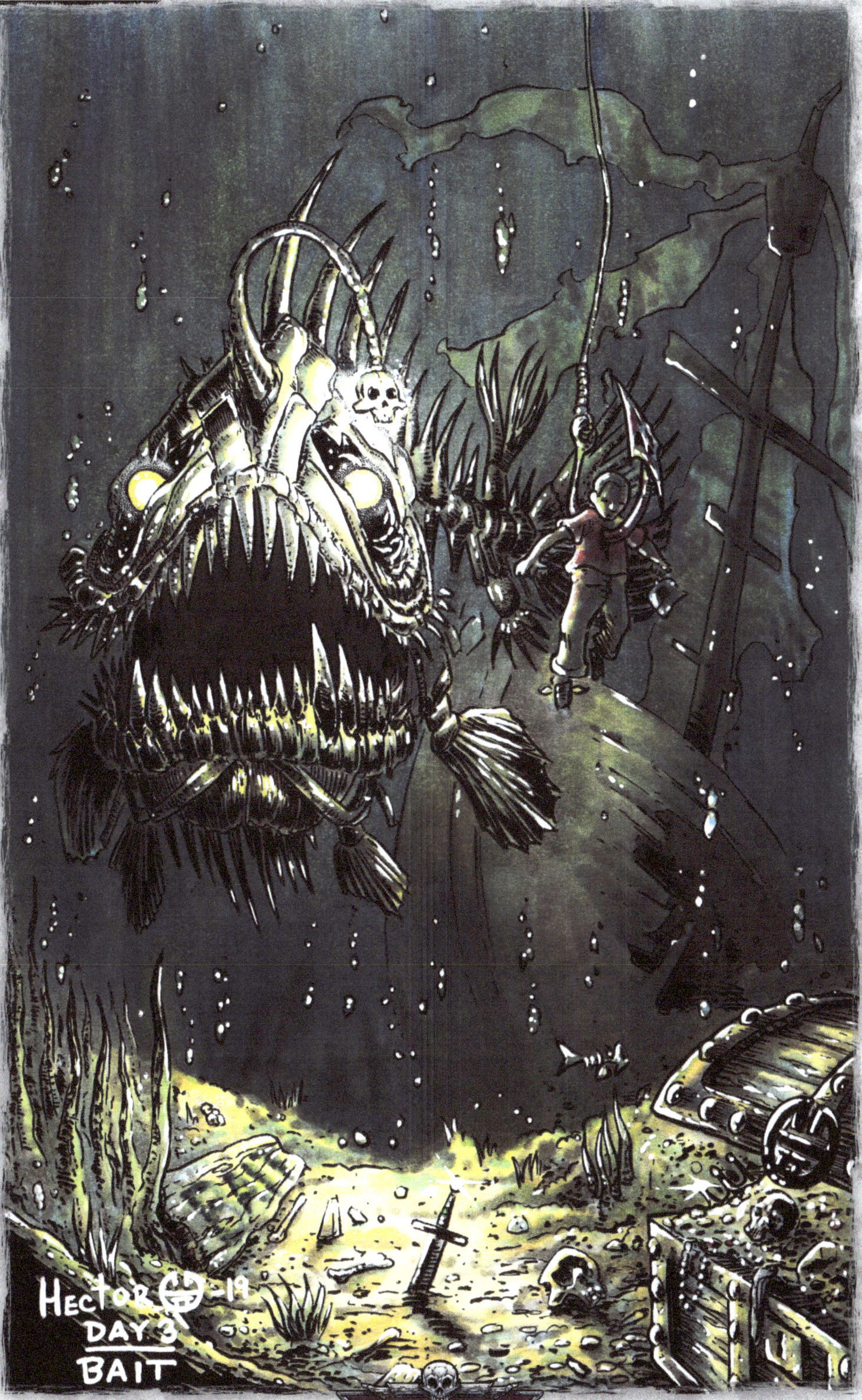

Hector -19
DAY 3
BAIT

- DAY 4 -

FREEZE

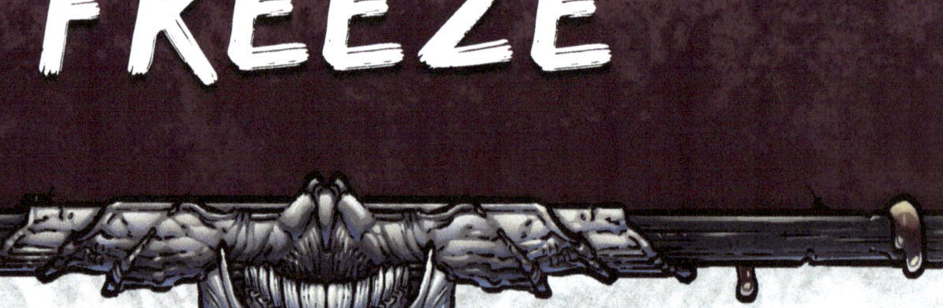

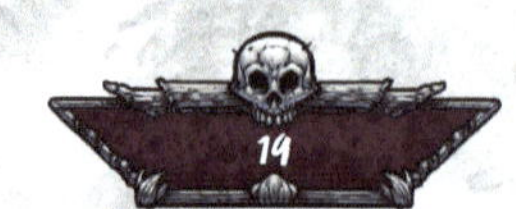

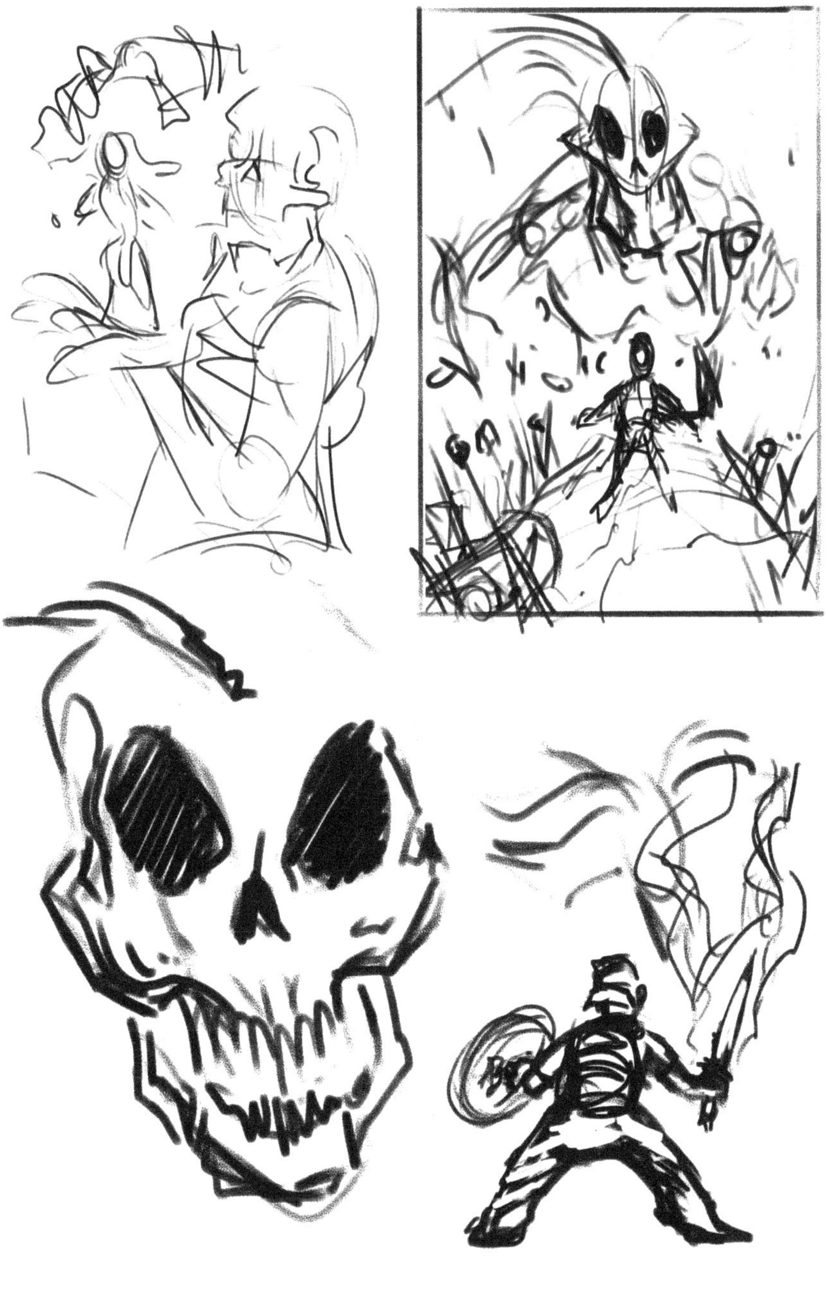

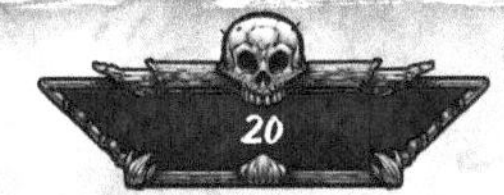

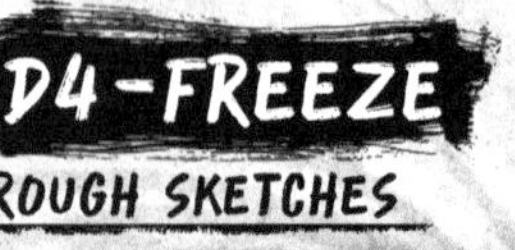
D4-FREEZE
ROUGH SKETCHES

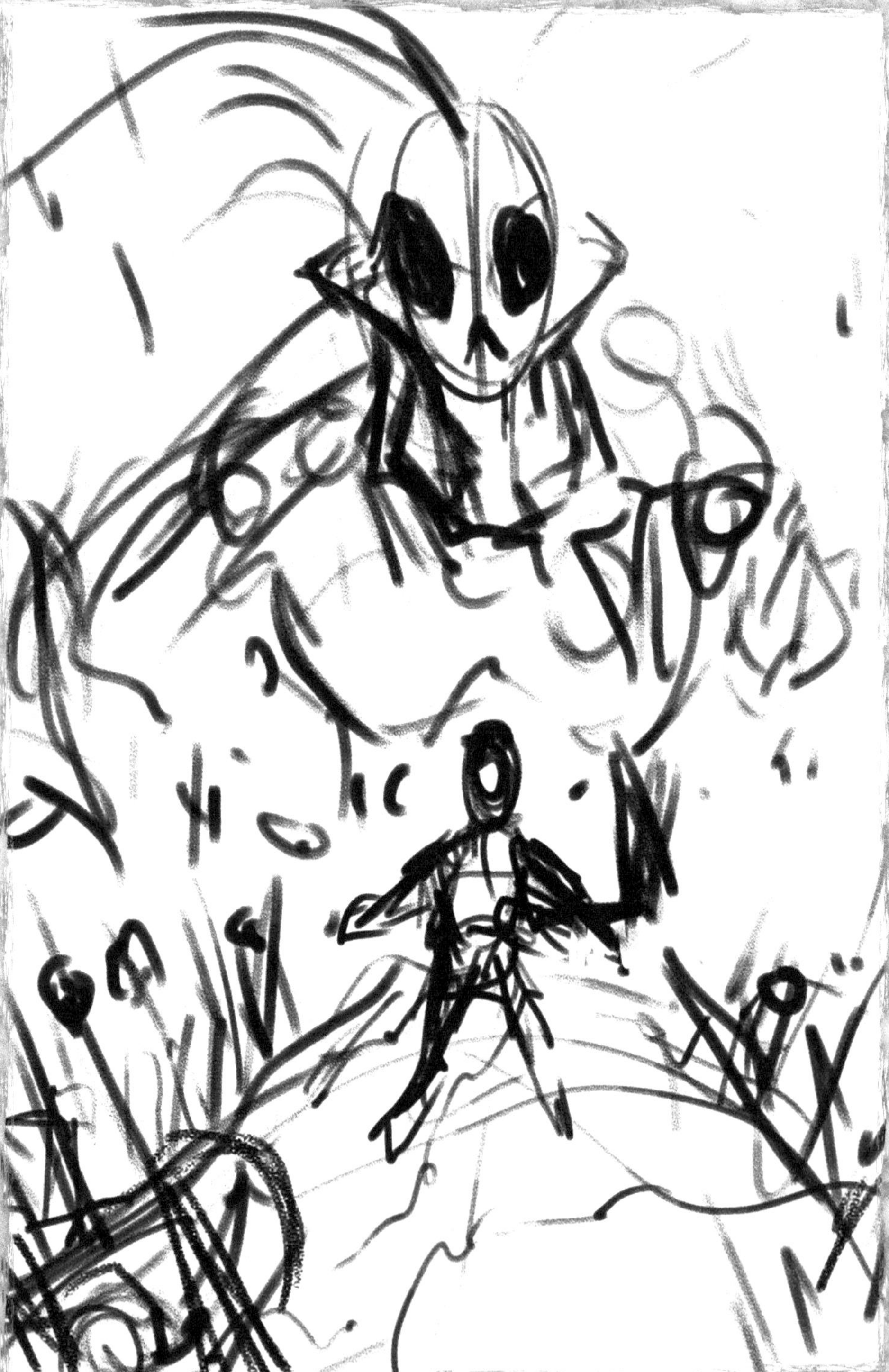

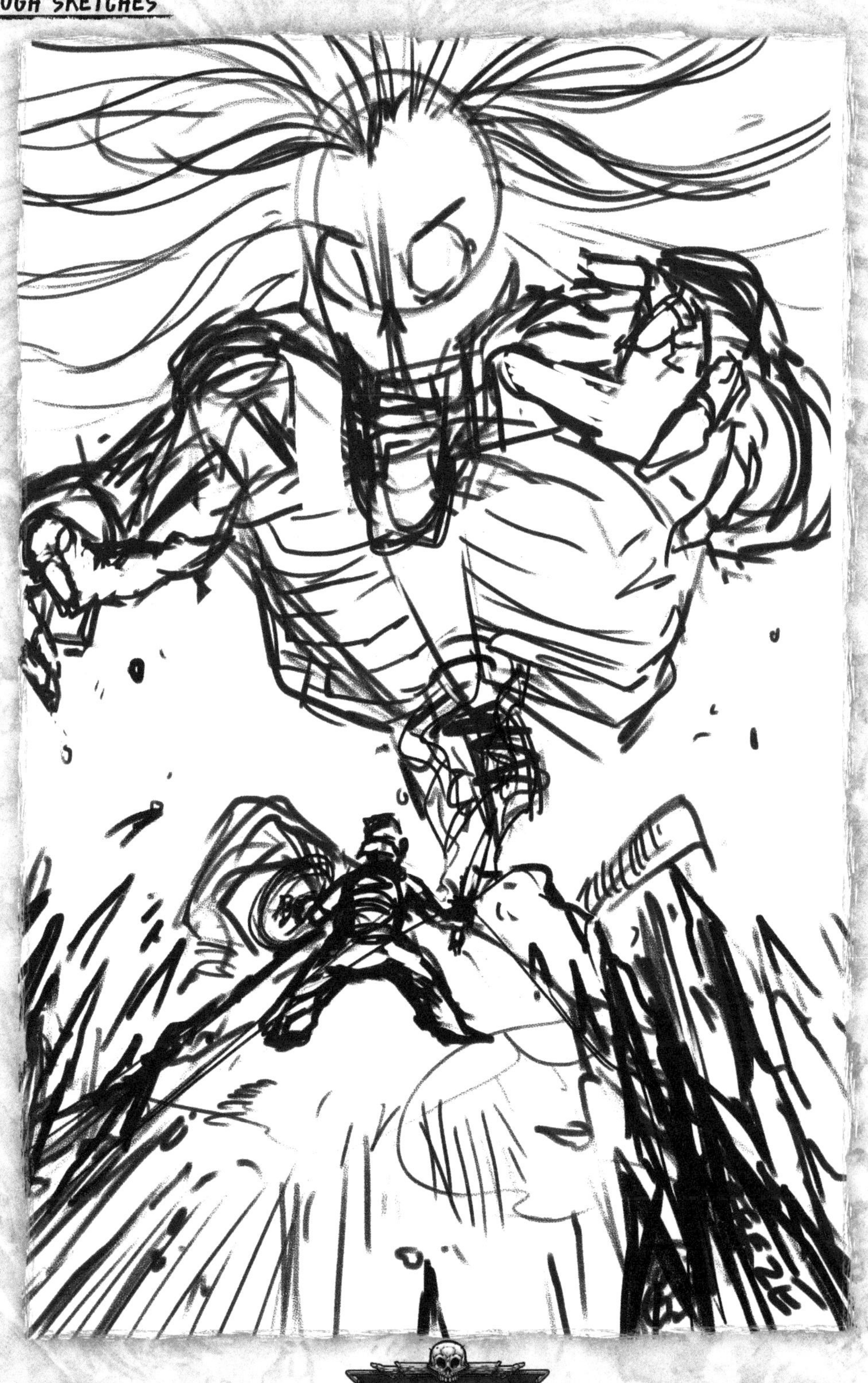

D4-FREEZE

FINAL LINE ART

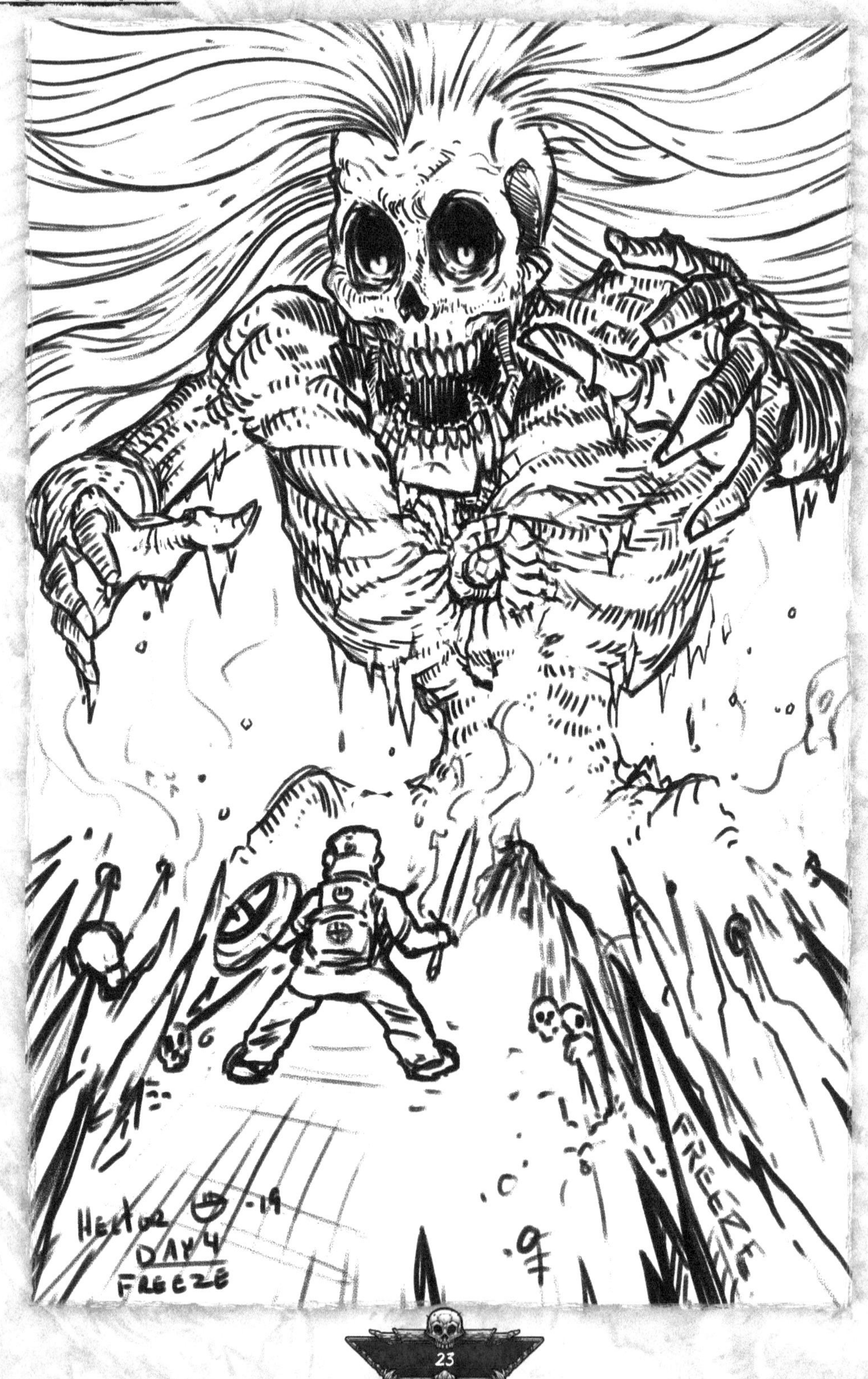

FINAL ILLUSTRATION

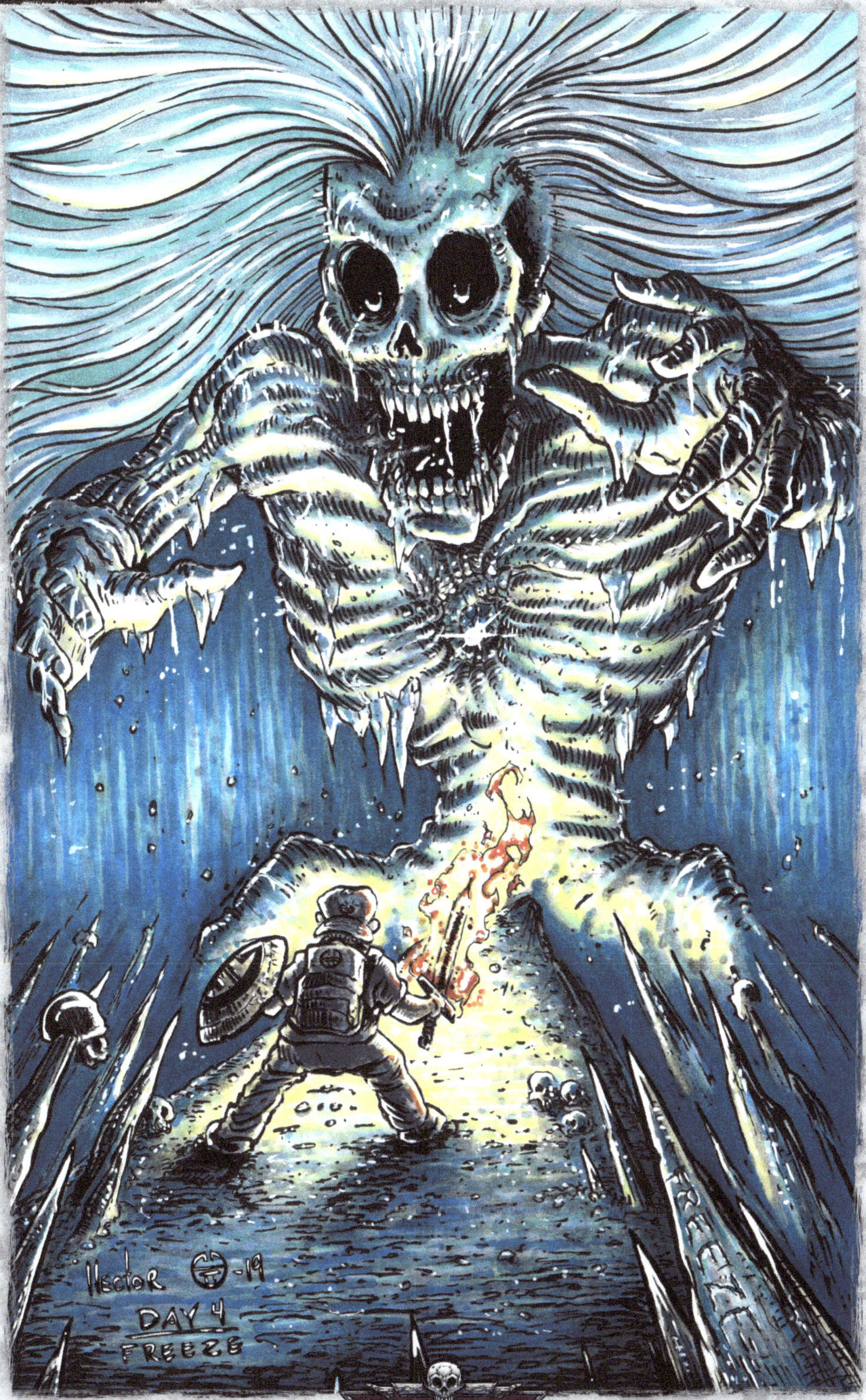

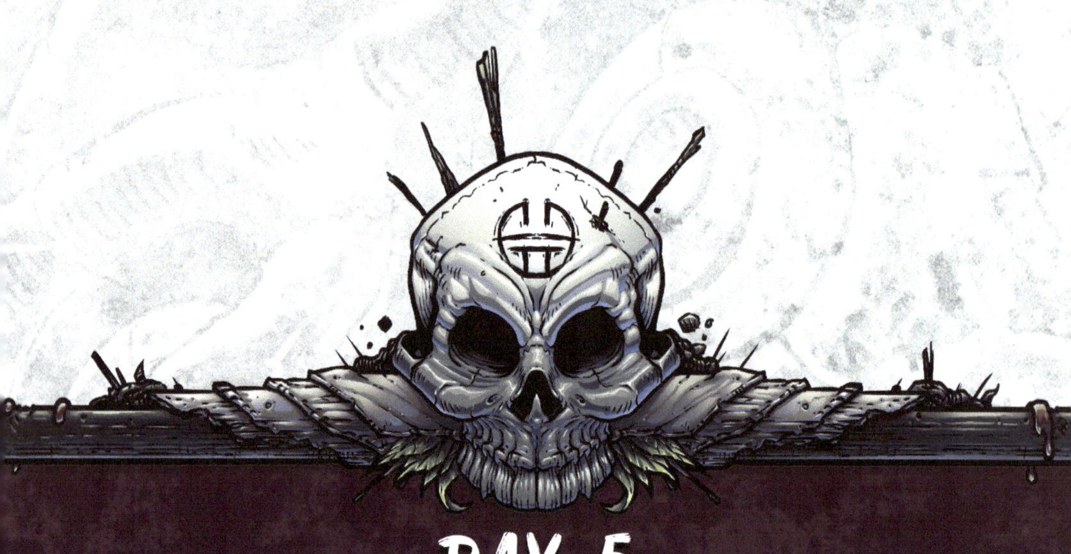

– DAY 5 –
BUILD

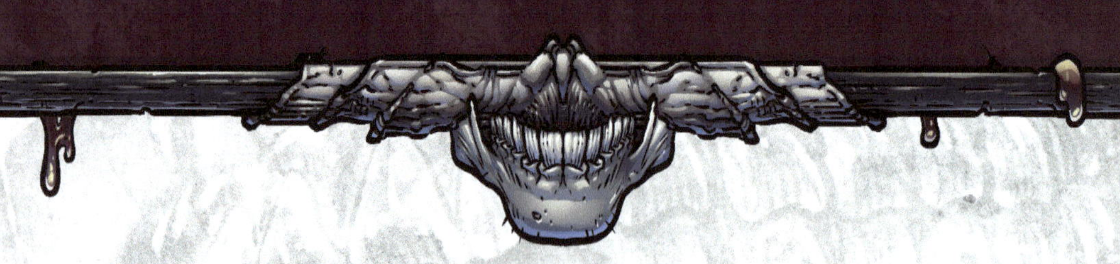

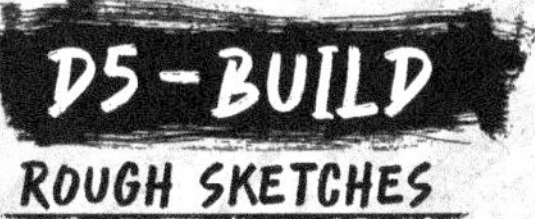

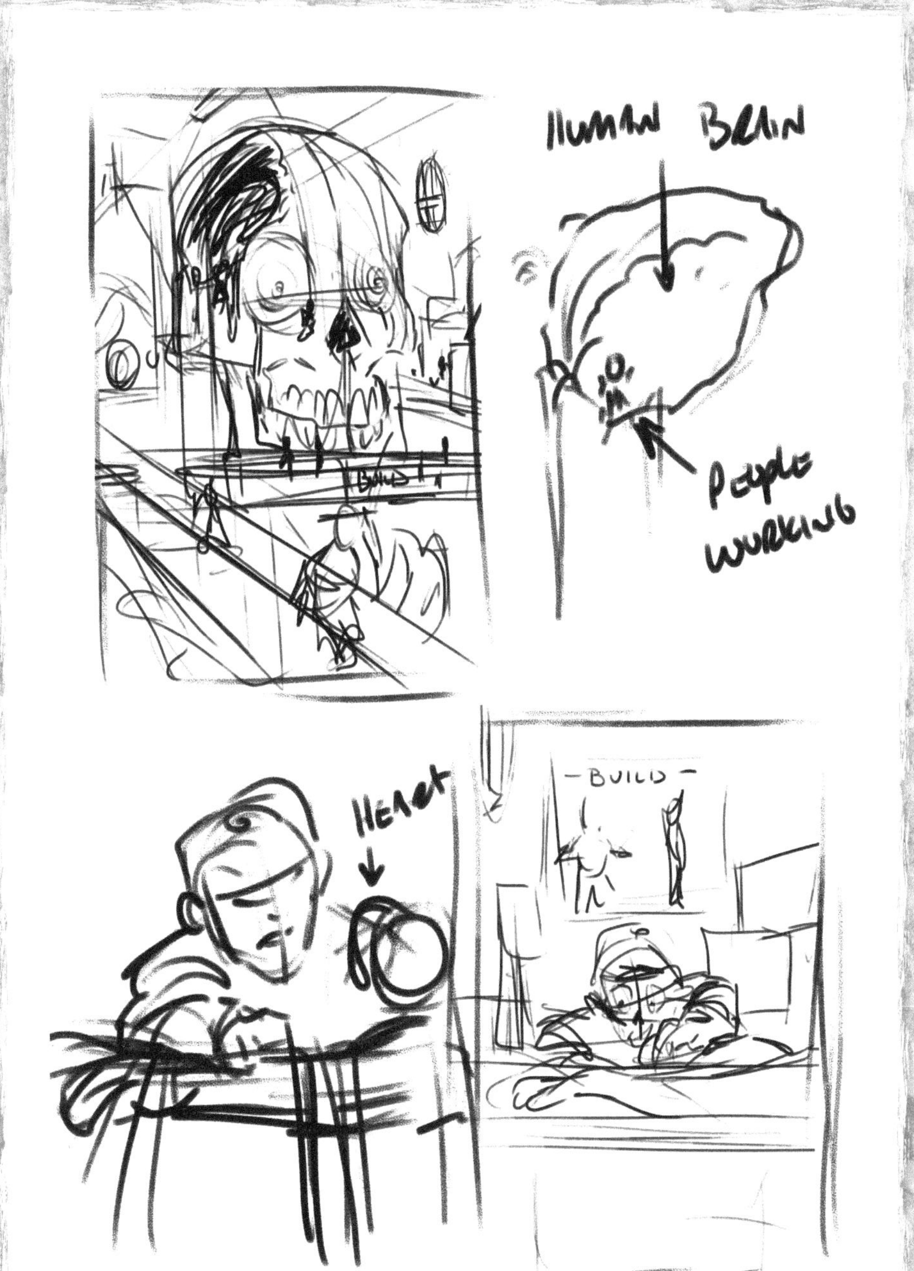

D5 – BUILD

ROUGH SKETCHES

HUMAN BRAIN
PEOPLE WORKING
BUILD
HEART
– BUILD –

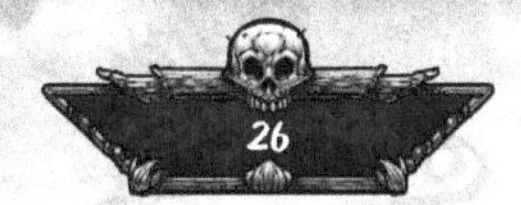

D5 - BUILD

FINAL LINE ART

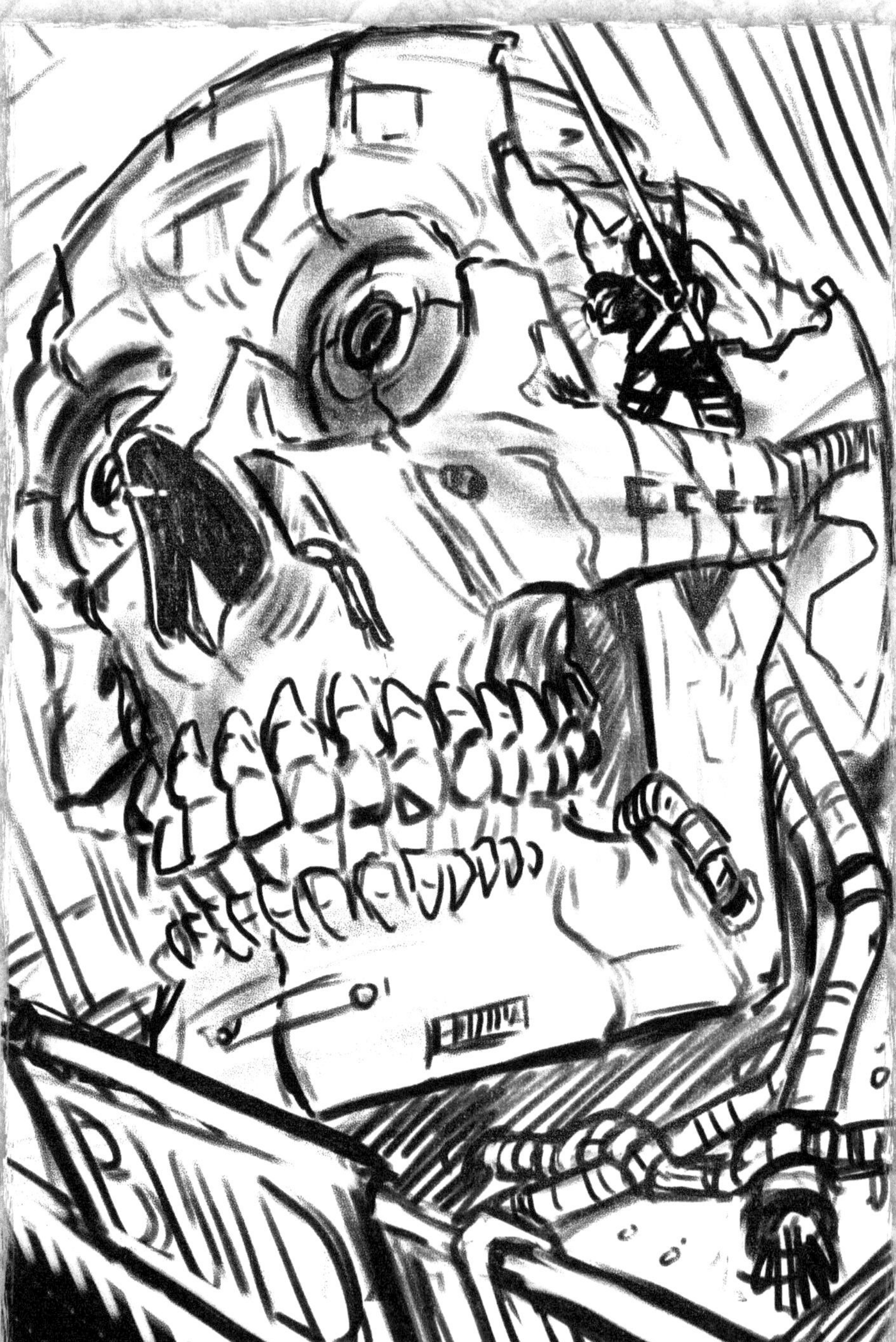

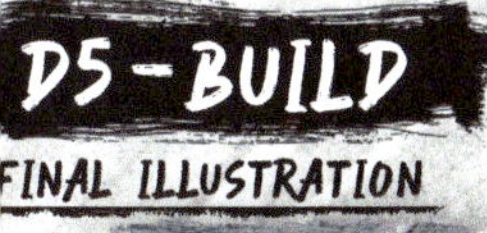

D5 - BUILD

FINAL ILLUSTRATION

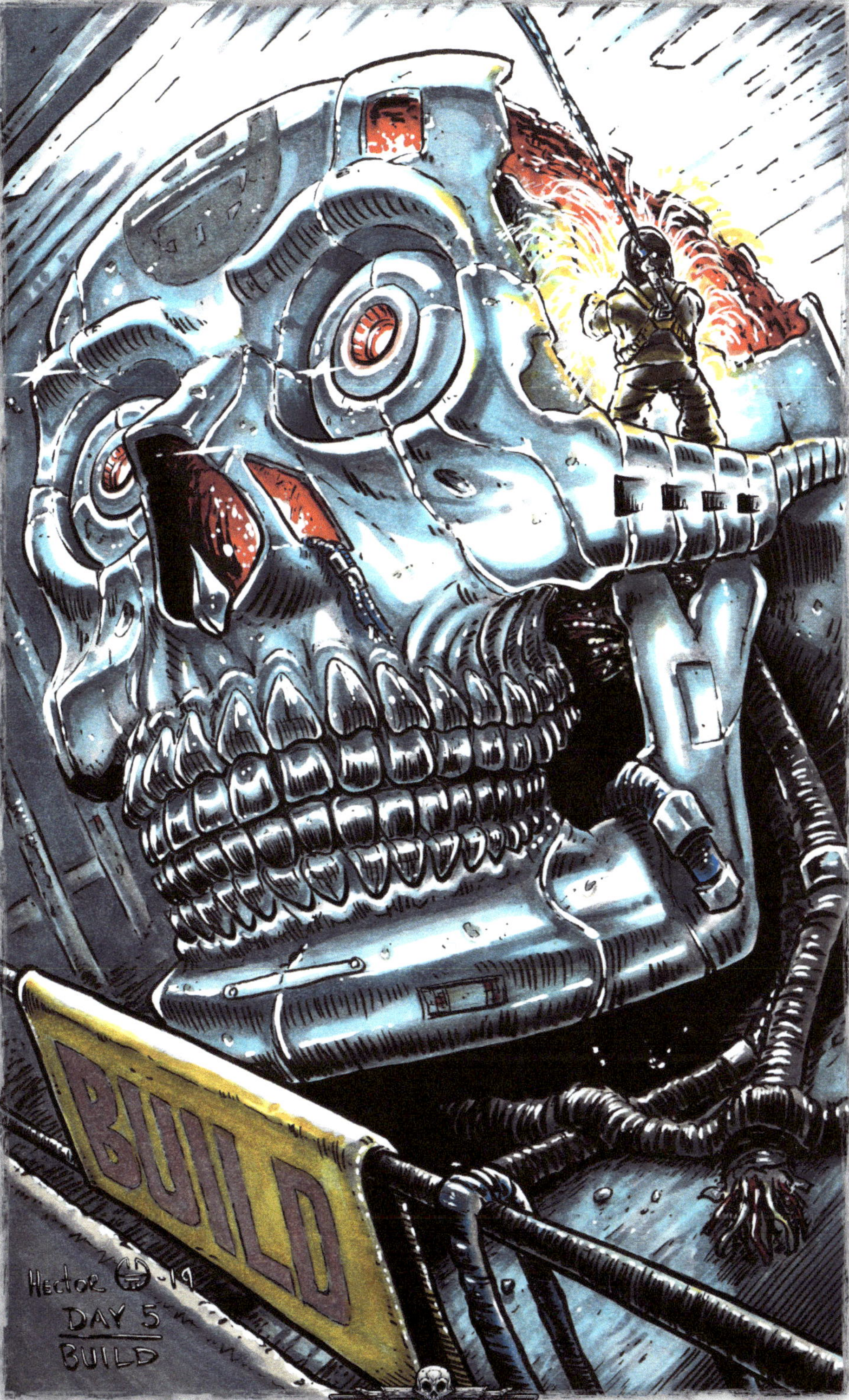

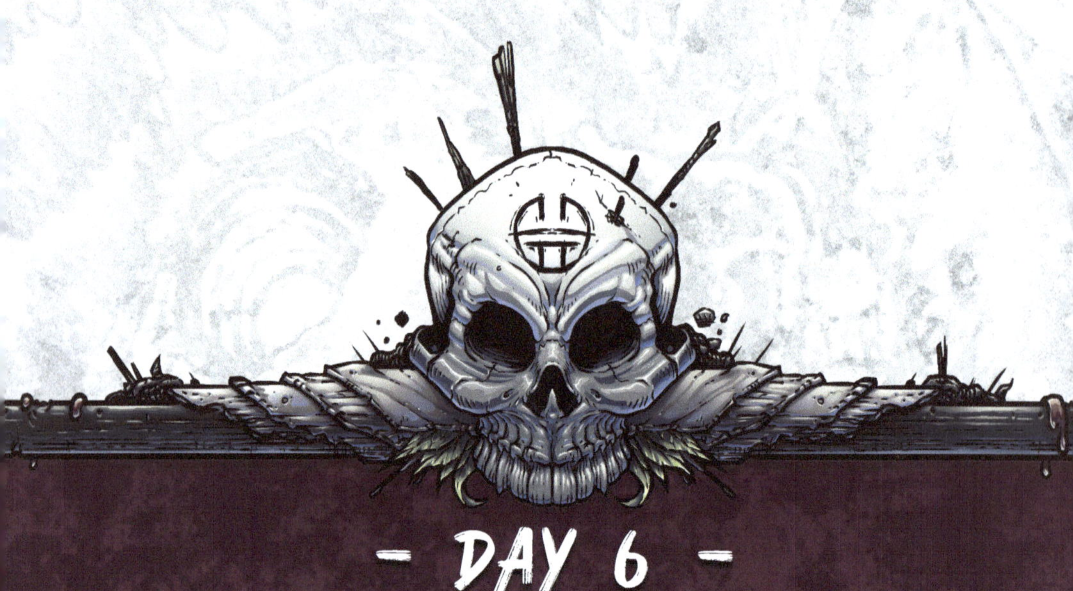

- DAY 6 -
HUSKY

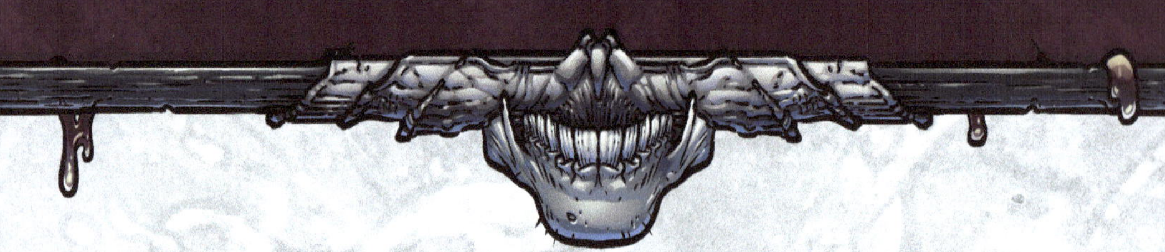

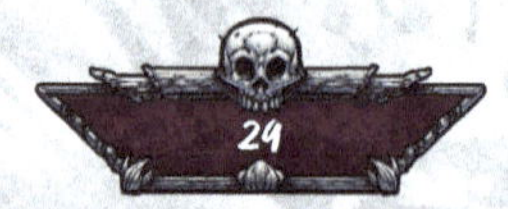

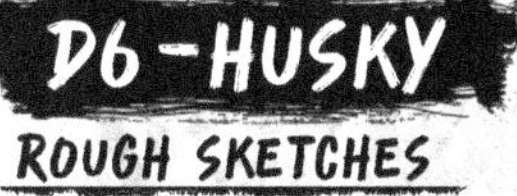

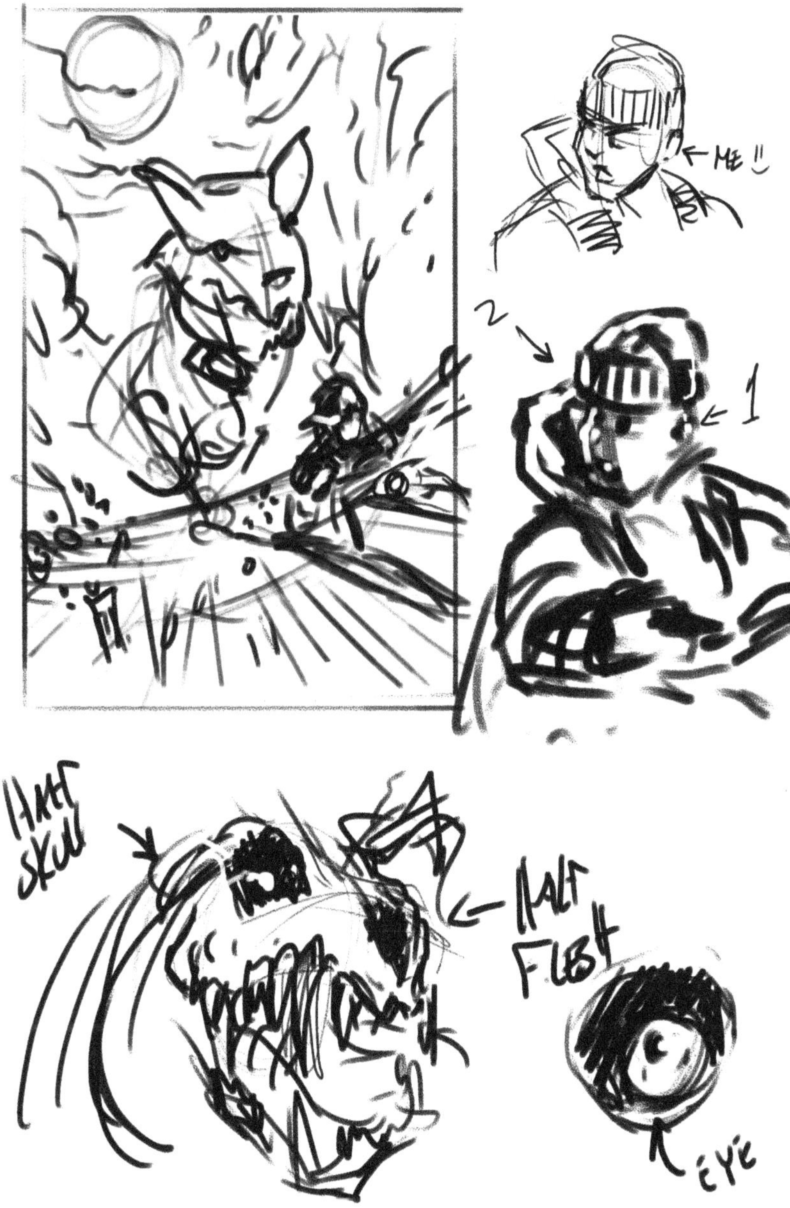

ME !!
2
1
HALF SKULL
HALF FLESH
EYE

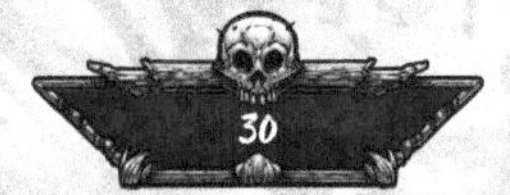

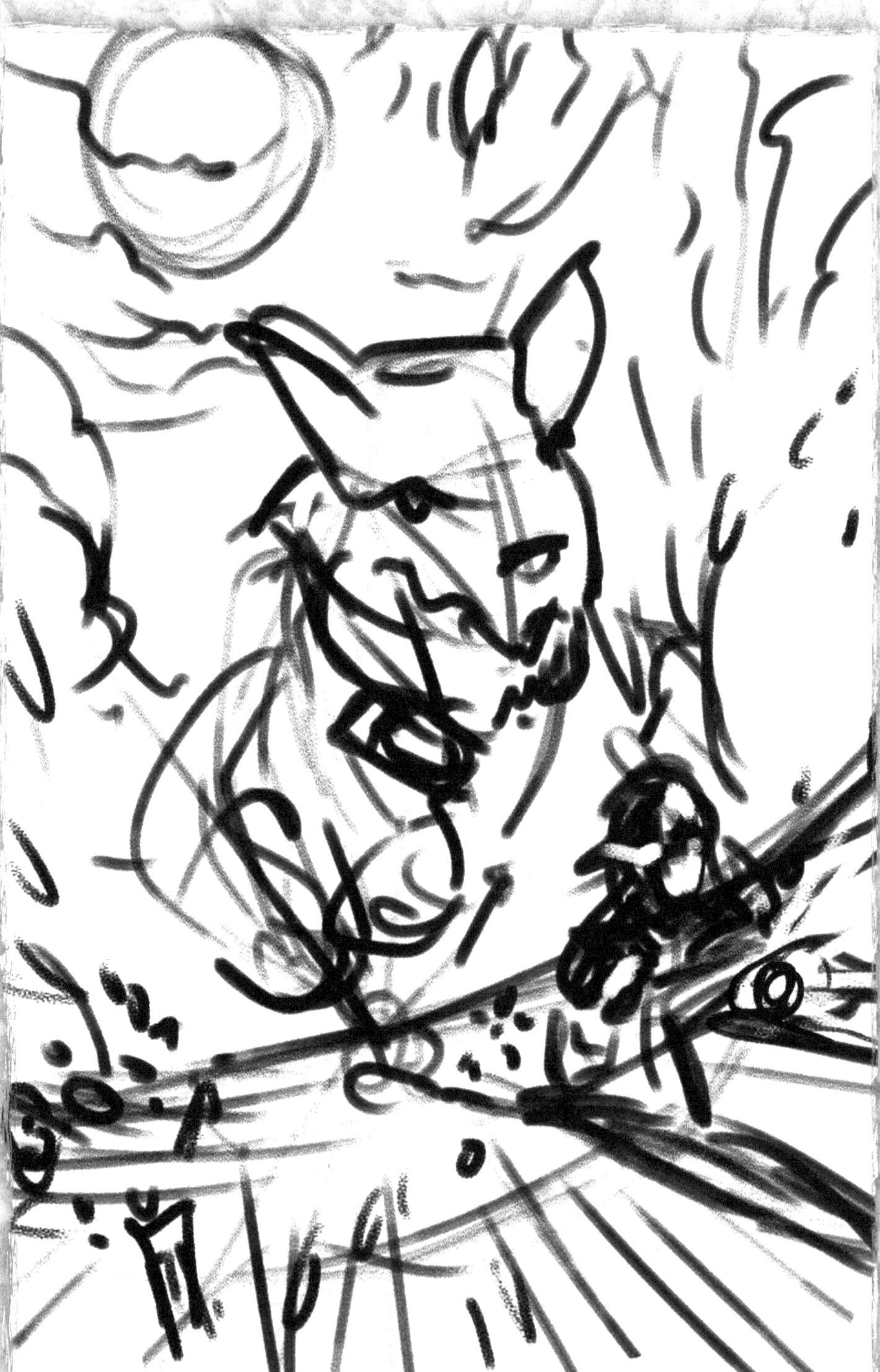

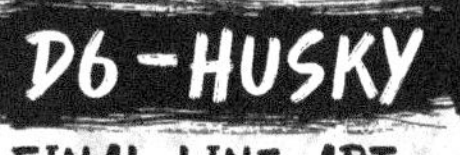

FINAL LINE ART

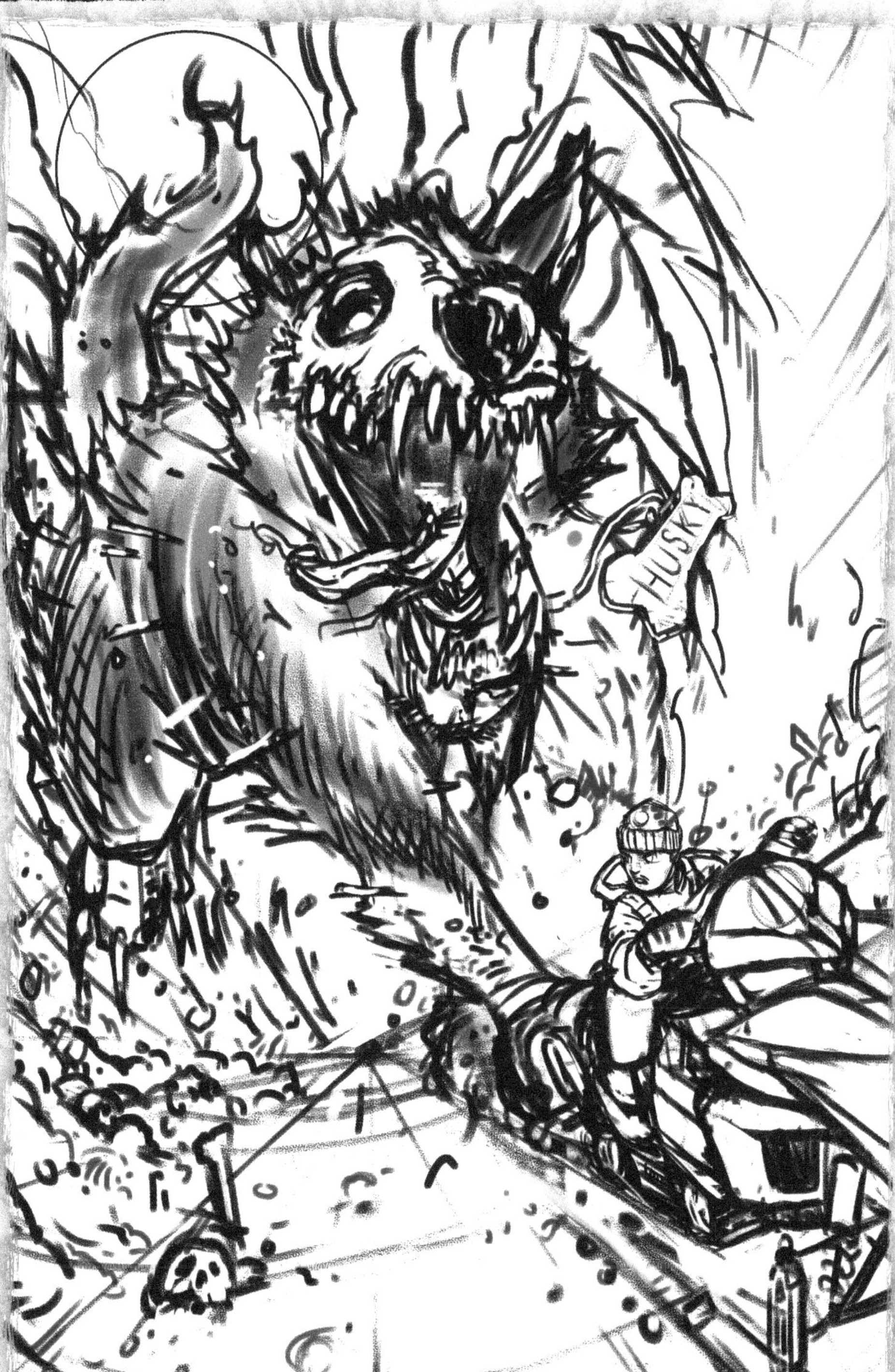

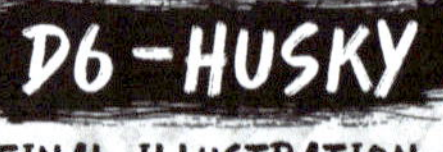

FINAL ILLUSTRATION

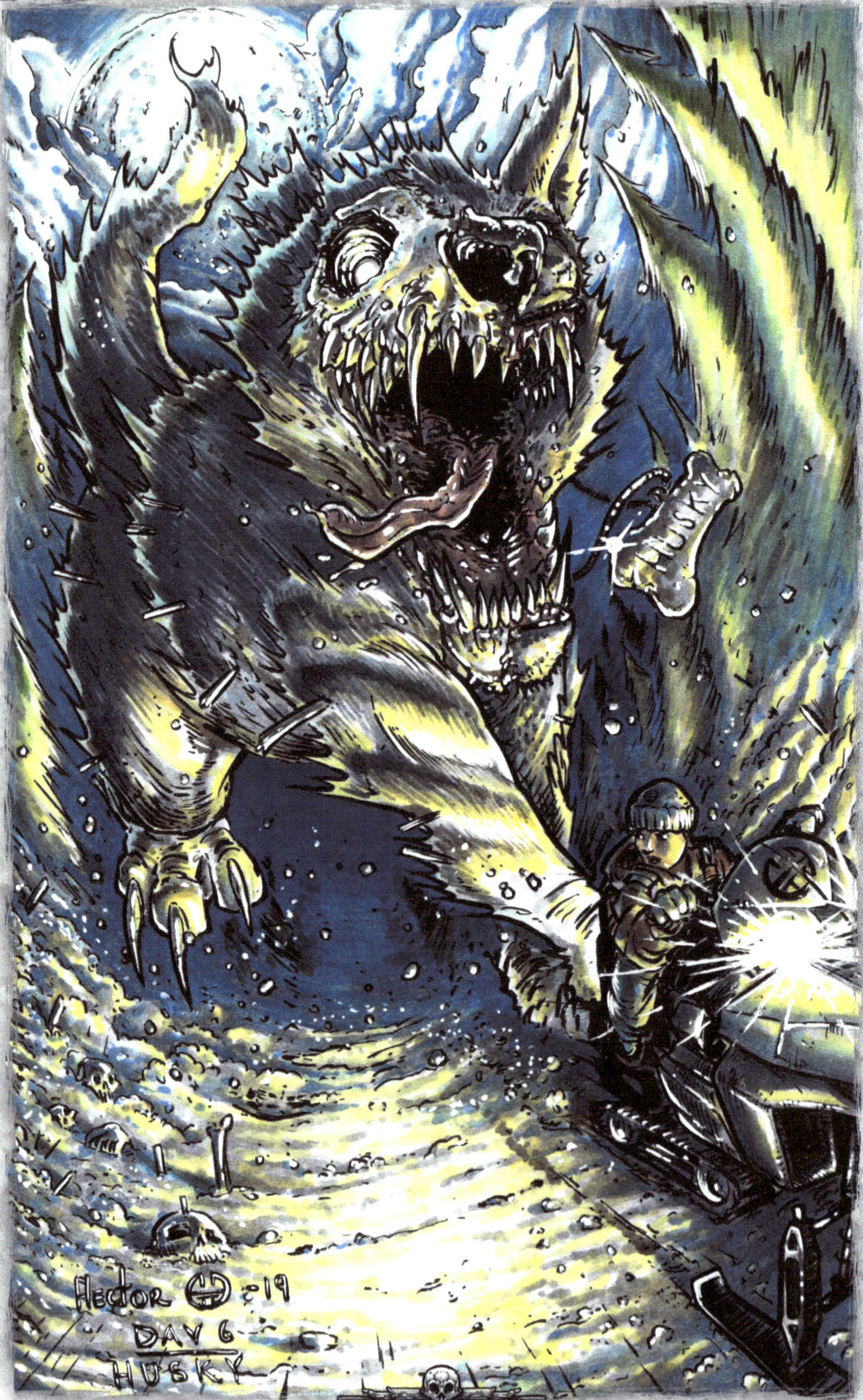

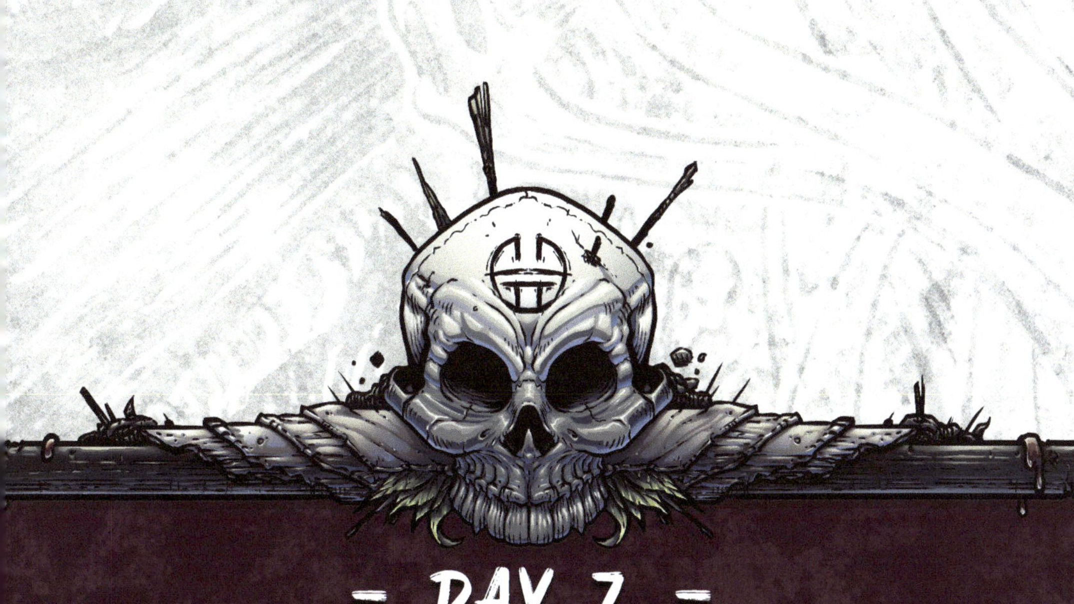

- DAY 7 -
ENCHANTED

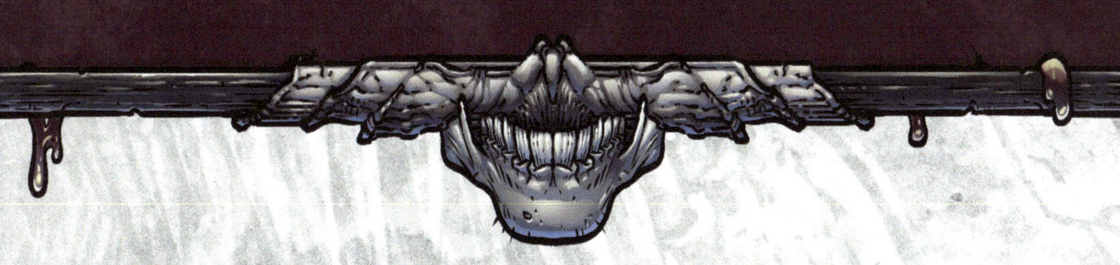

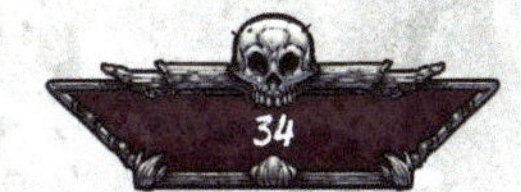

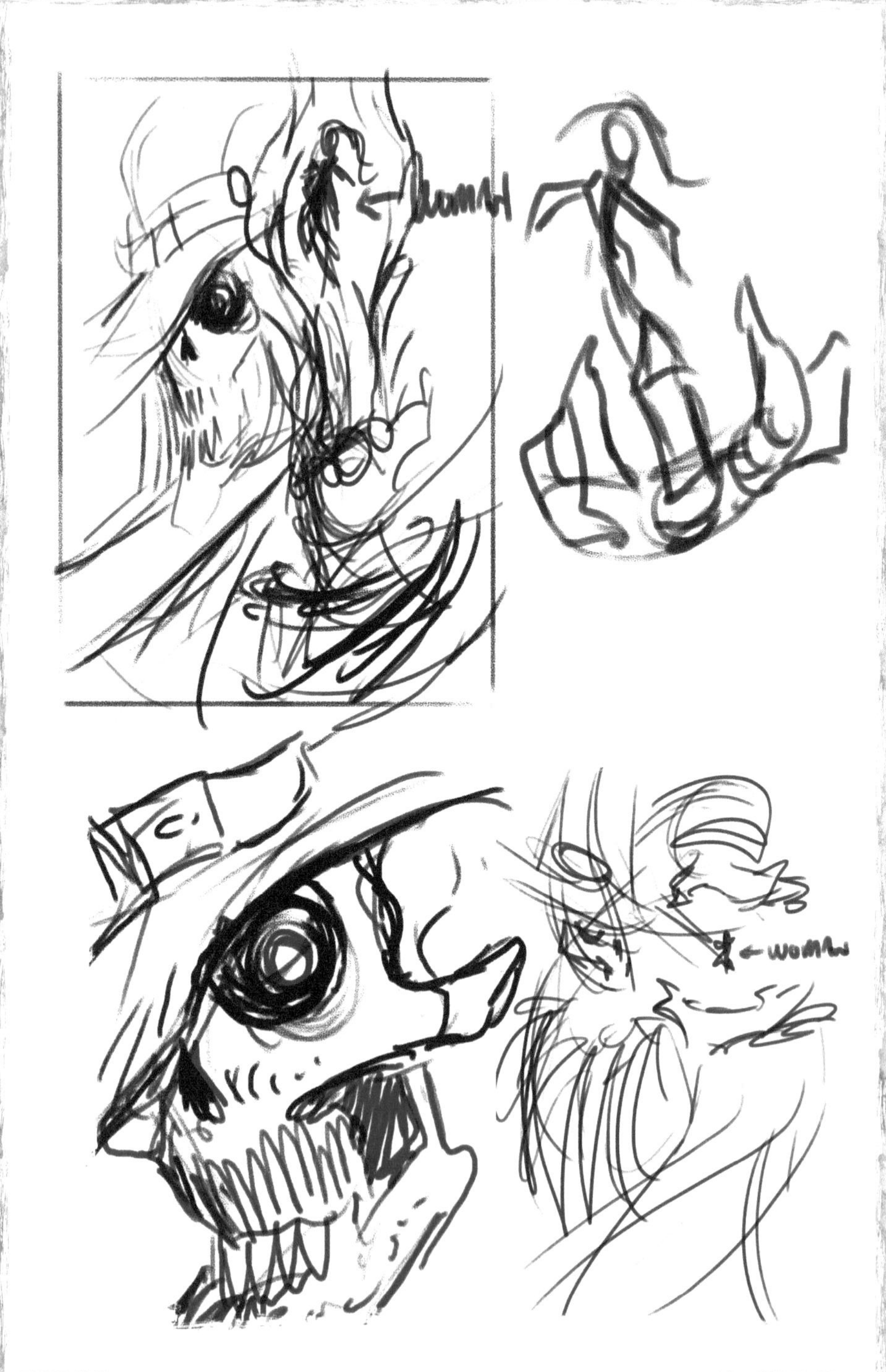

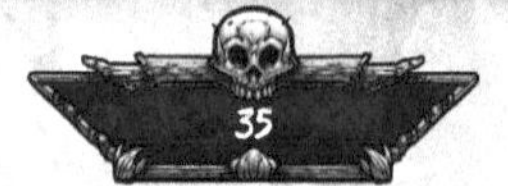

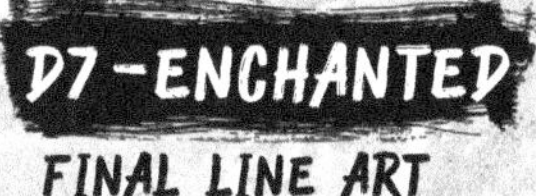
D7-ENCHANTED
FINAL LINE ART

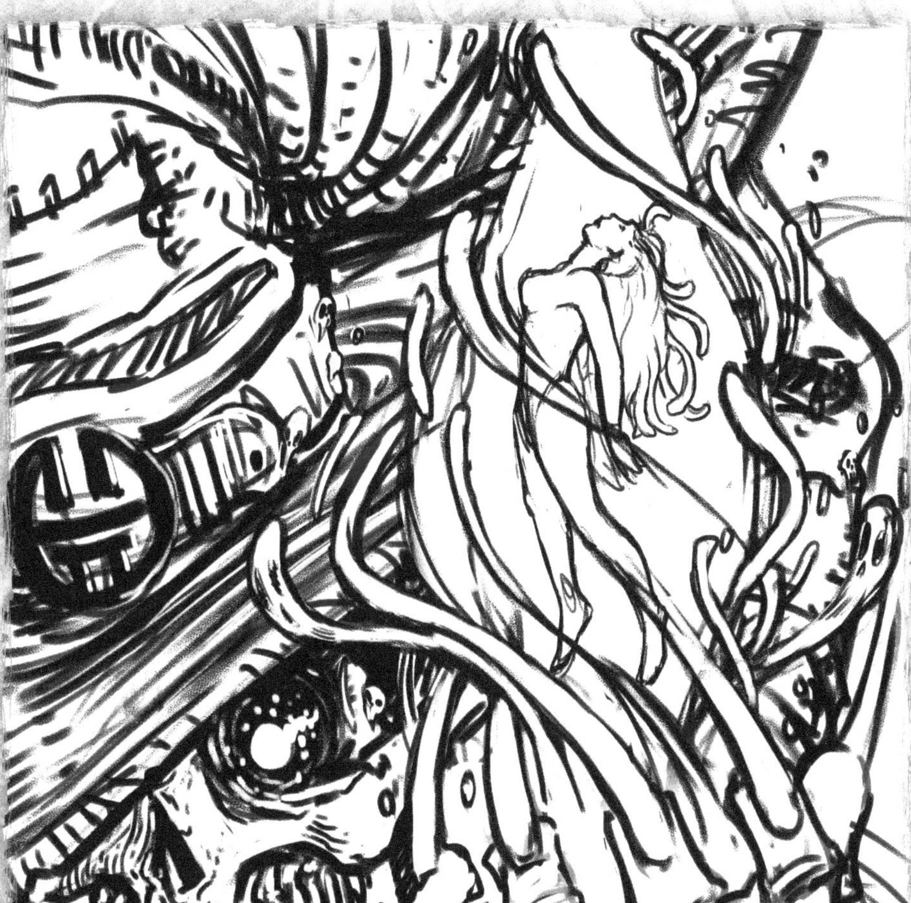

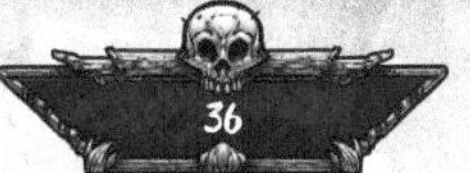

FINAL ILLUSTRATION

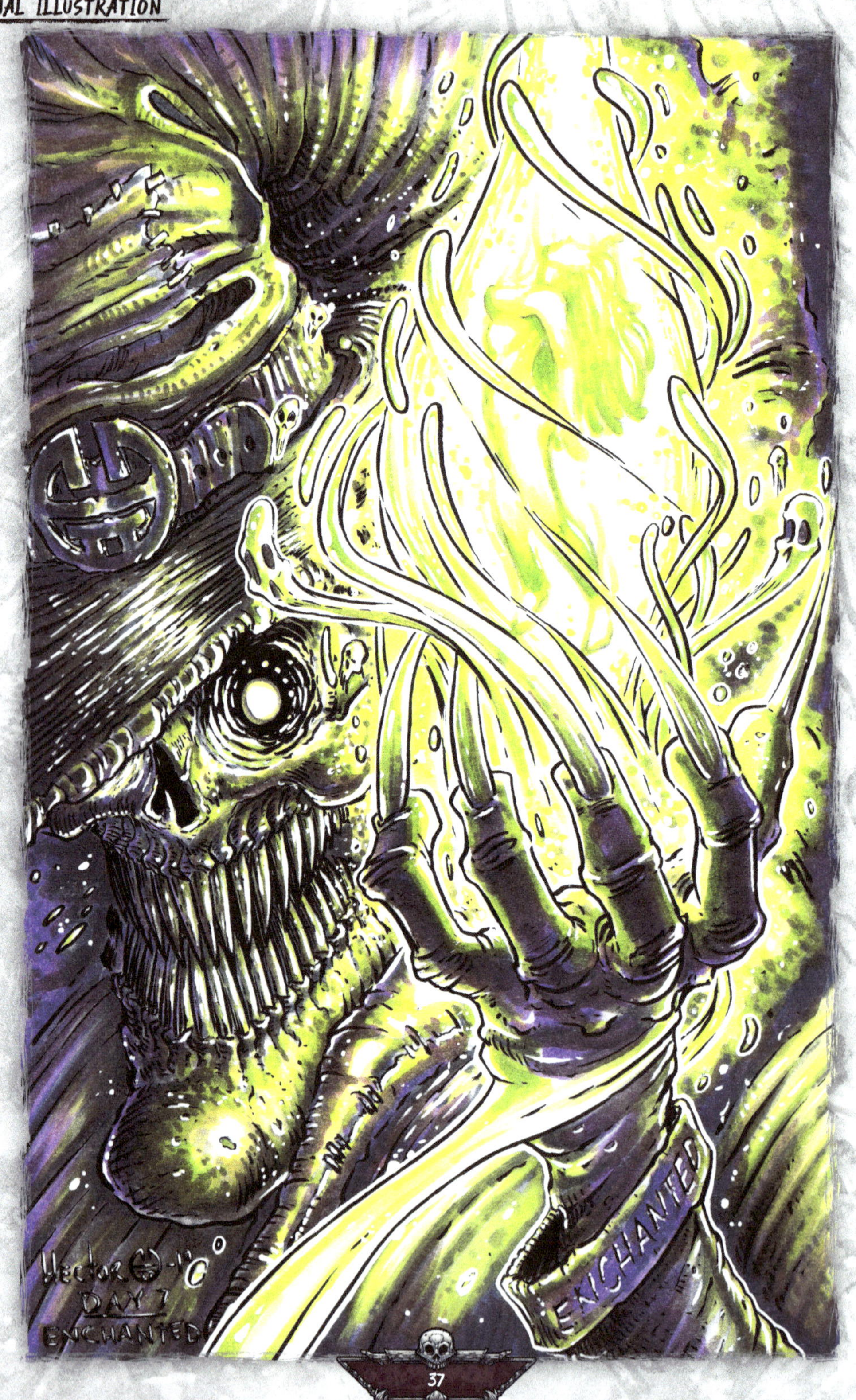

- DAY 8 -

FRAIL

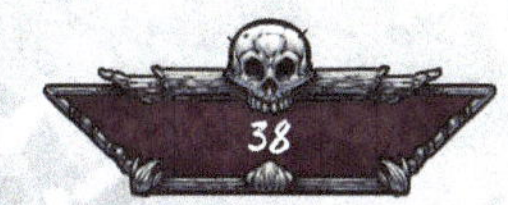

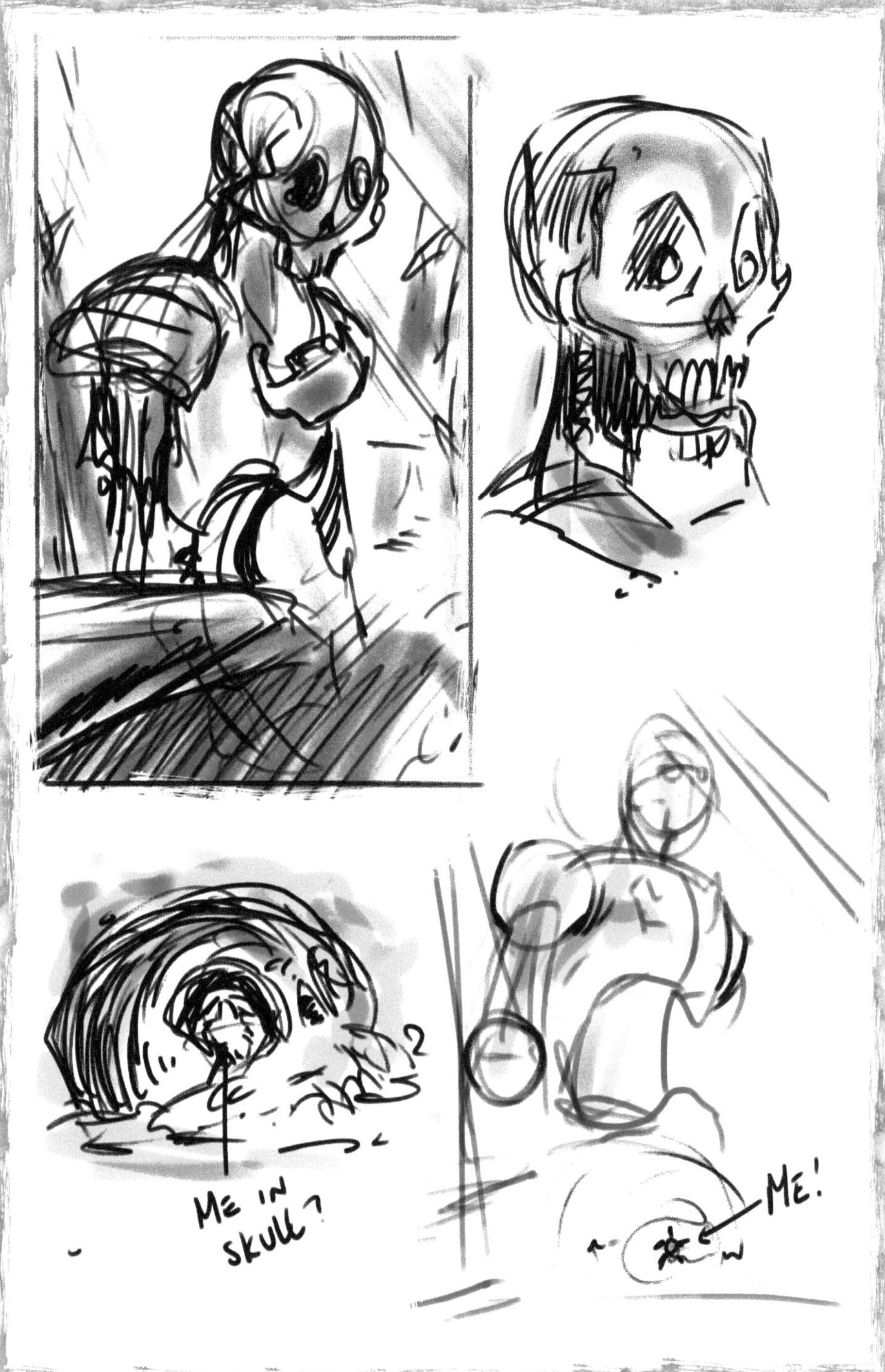

D8 - FRAIL

ROUGH SKETCHES

ME IN SKULL?

ME!

D8 – FRAIL

FINAL LINE ART

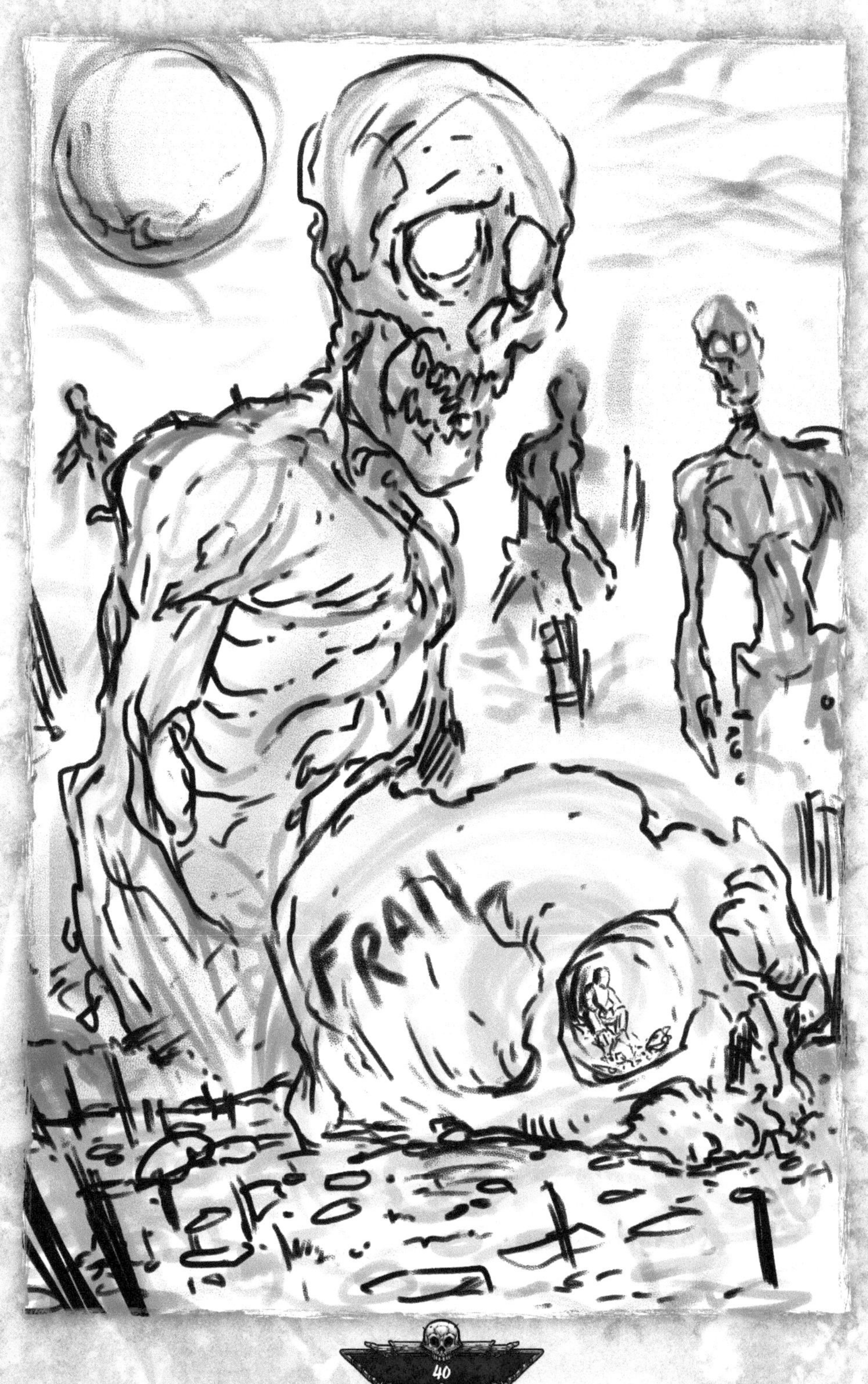

D8 - FRAIL

FINAL ILLUSTRATION

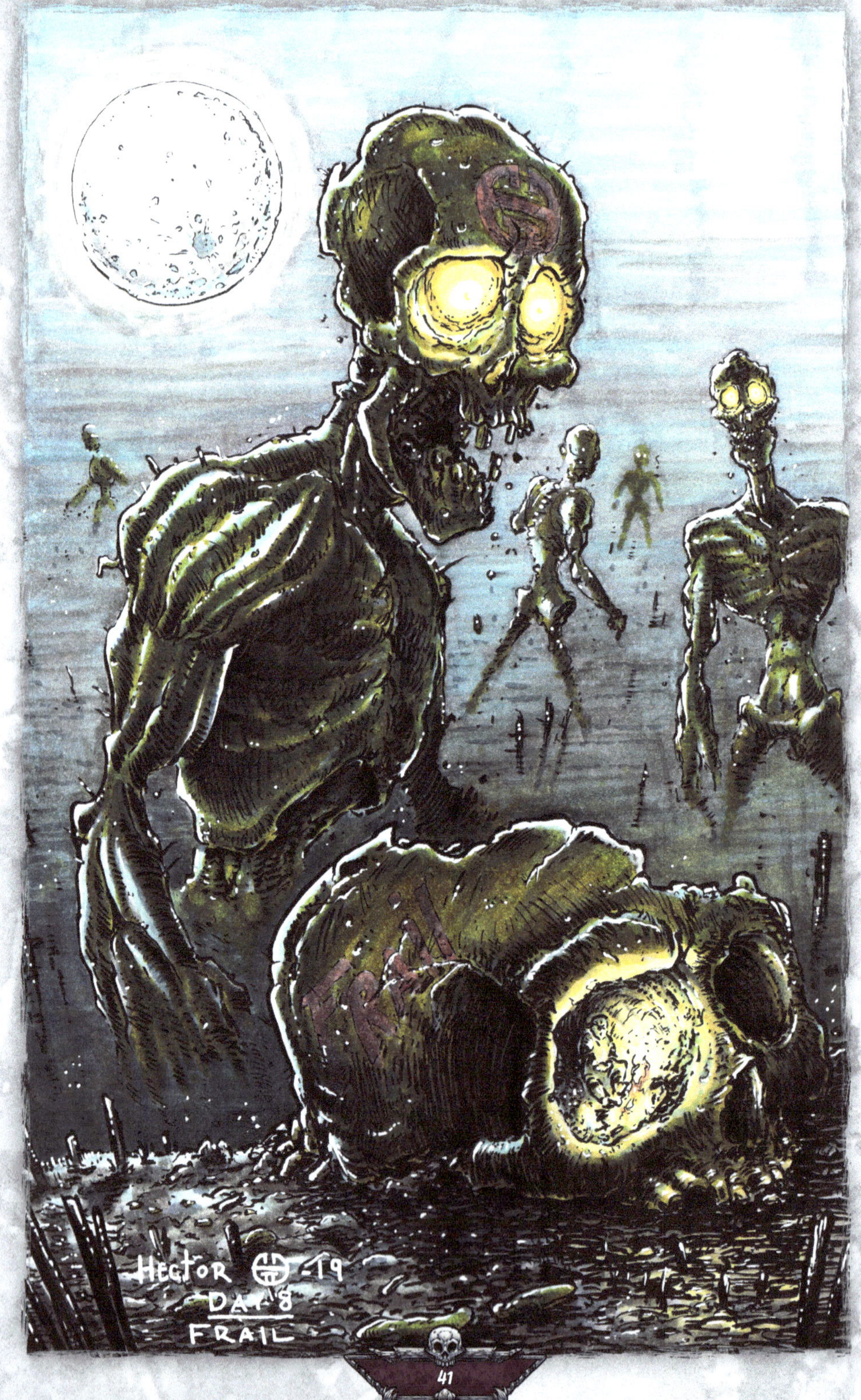

- DAY 9 -
SWING

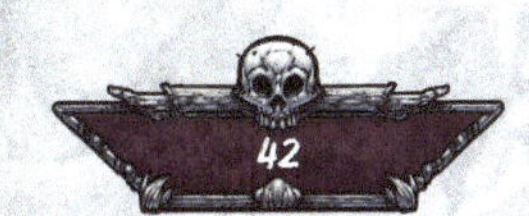

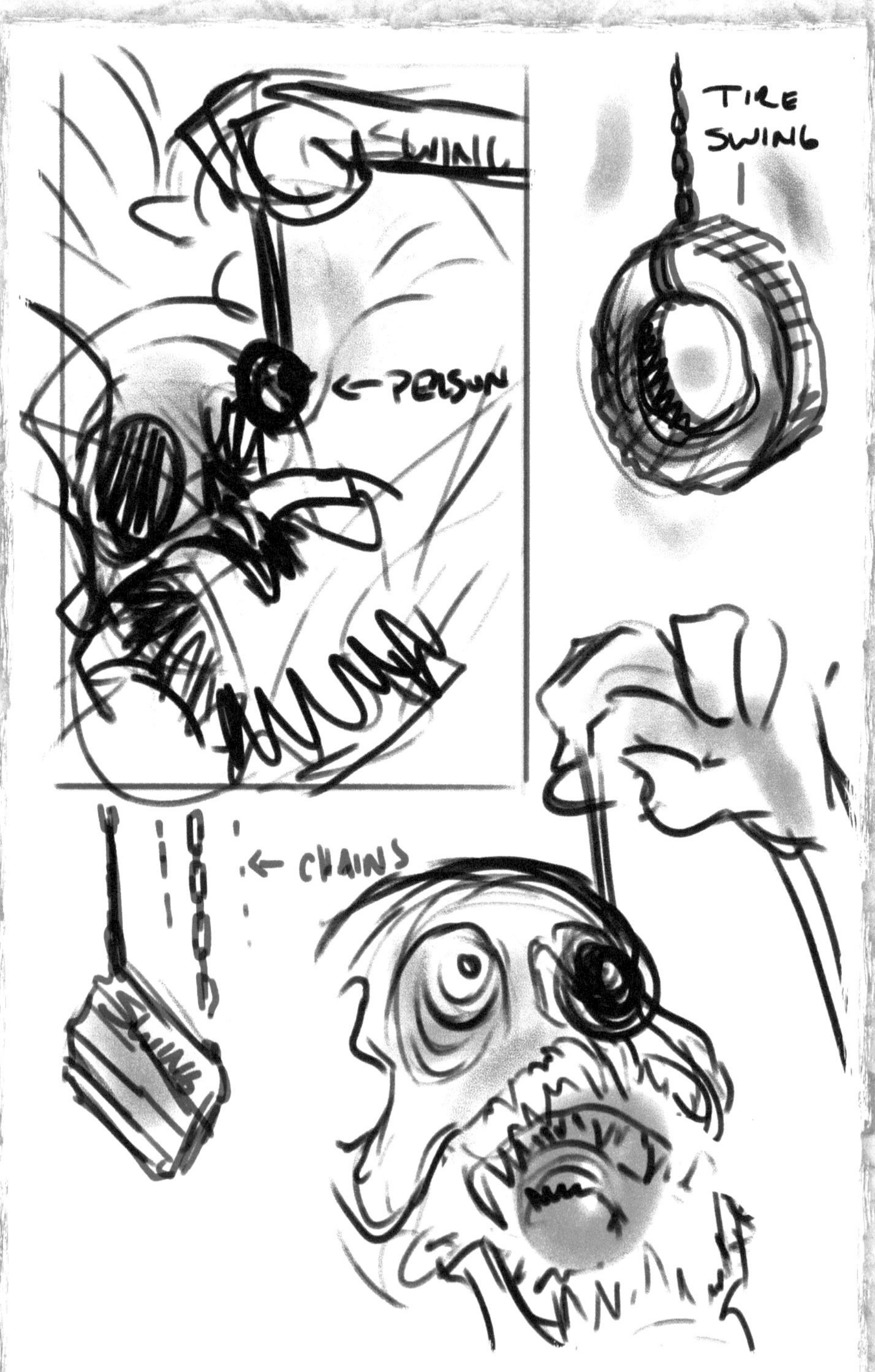

D9 – SWING

ROUGH SKETCHES

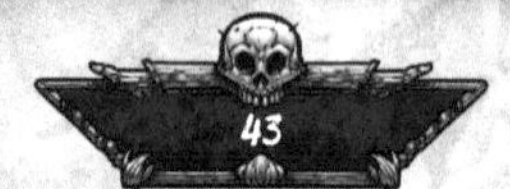

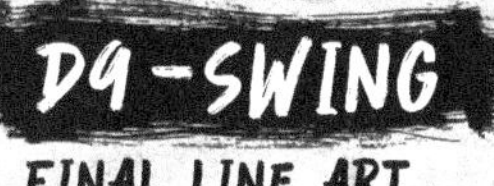

FINAL LINE ART

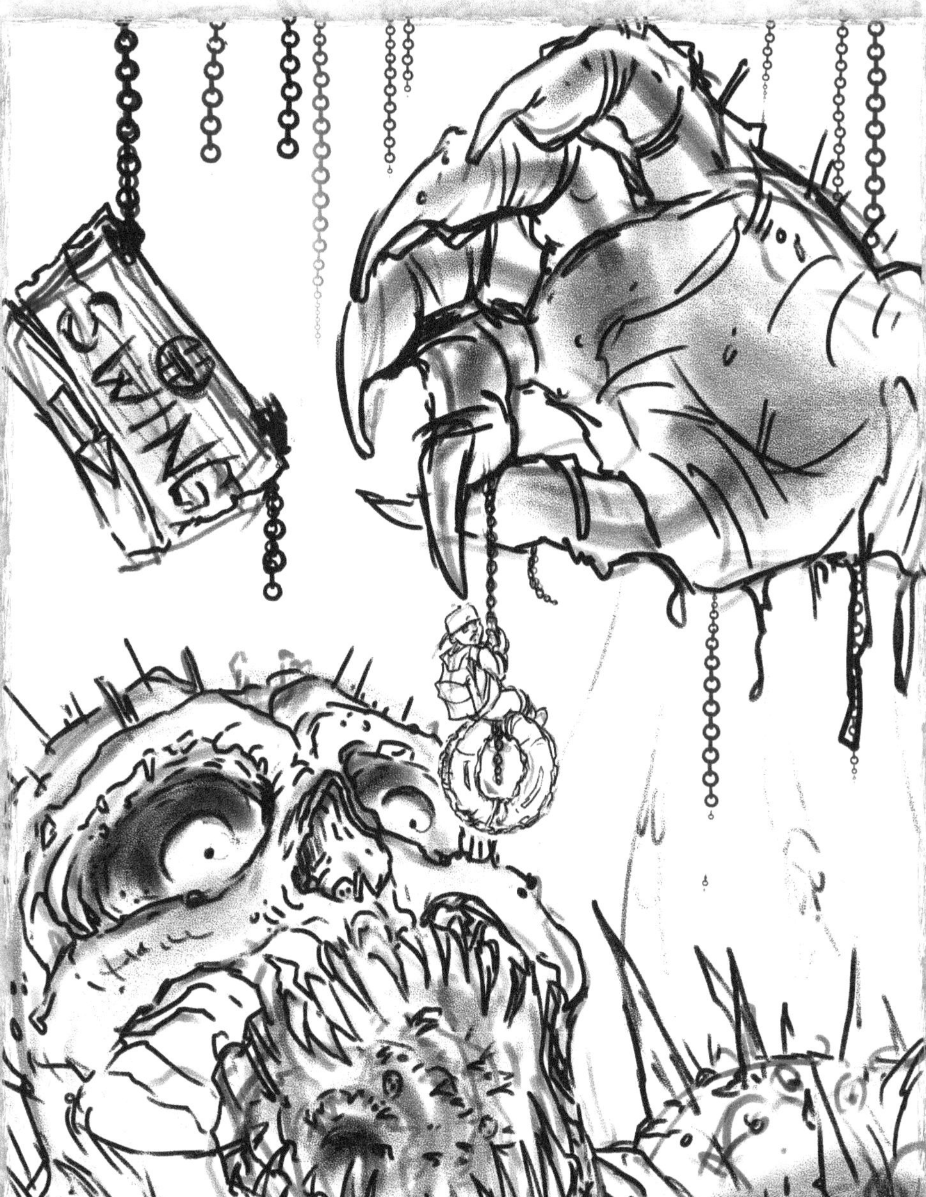

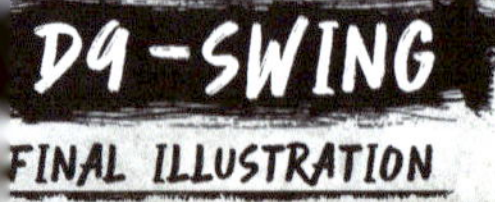

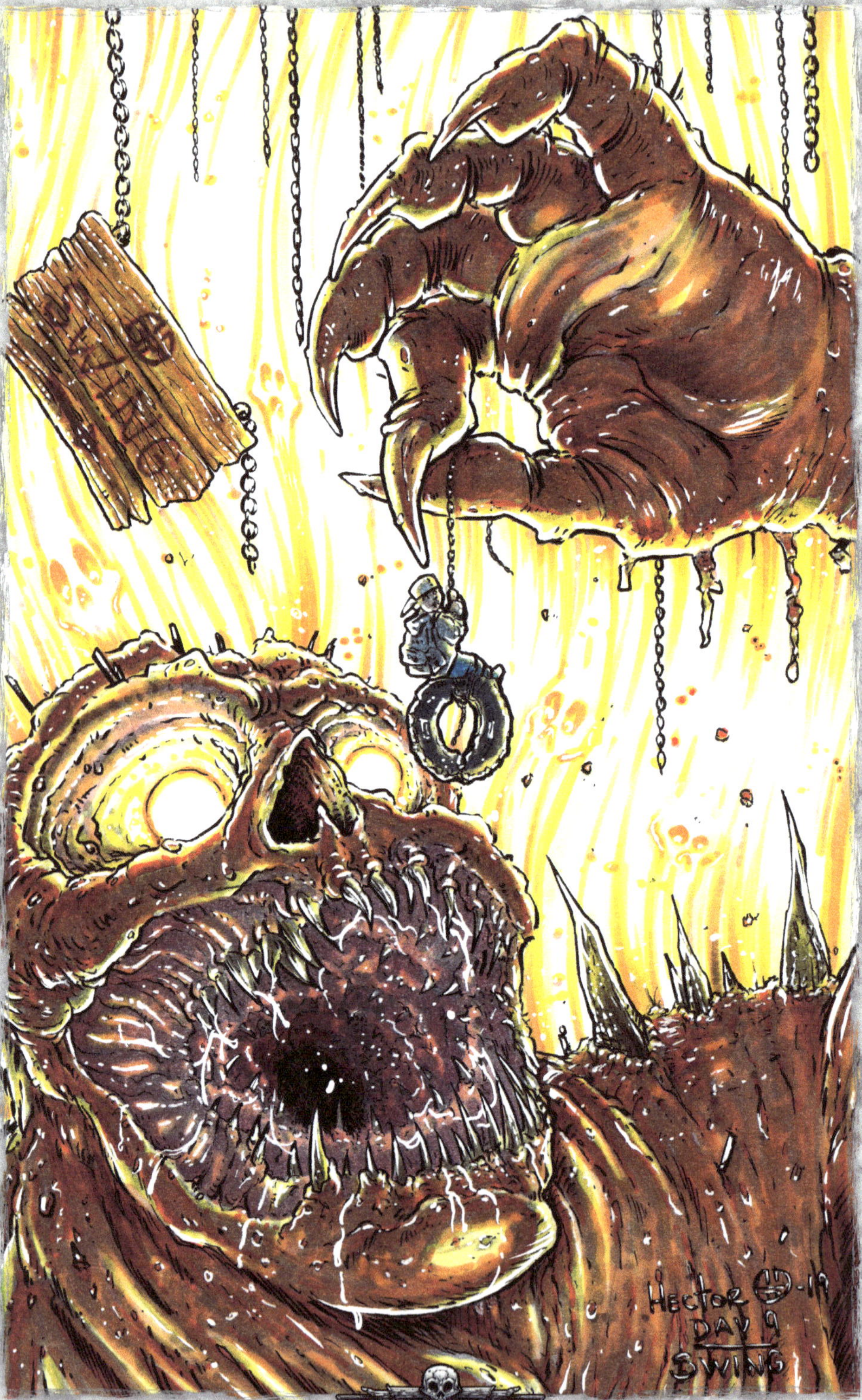

FINAL ILLUSTRATION

- DAY 10 -

PATTERN

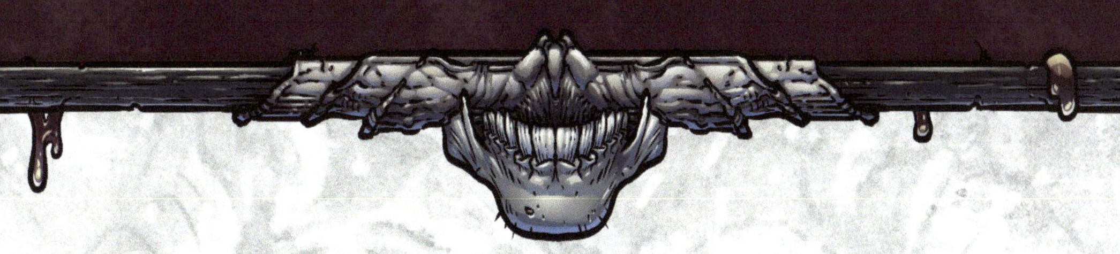

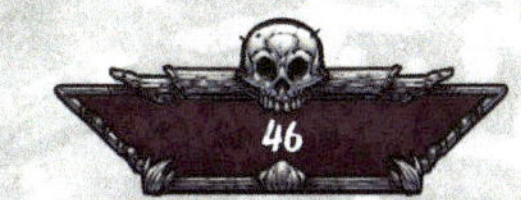

D10 - PATTERN

ROUGH SKETCHES

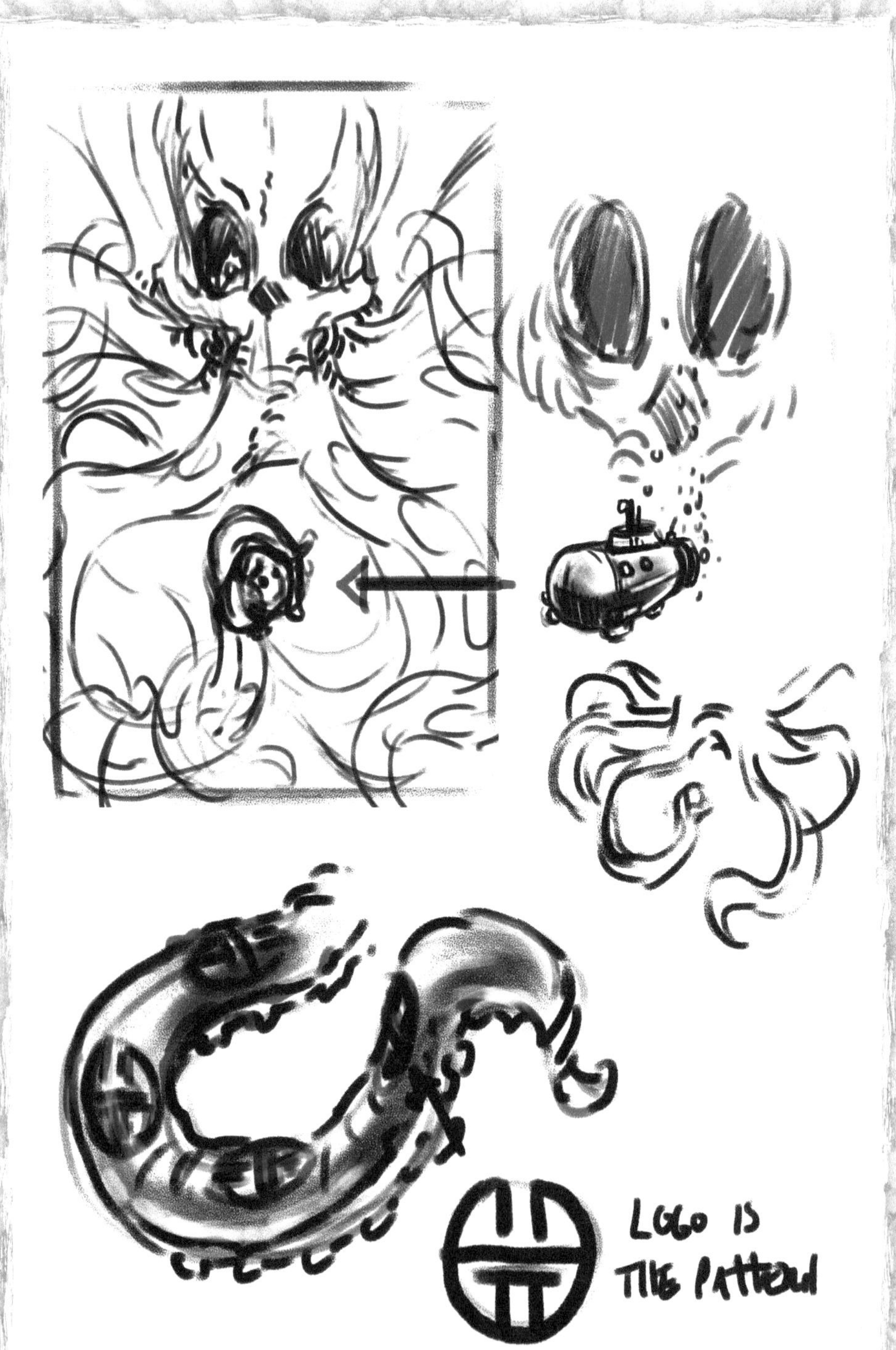

LOGO IS THE PATTERN

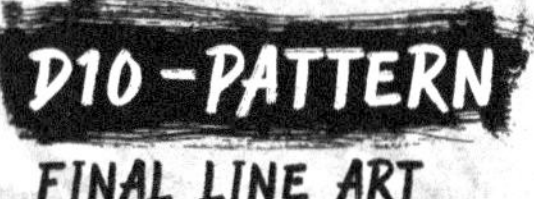
D10 - PATTERN
FINAL LINE ART

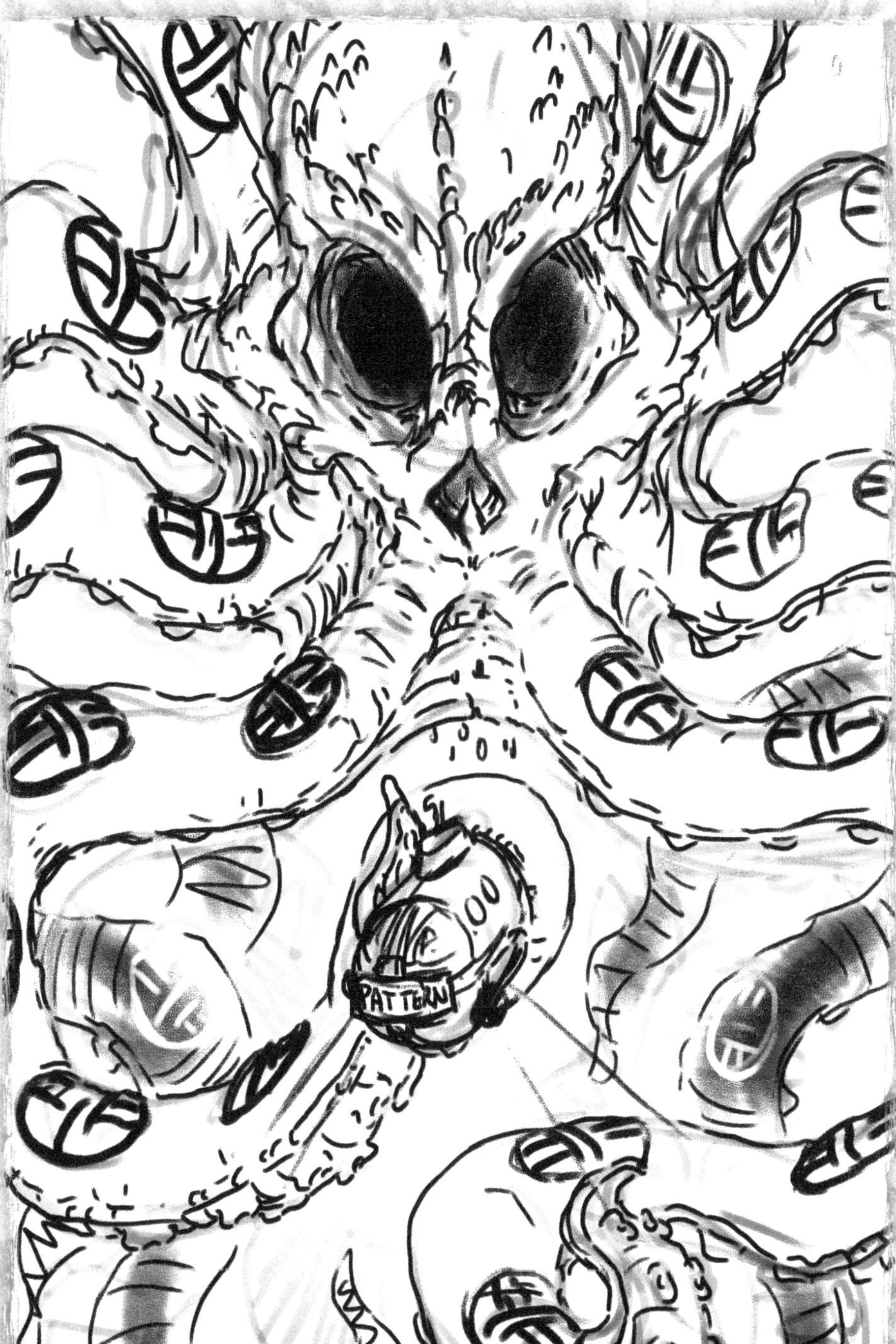

D10 - PATTERN

FINAL ILLUSTRATION

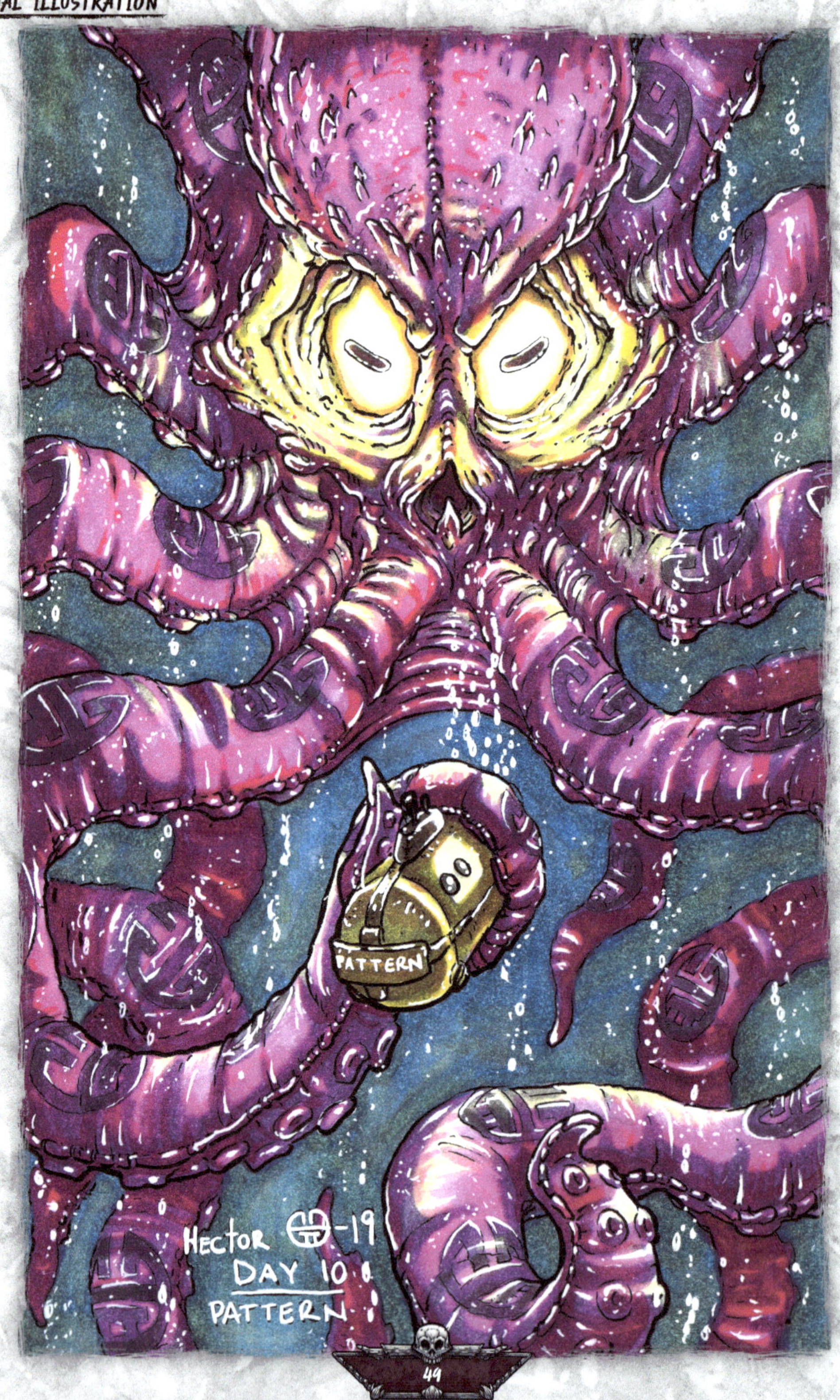

– DAY 11 –
SNOW

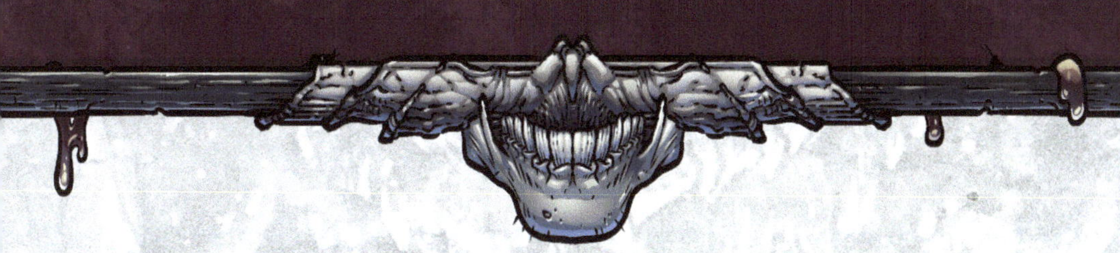

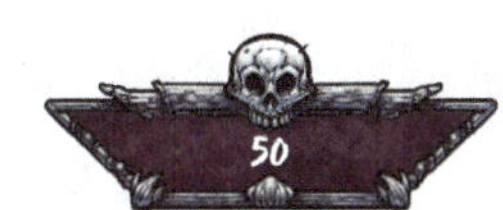

TOP HAT

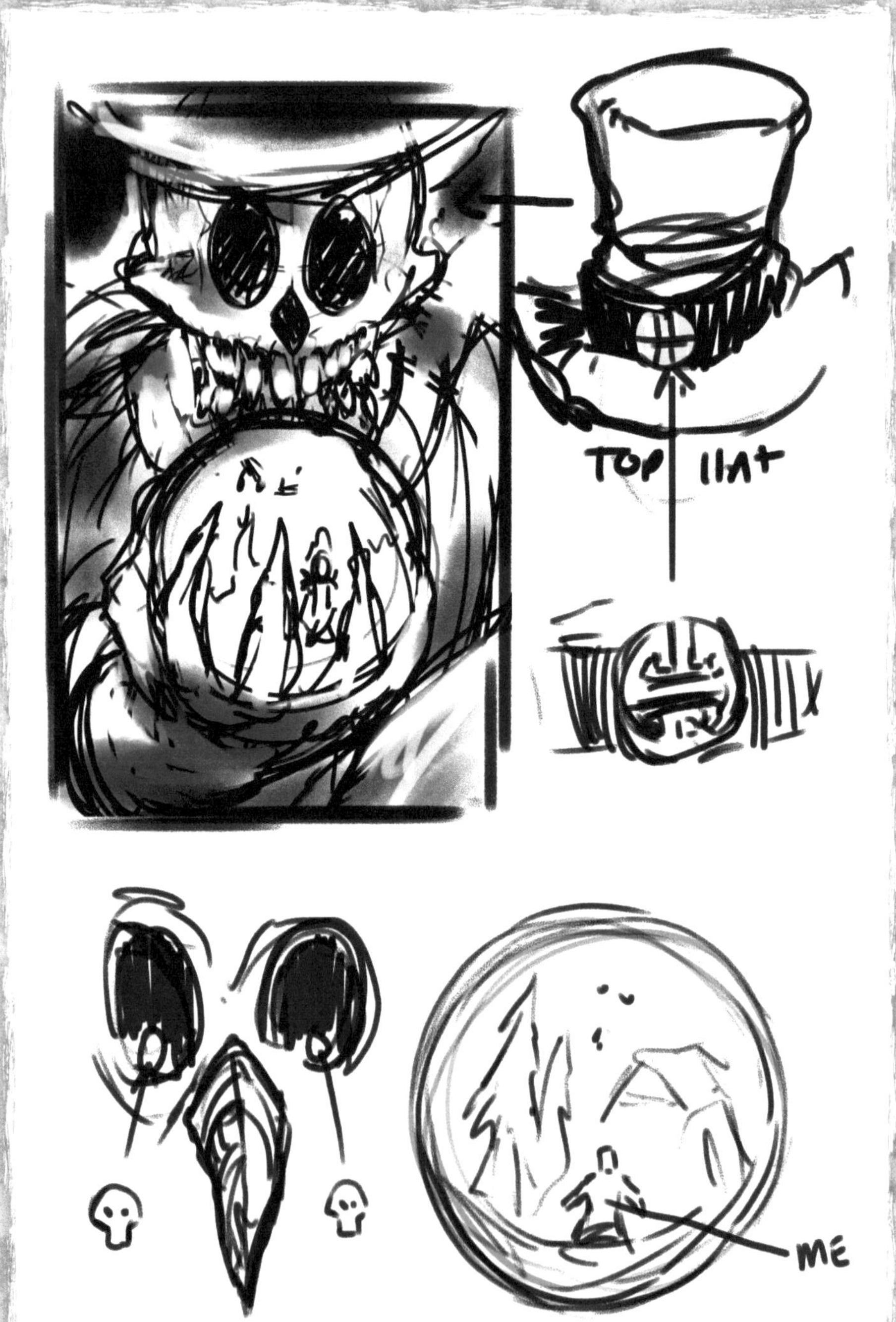

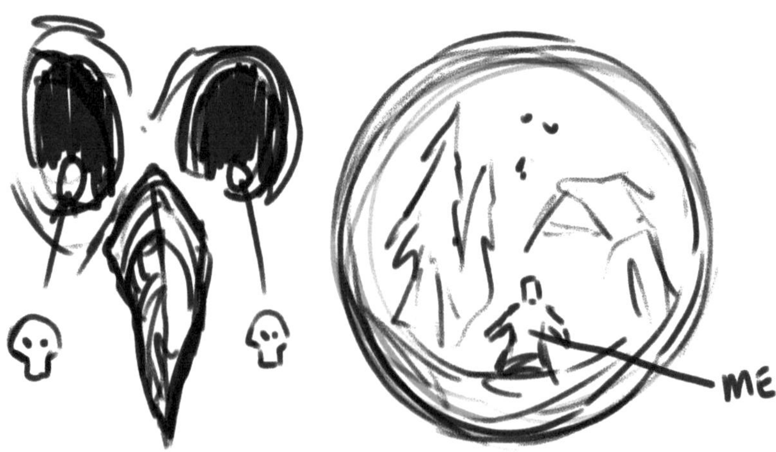

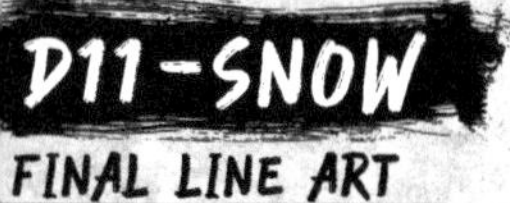

FINAL LINE ART

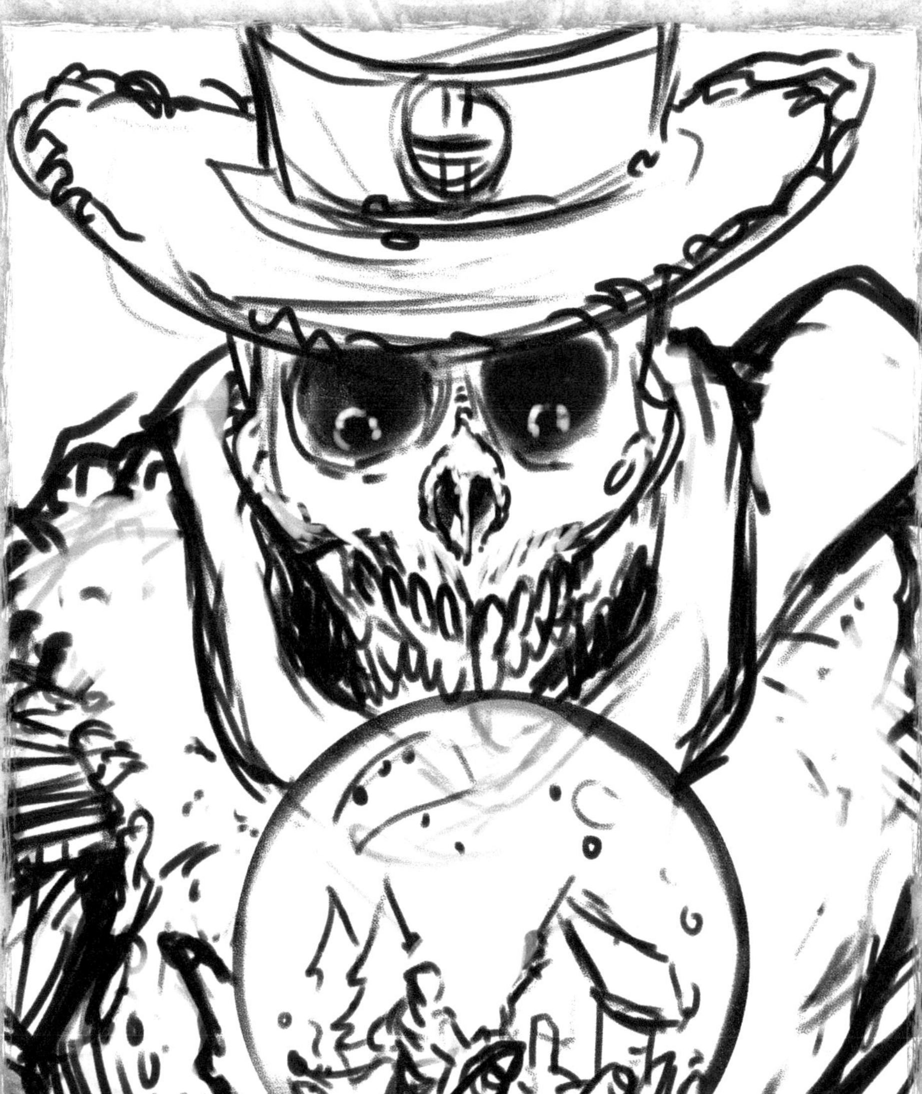

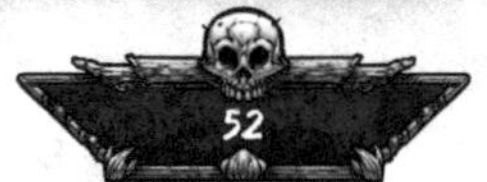

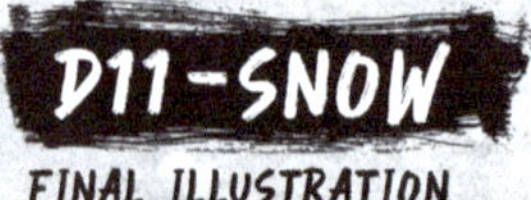

FINAL ILLUSTRATION

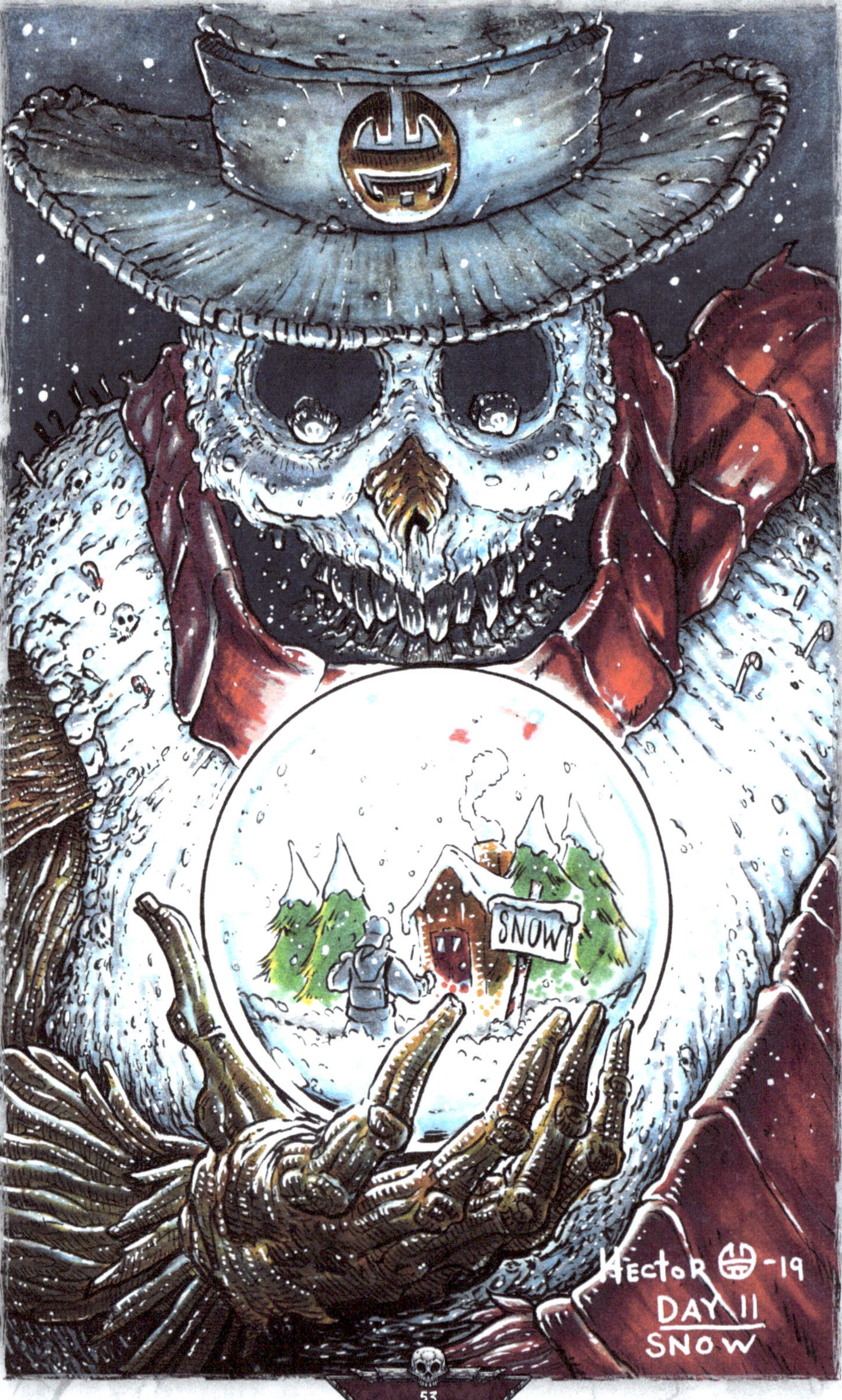

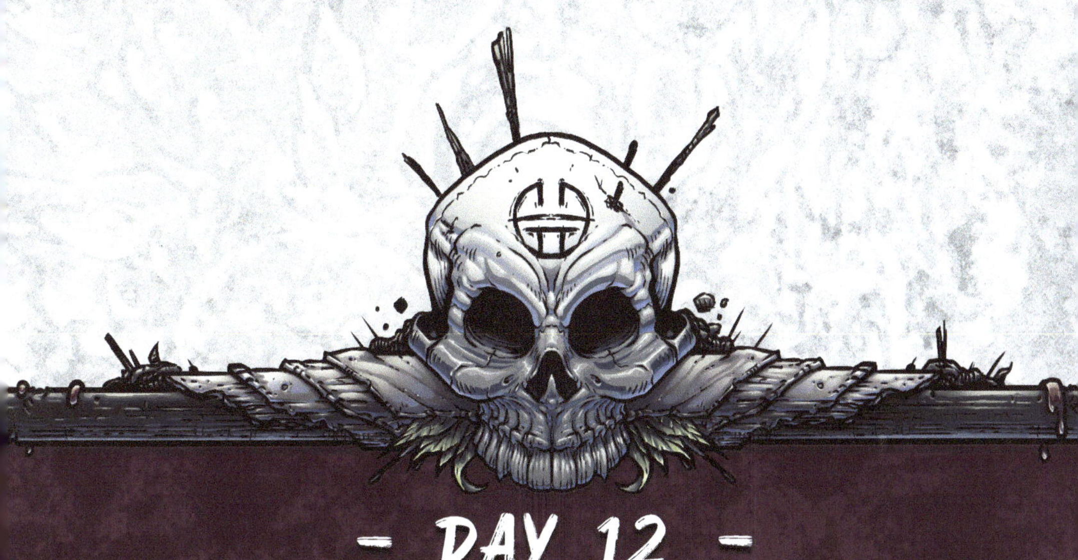

- DAY 12 -
DRAGON

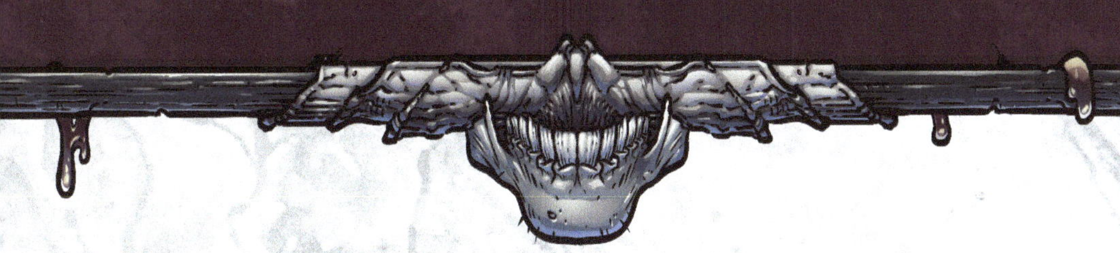

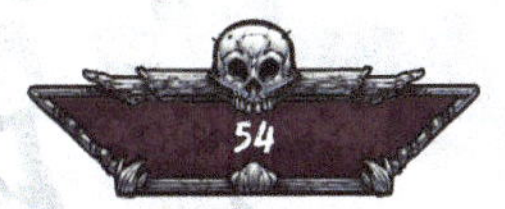

D12 - DRAGON

ROUGH SKETCHES

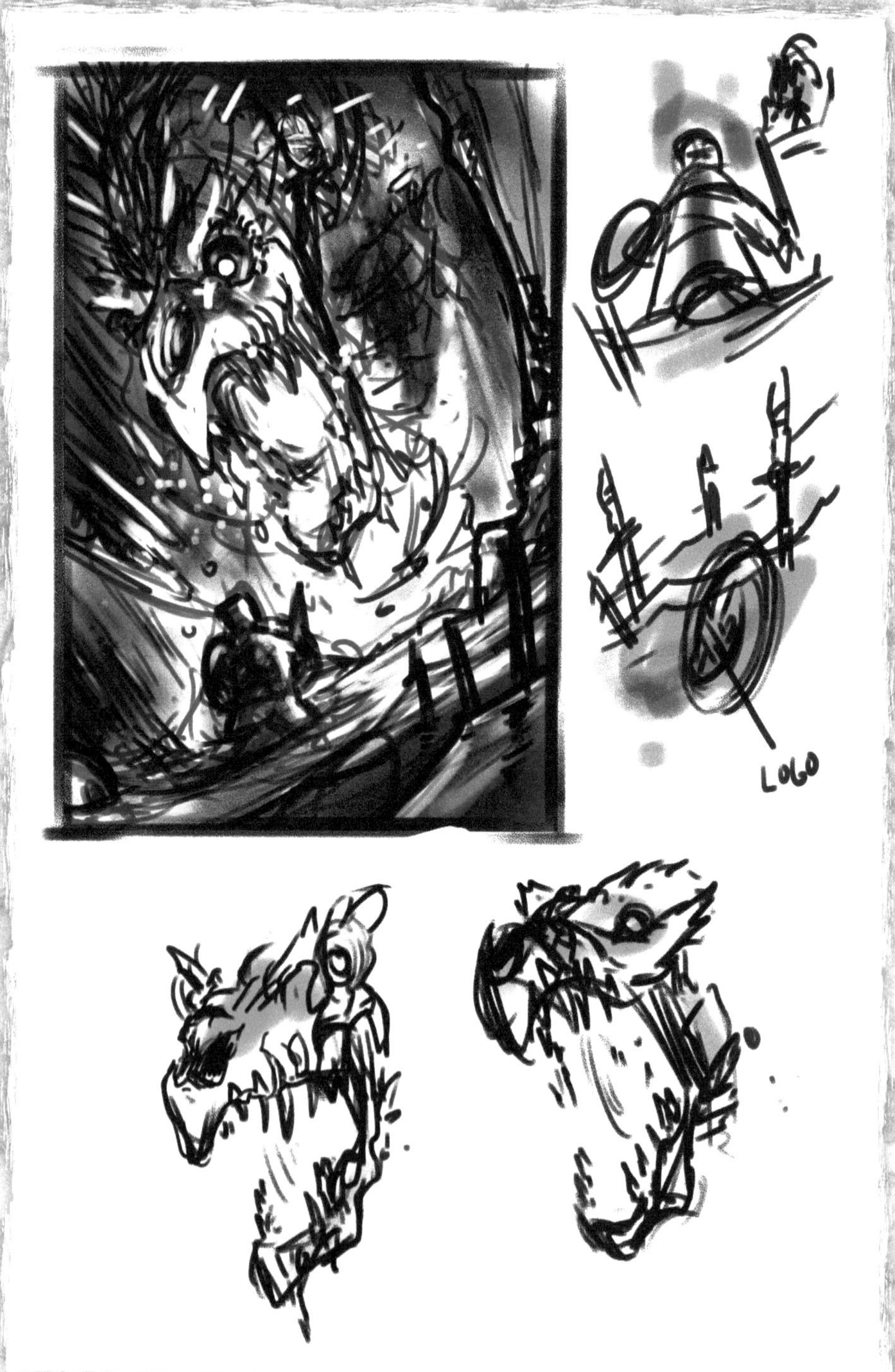

LOGO

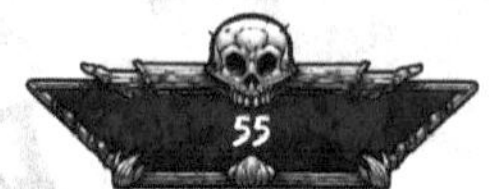

D12 - DRAGON

ROUGH SKETCHES

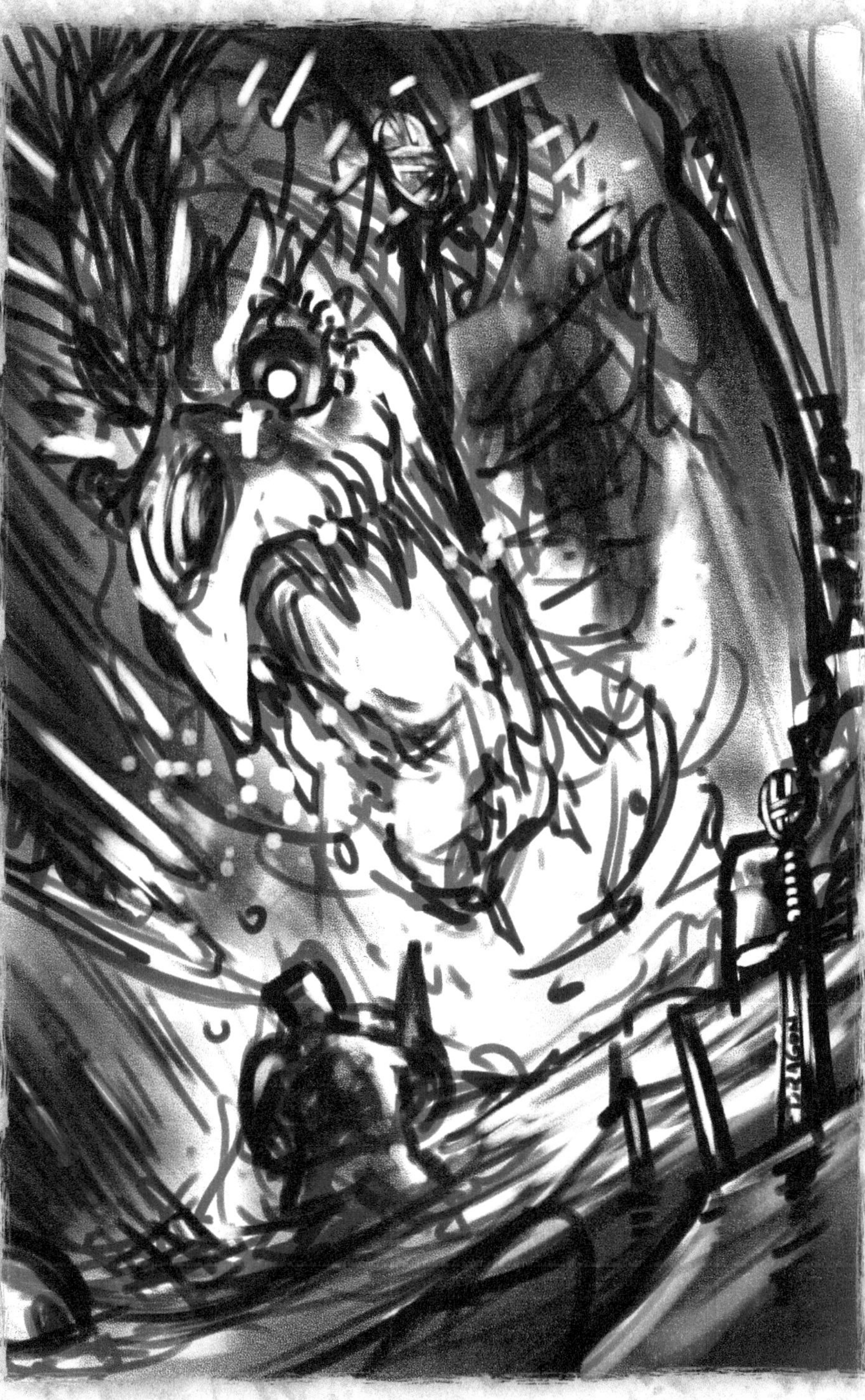

D12-DRAGON

FINAL LINE ART

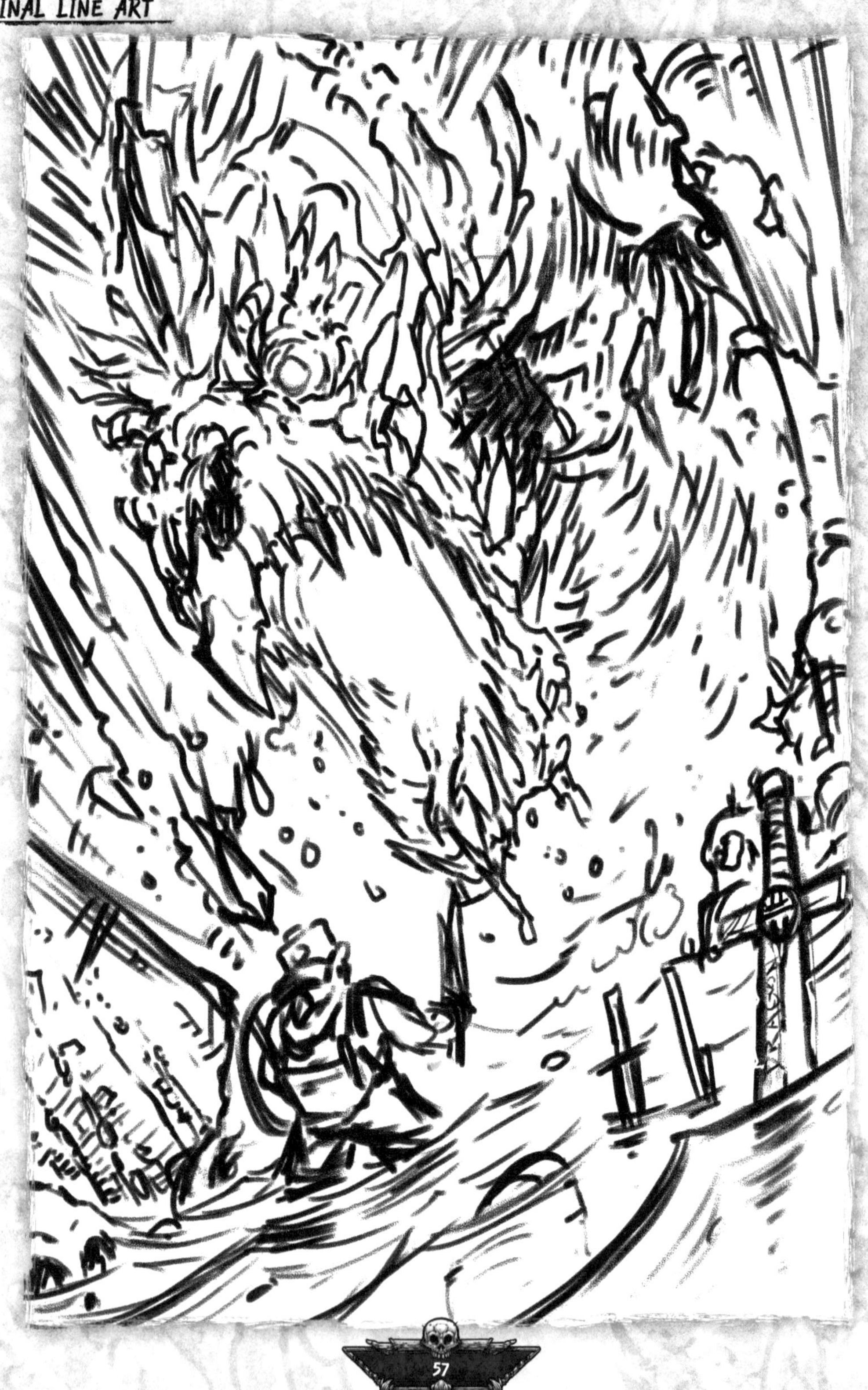

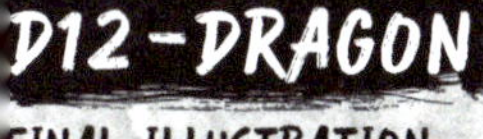

FINAL ILLUSTRATION

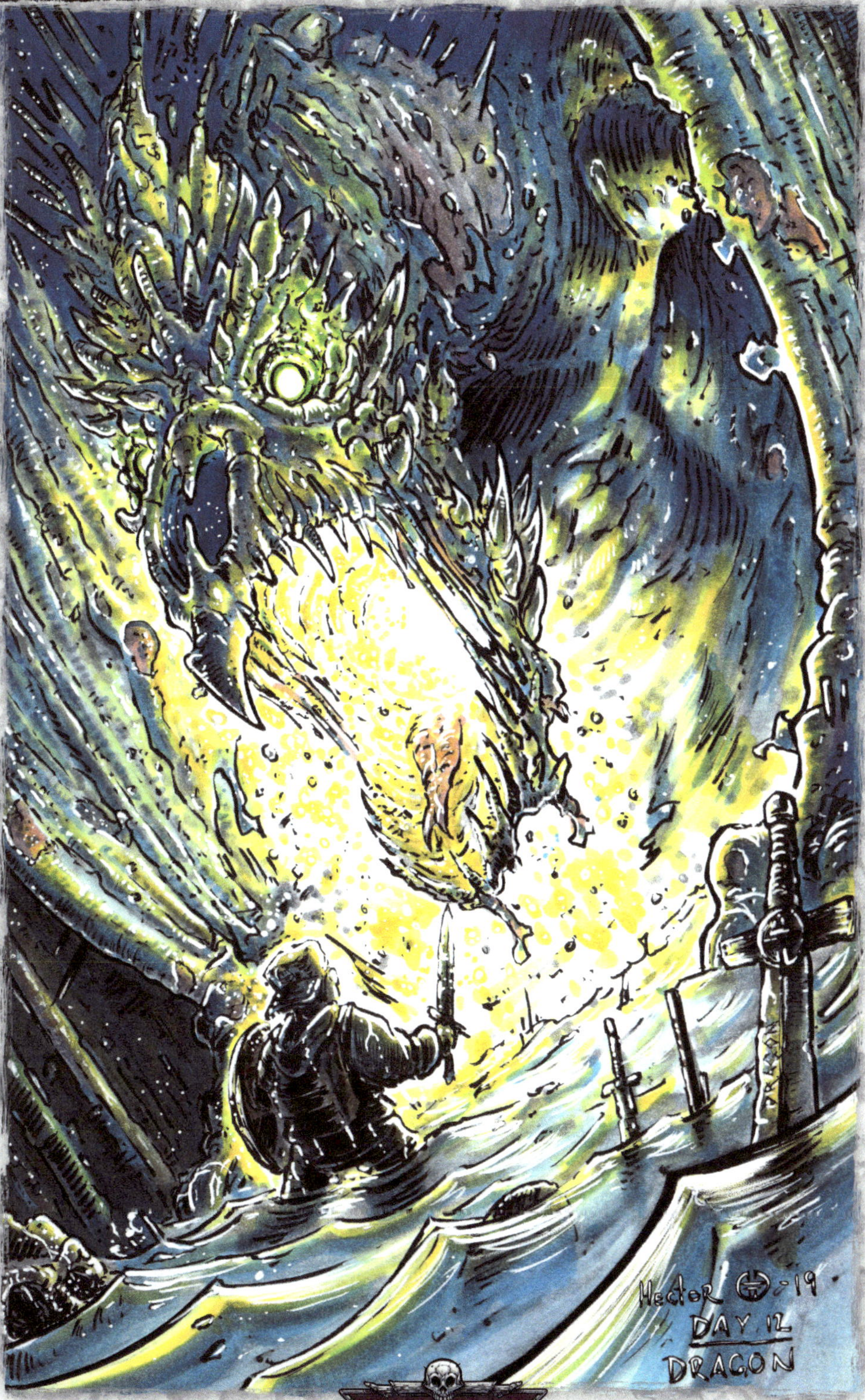

- DAY 13 -
ASH

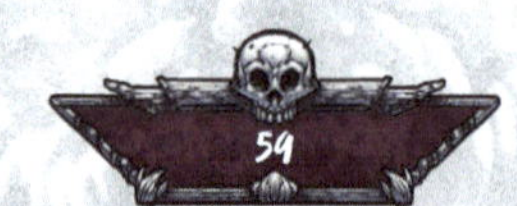

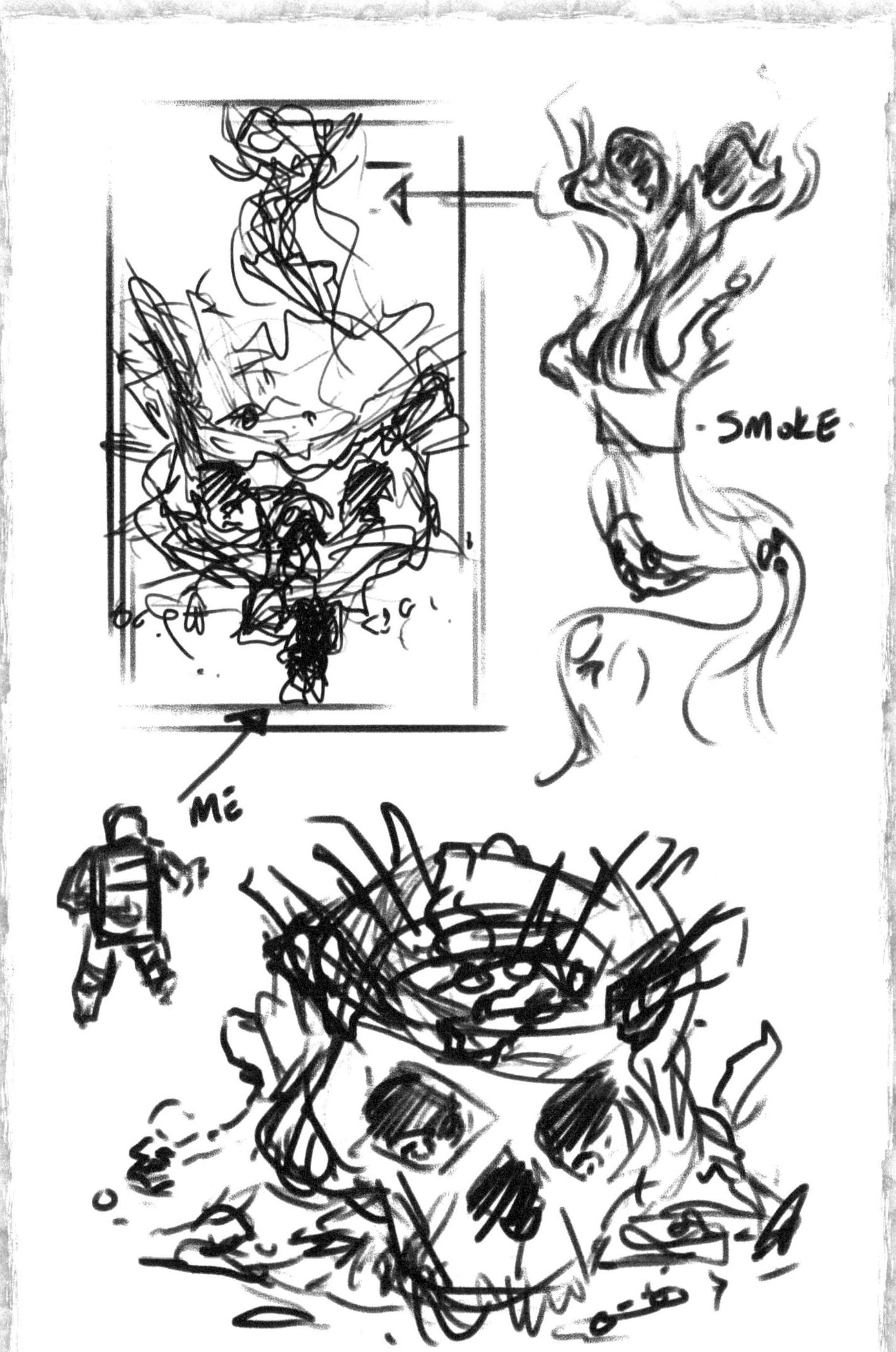

D13-ASH

ROUGH SKETCHES

SMOKE

ME

D13-ASH

FINAL LINE ART

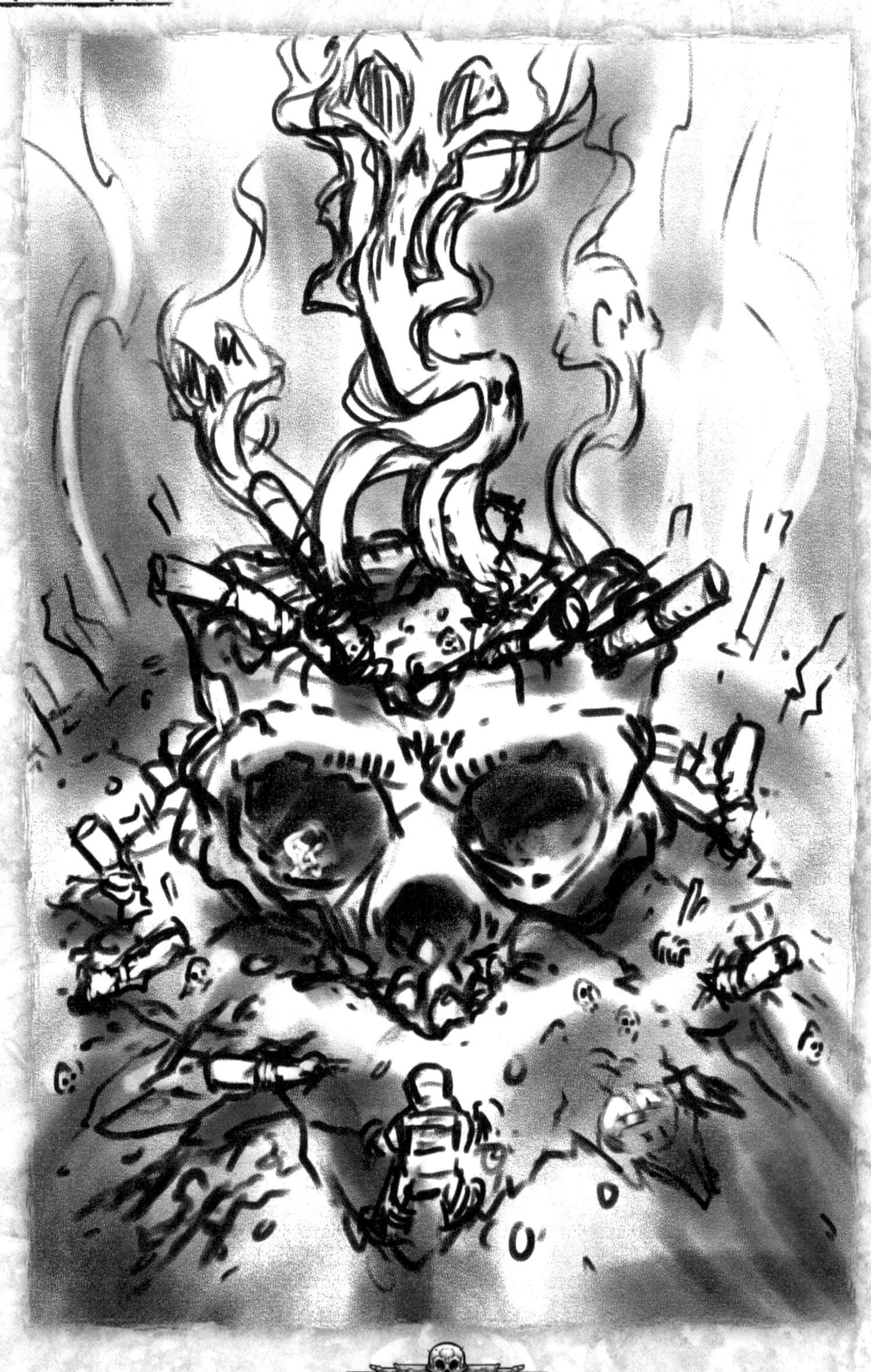

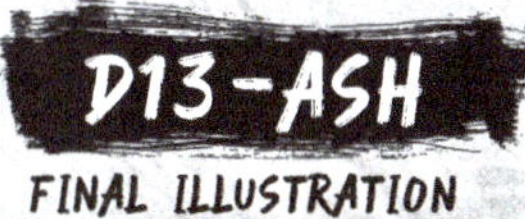

FINAL ILLUSTRATION

Hector -19
DAY 13
ASH

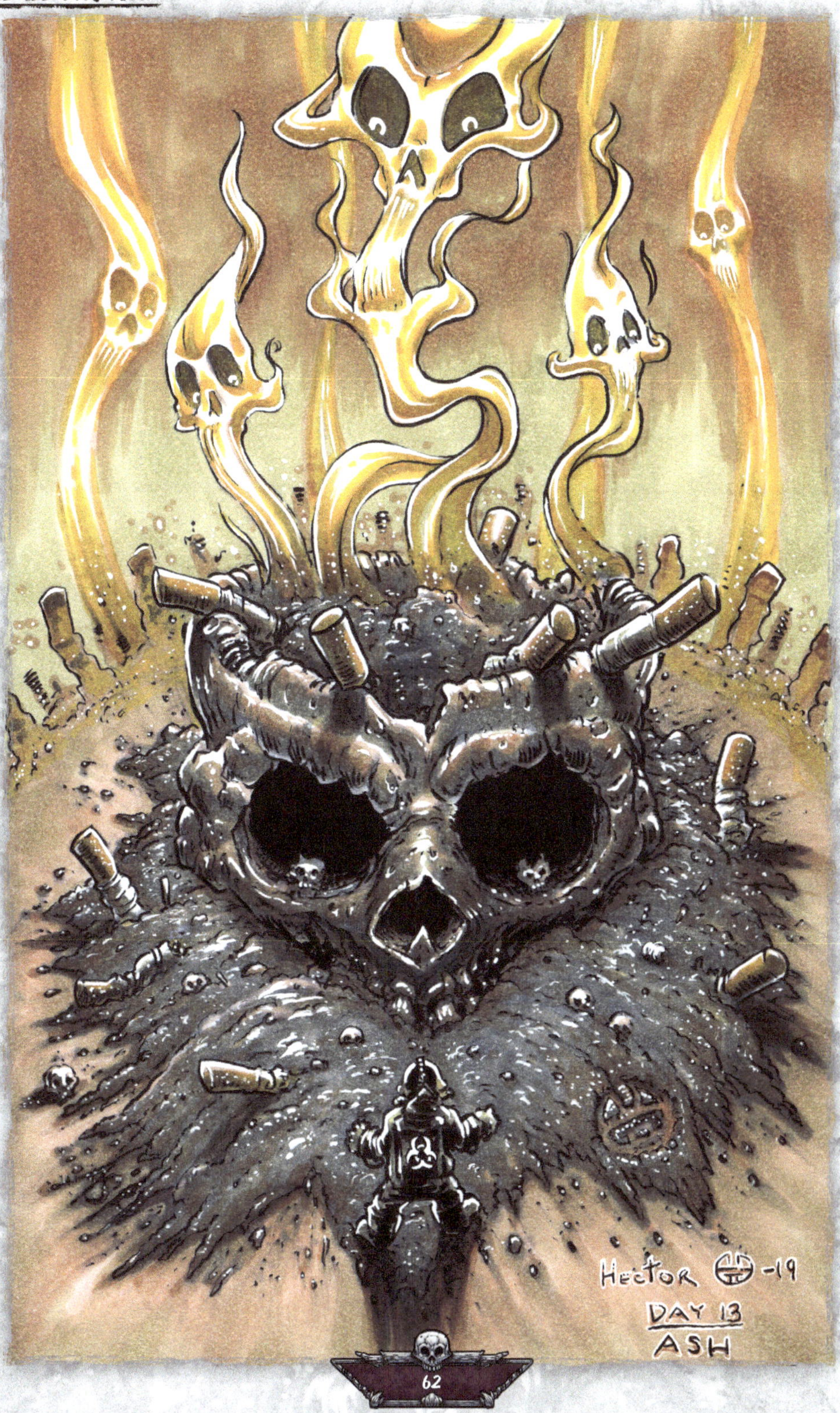

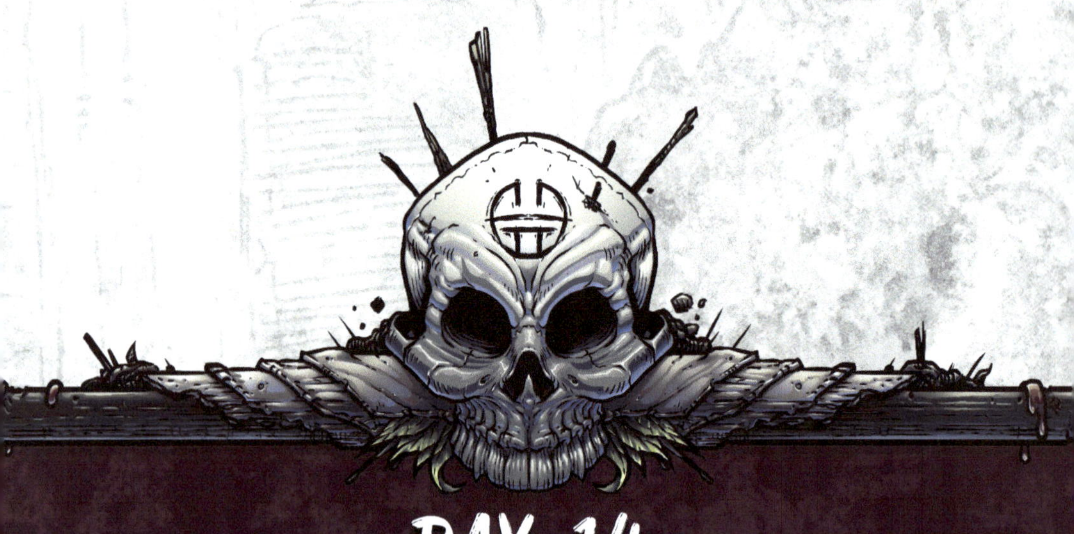

- DAY 14 -
OVERGROWN

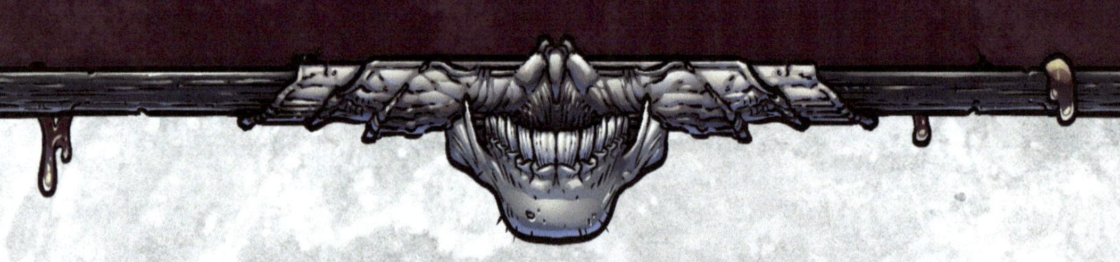

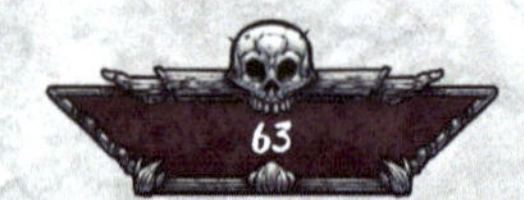

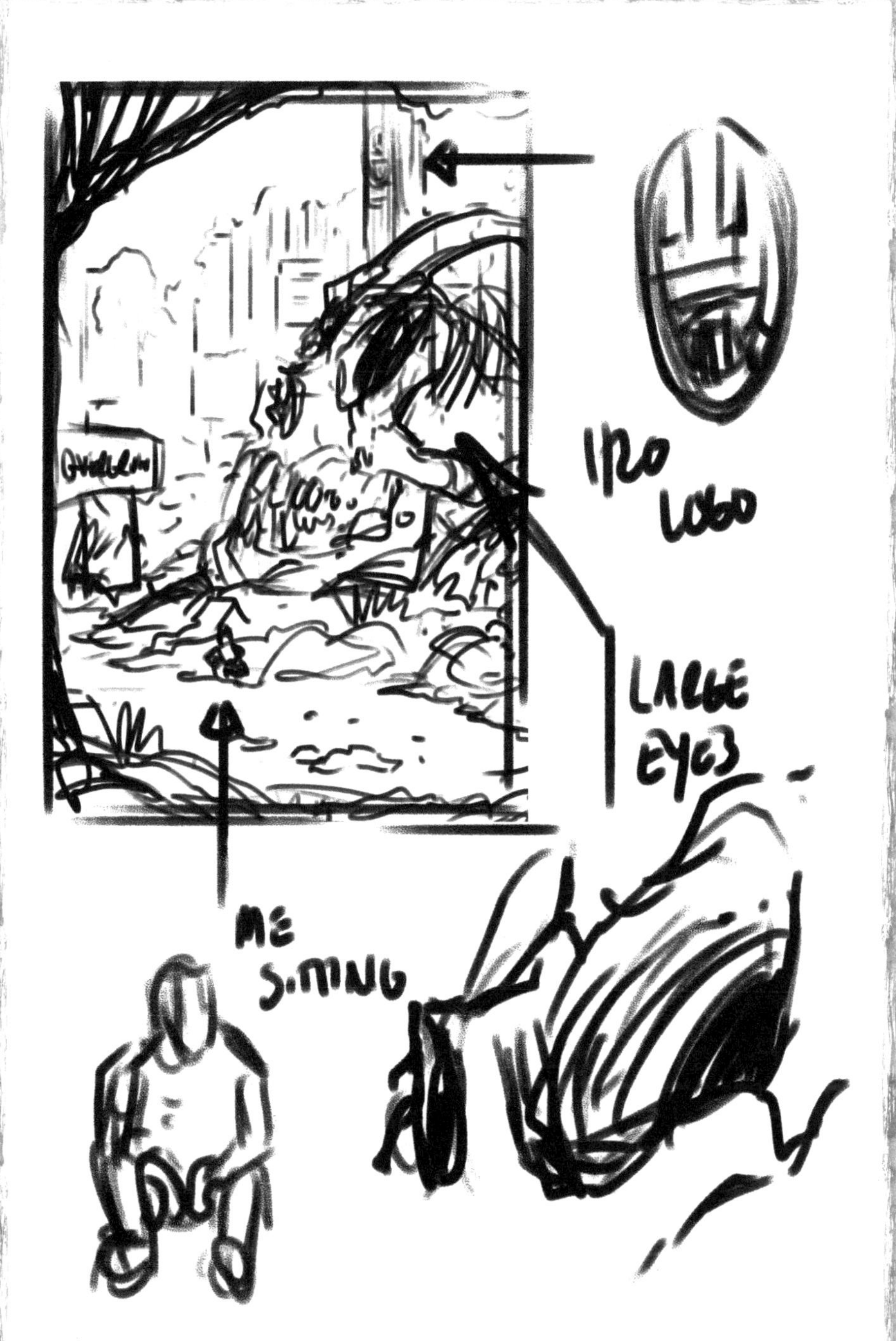

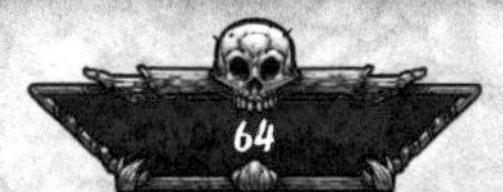

D14 - OVERGROWN

FINAL LINE ART

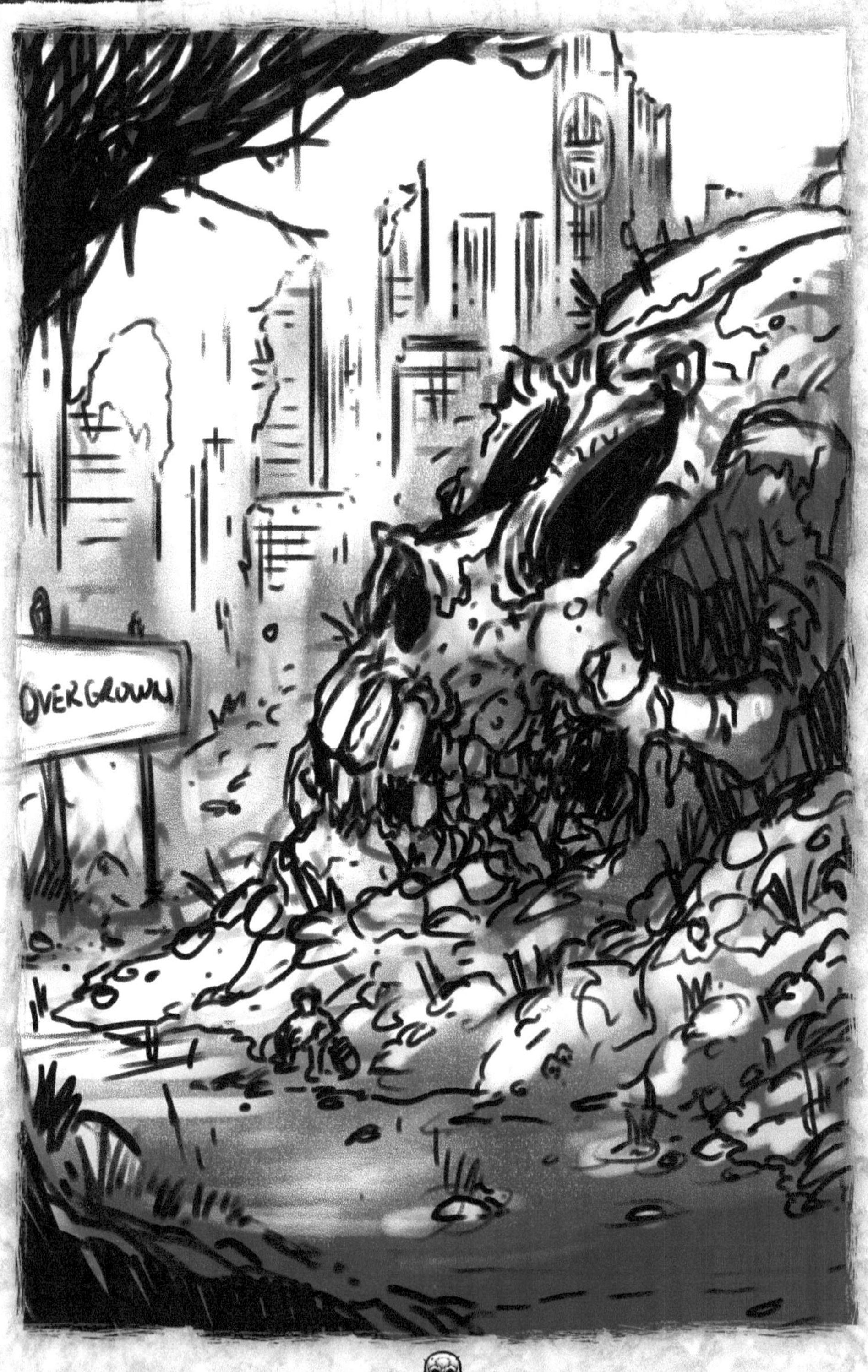

D14 – OVERGROWN

FINAL ILLUSTRATION

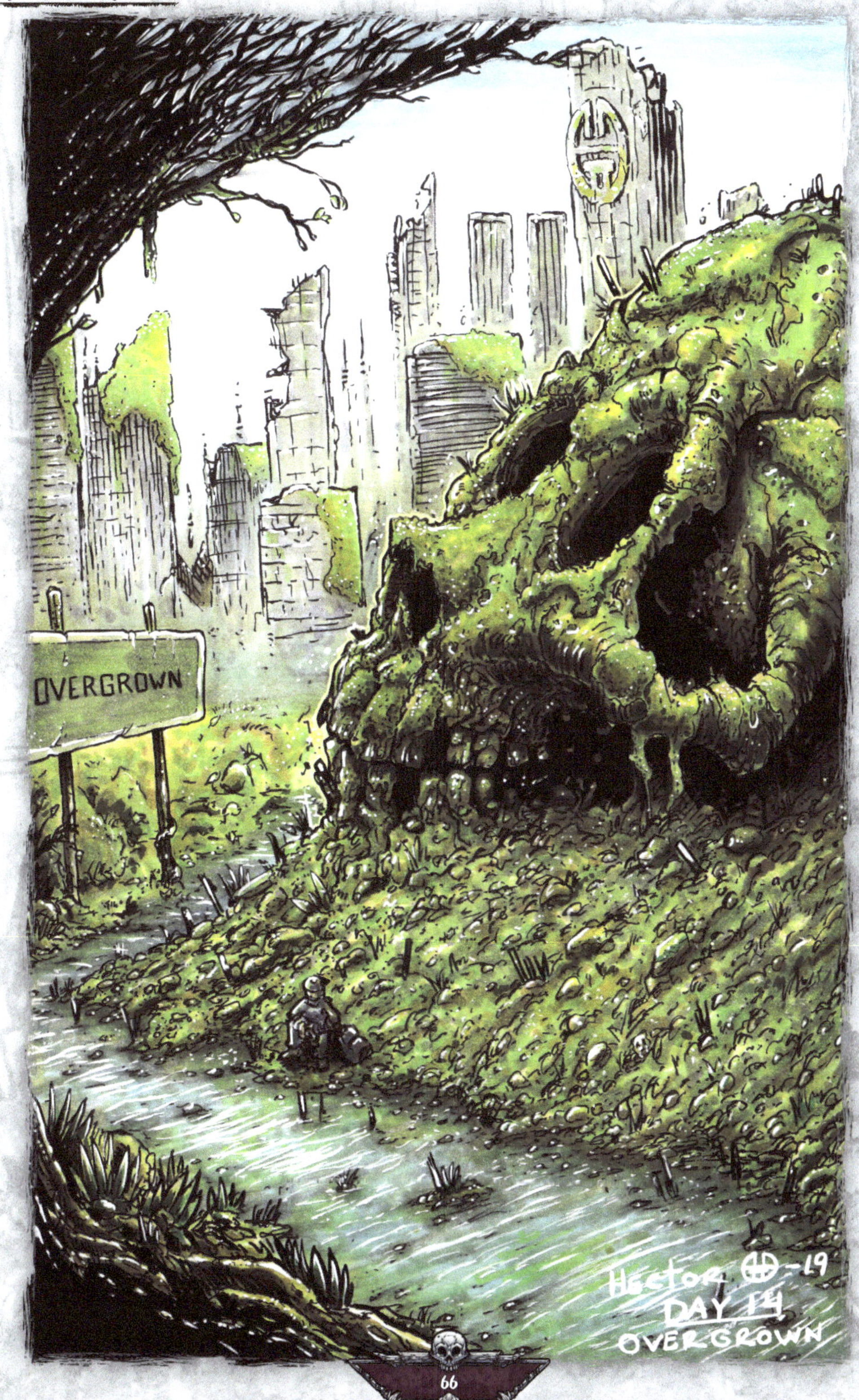

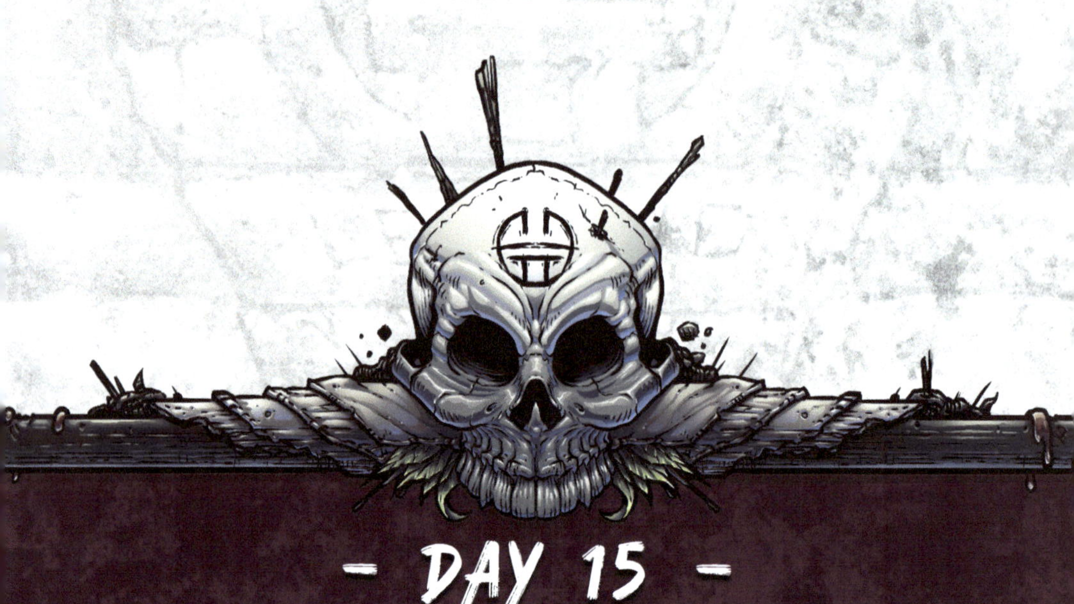

- DAY 15 -

LEGEND

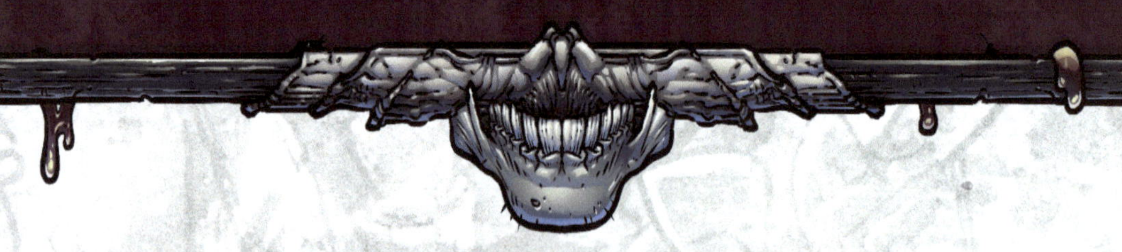

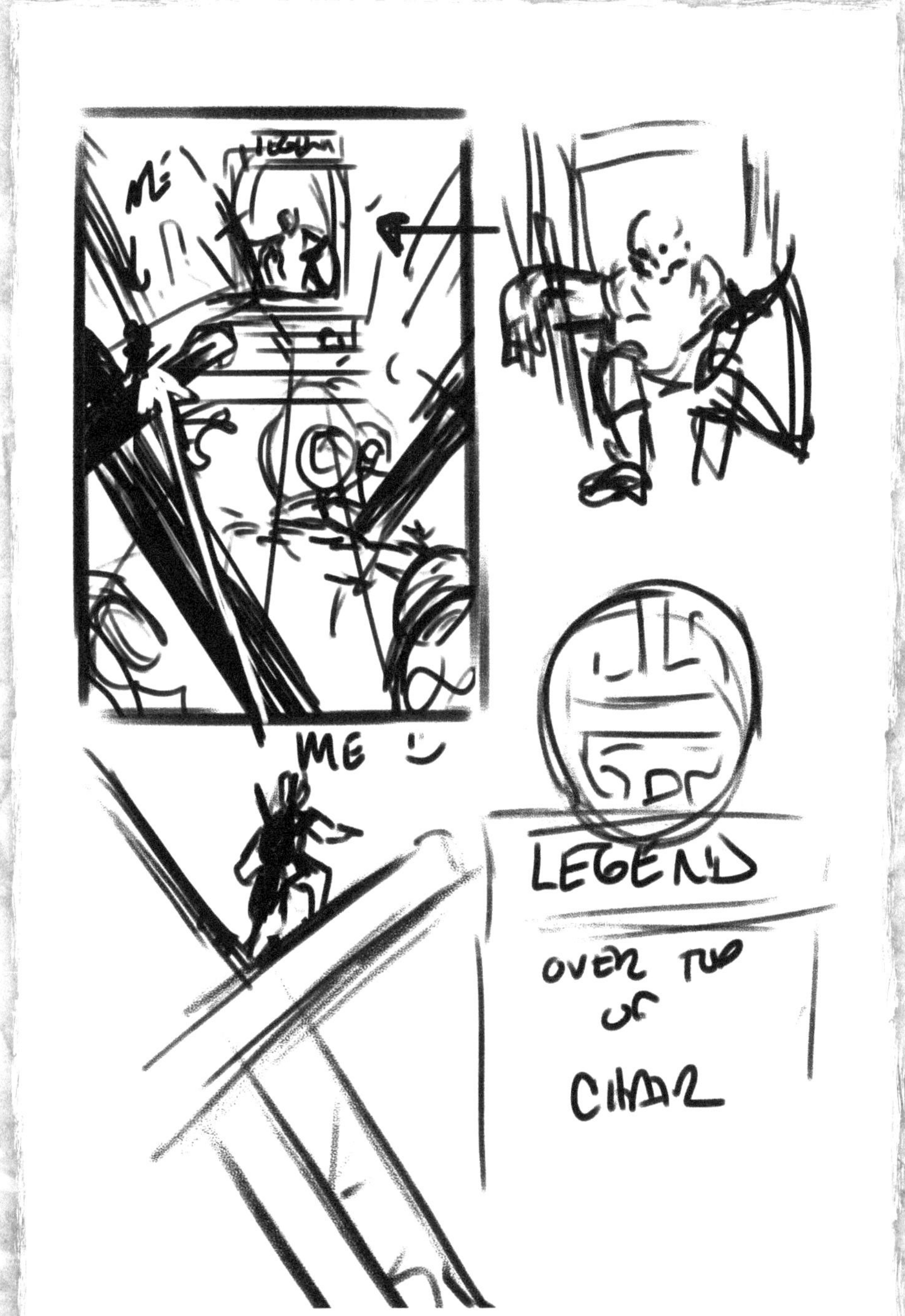

D15 - LEGEND

ROUGH SKETCHES

ME

ME :)

LEGEND

OVER TOP OF CHAIR

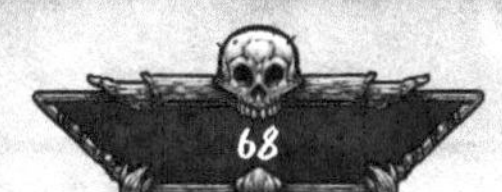

D15 - LEGEND

FINAL LINE ART

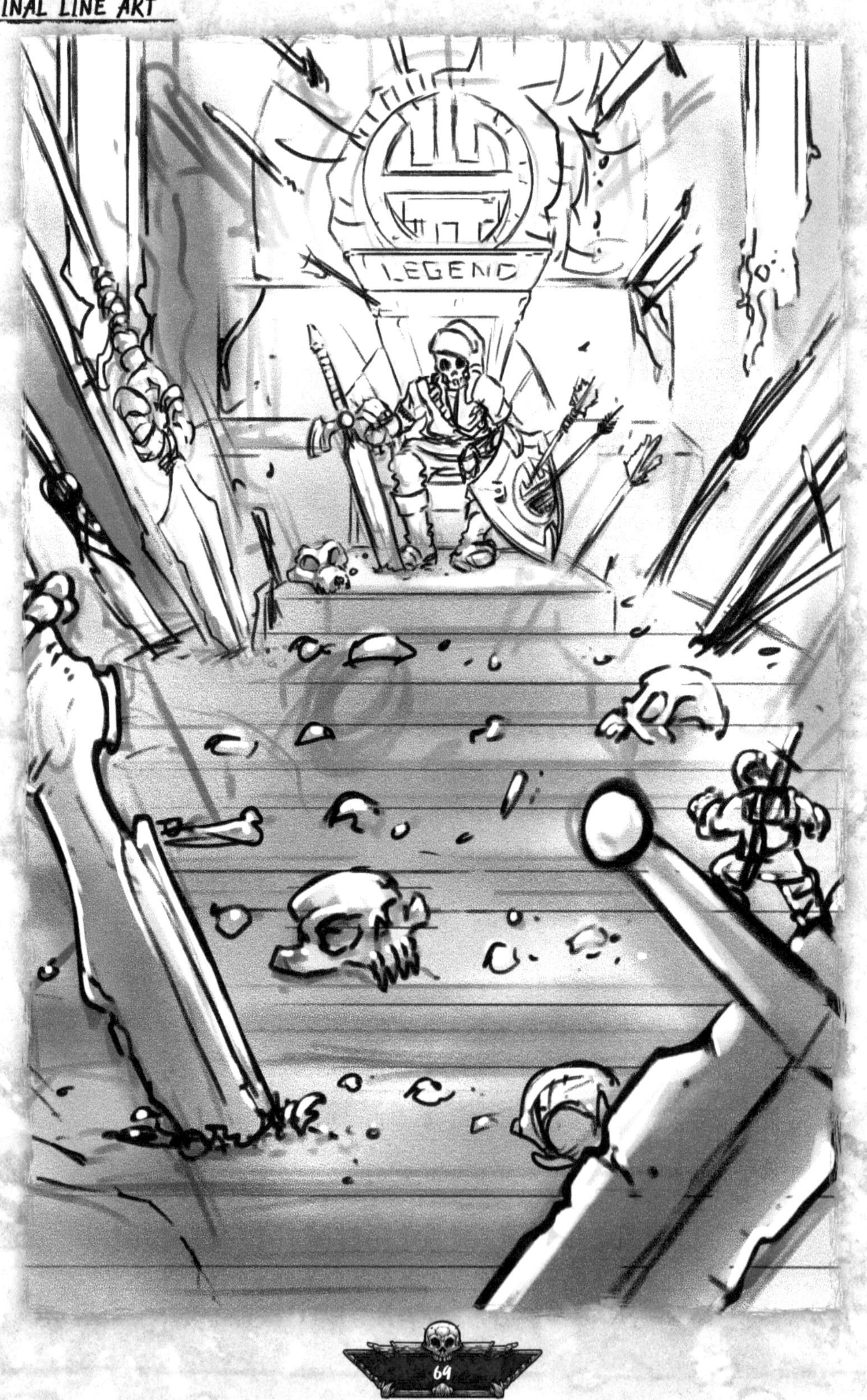

D15 - LEGEND

FINAL ILLUSTRATION

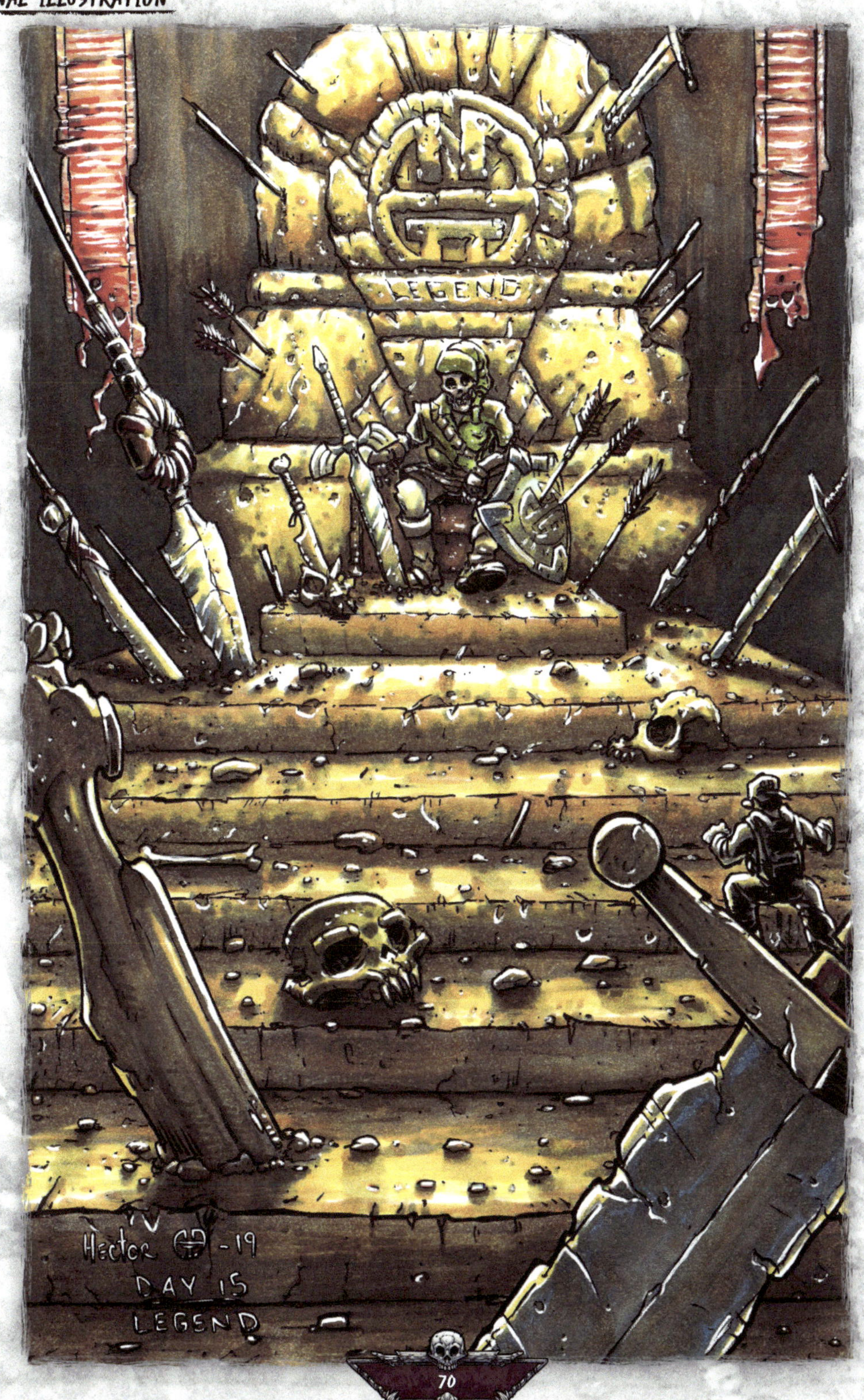

- DAY 16 -
WILD

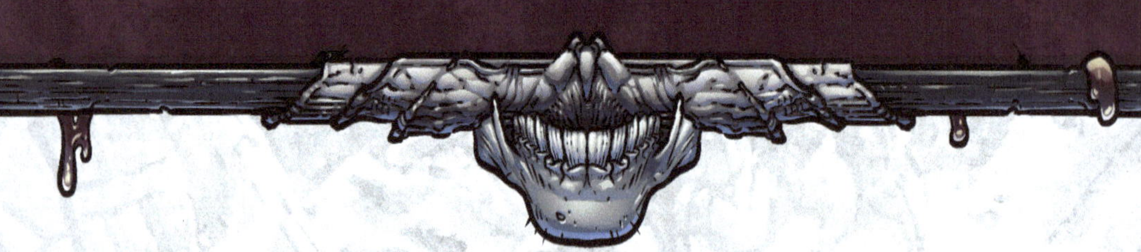

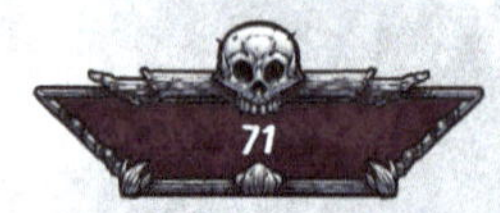

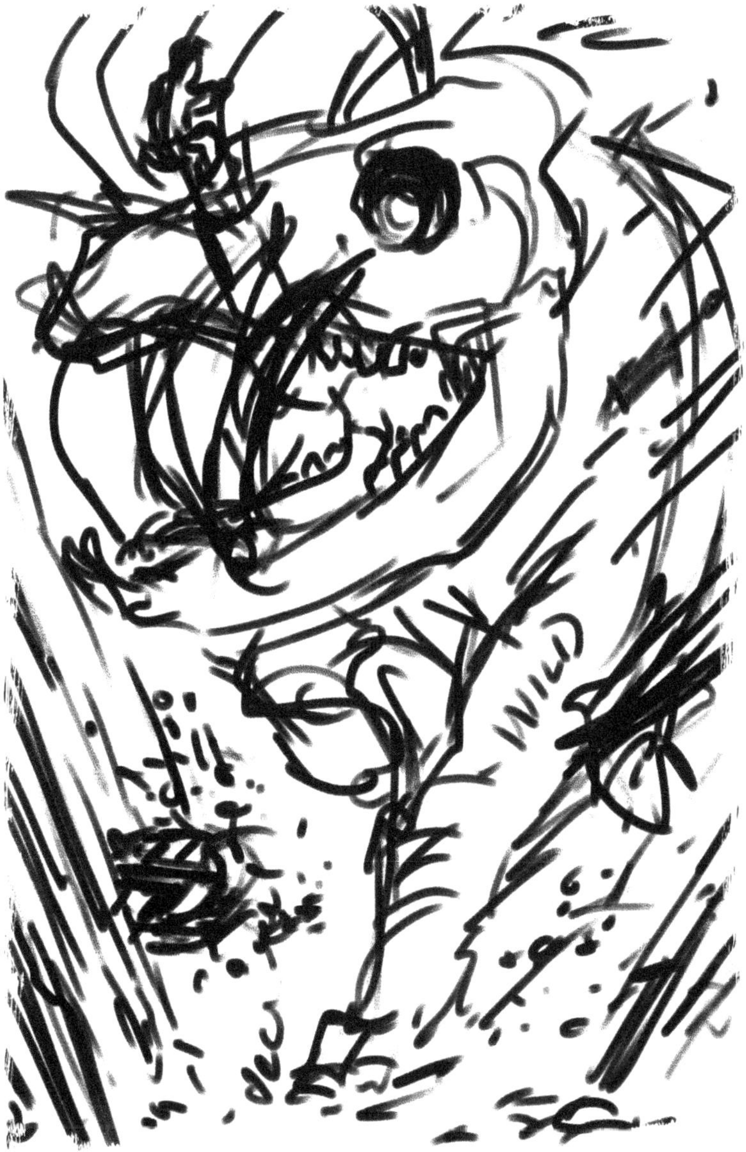

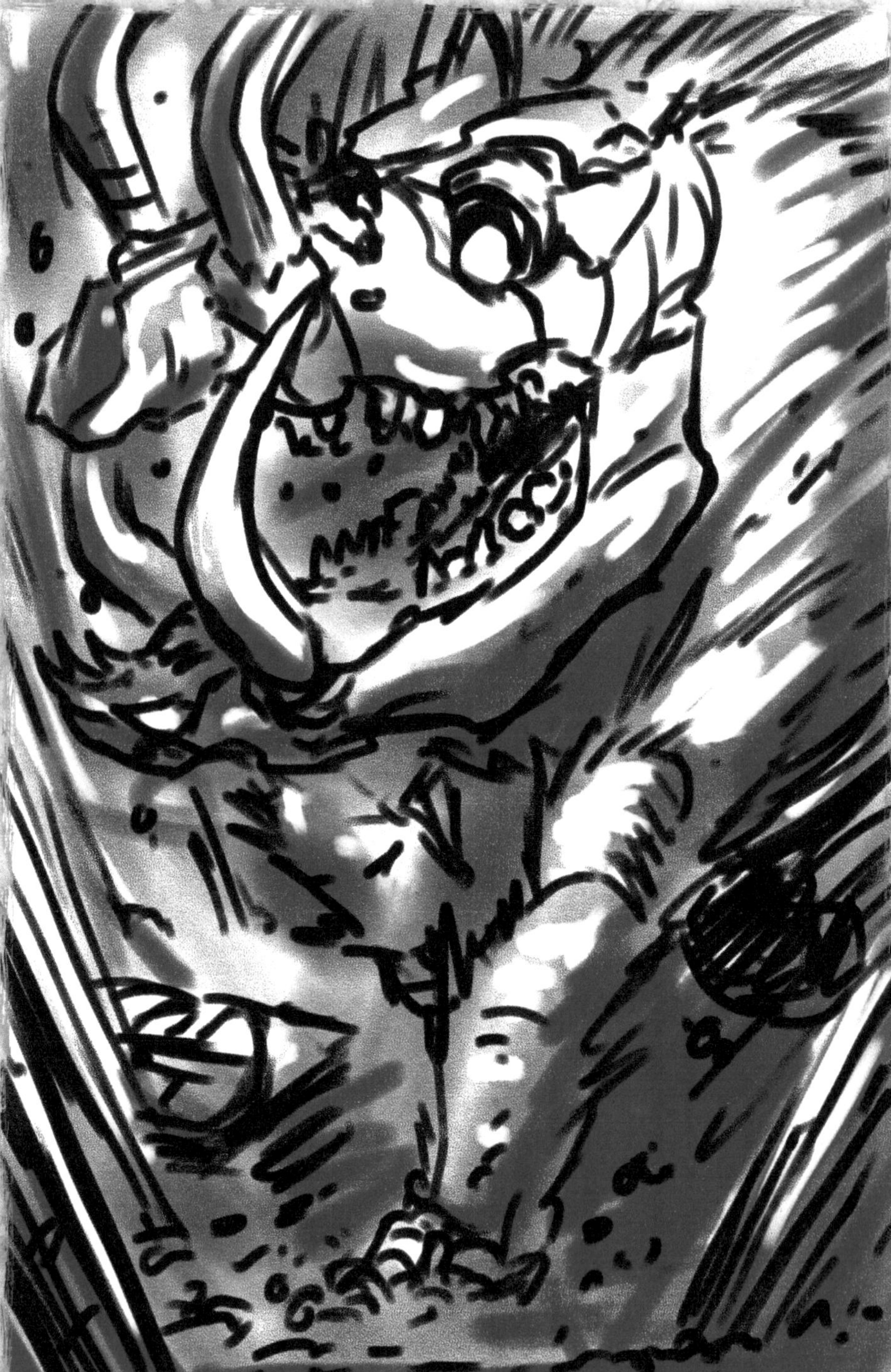

D16 - WILD

FINAL LINE ART

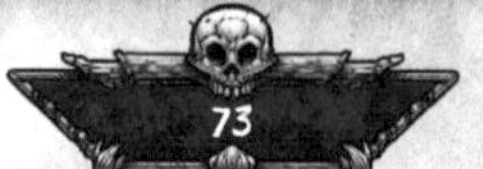

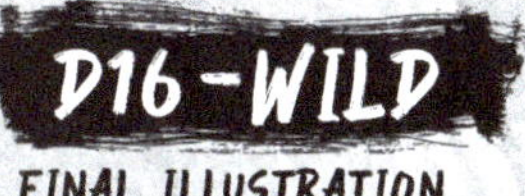

FINAL ILLUSTRATION

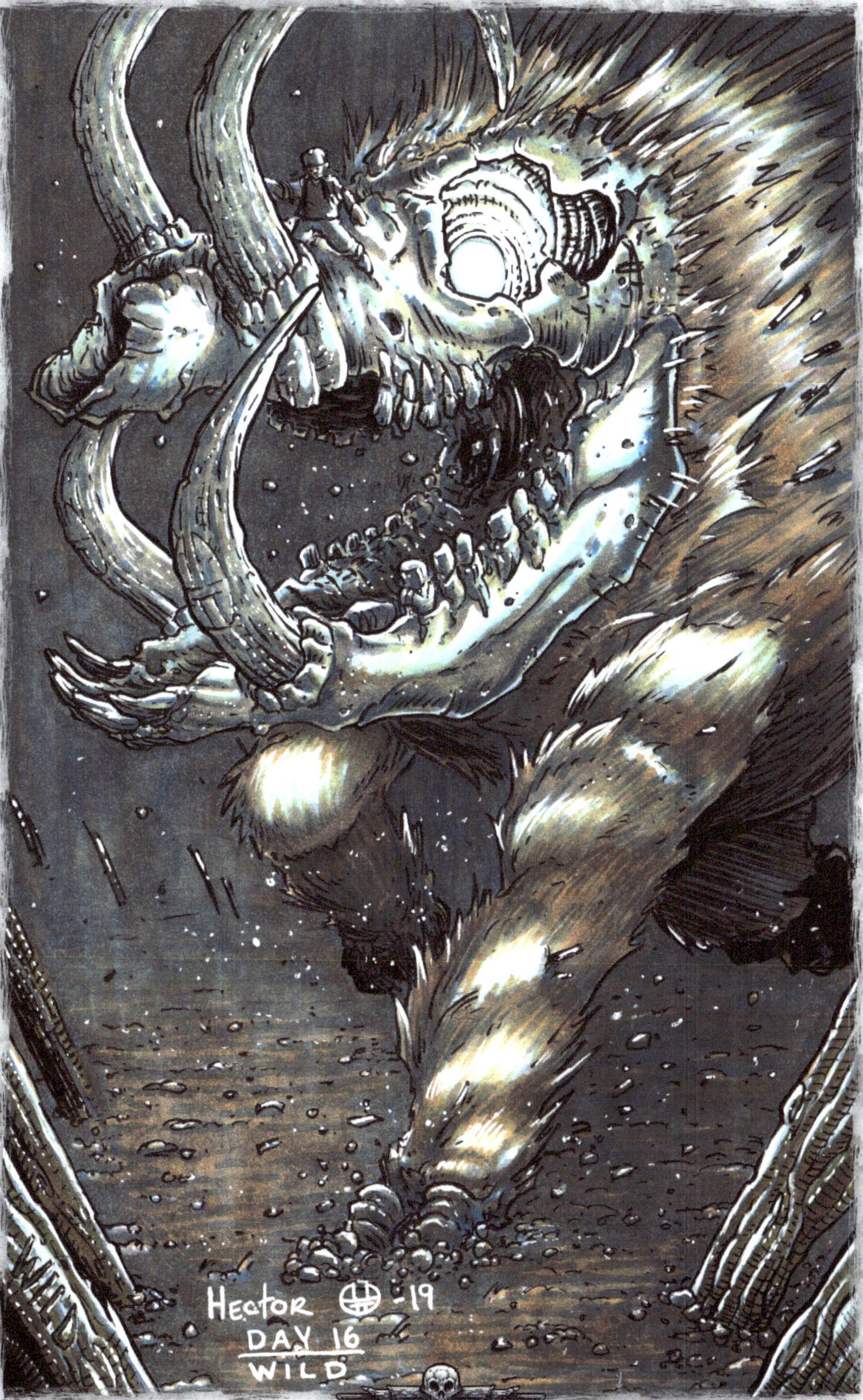

- DAY 18 -
ORNAMENT

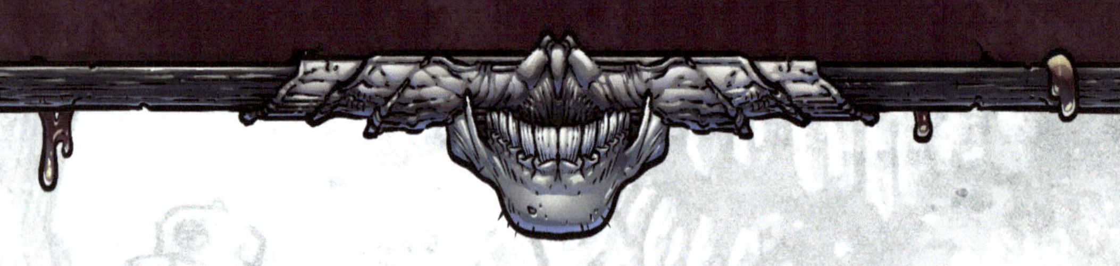

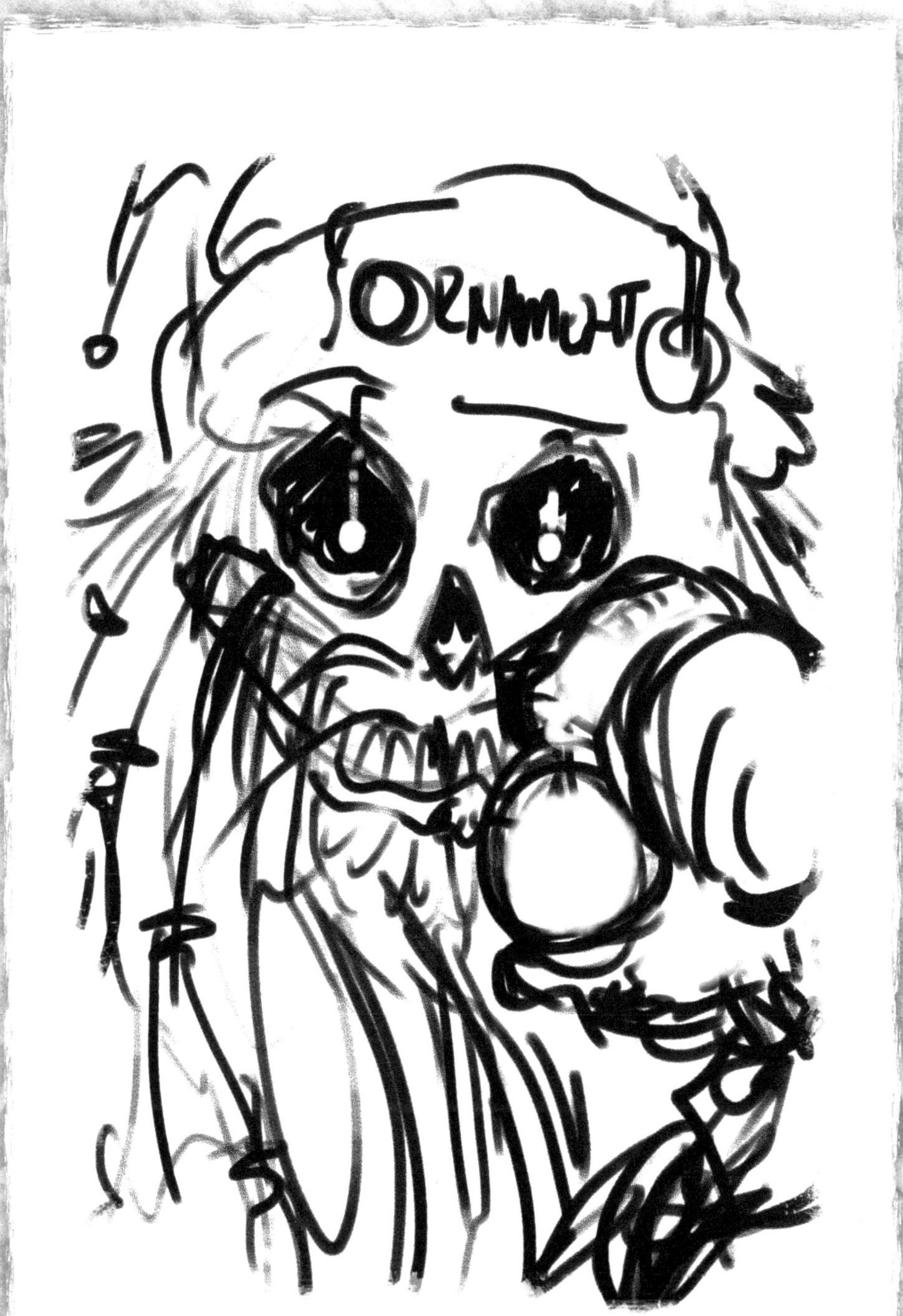

D17 - ORNAMENT

ROUGH SKETCHES

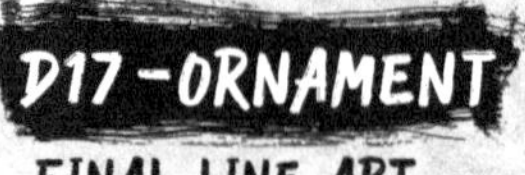

FINAL LINE ART

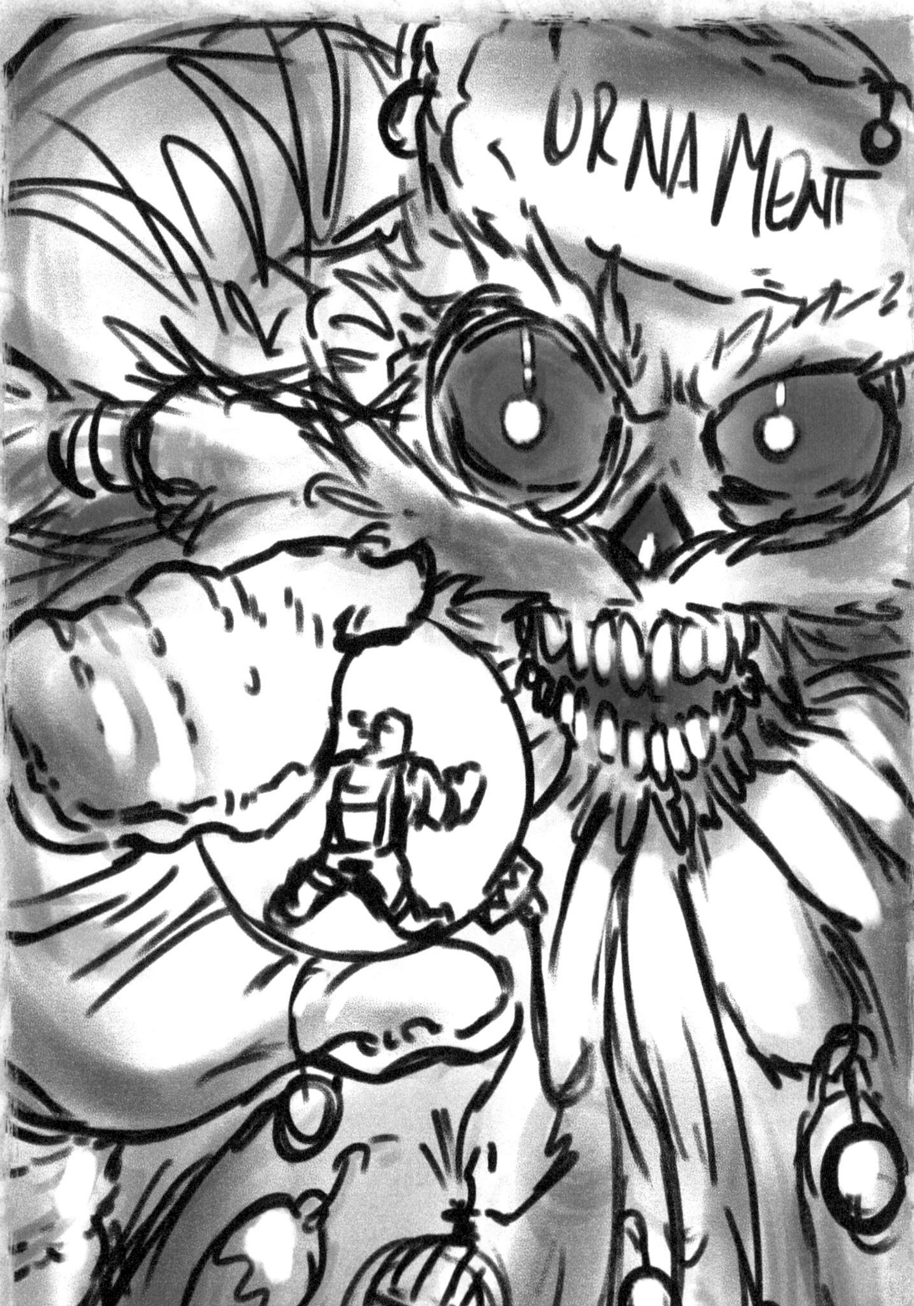

D17 - ORNAMENT

FINAL ILLUSTRATION

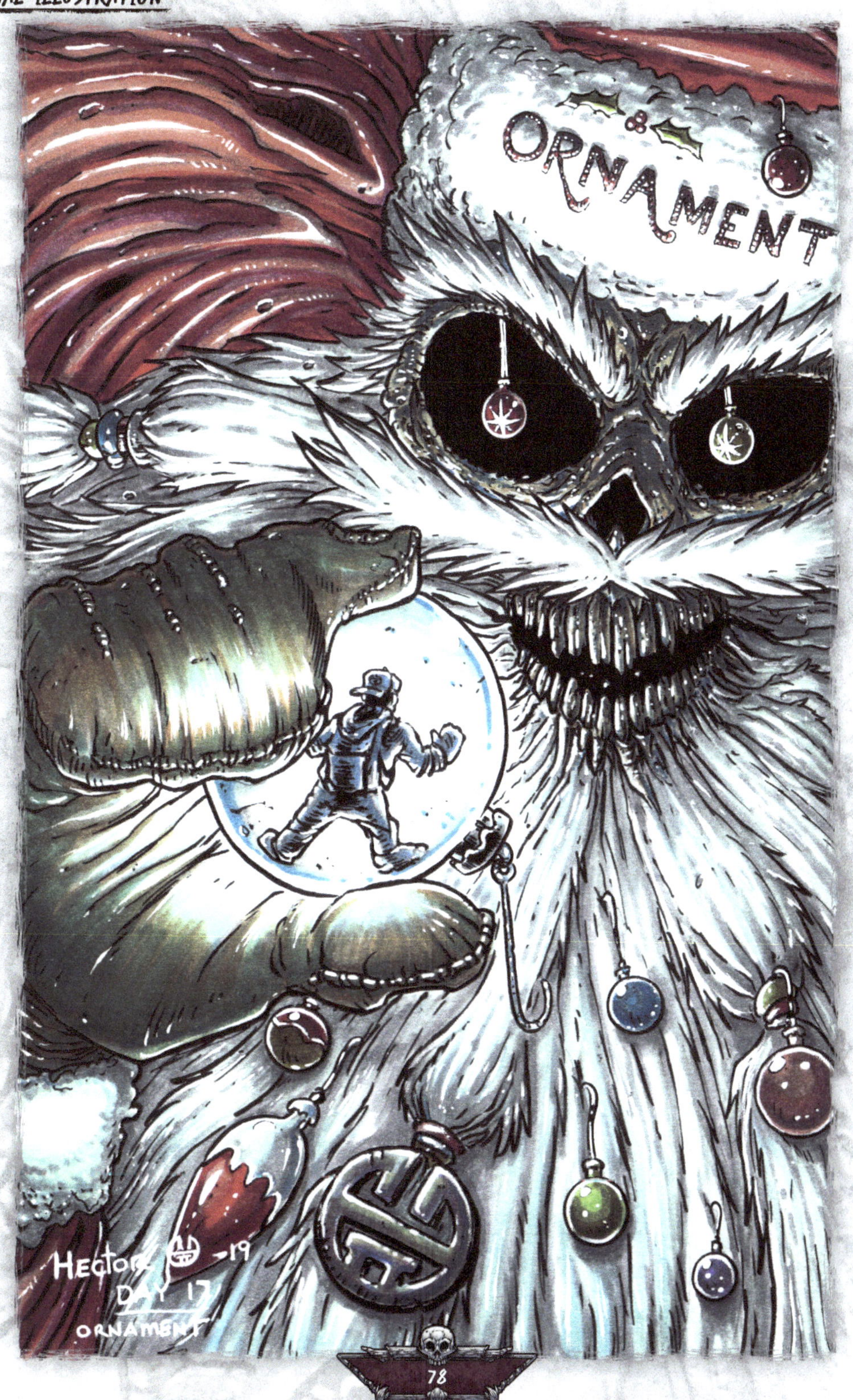

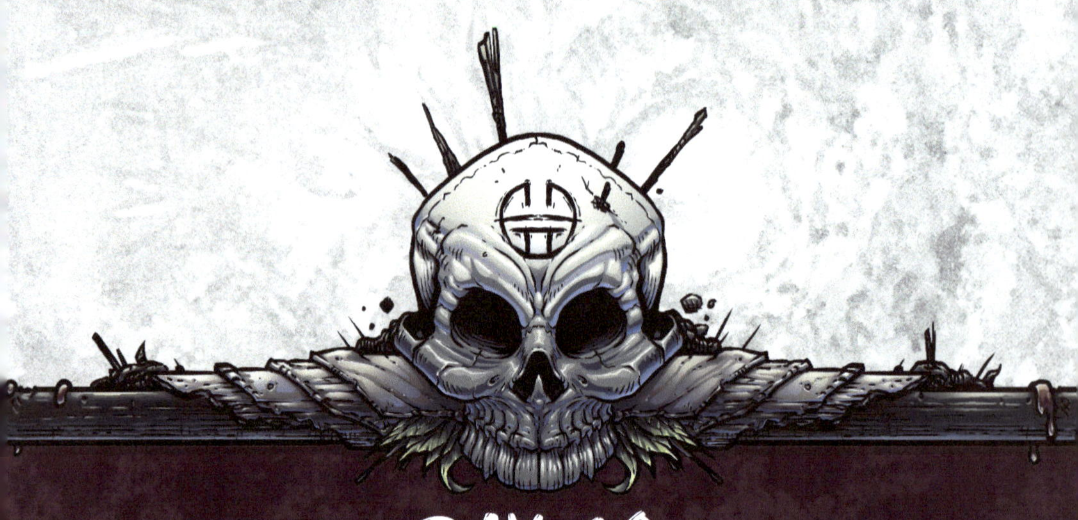

- DAY 18 -

MISFIT

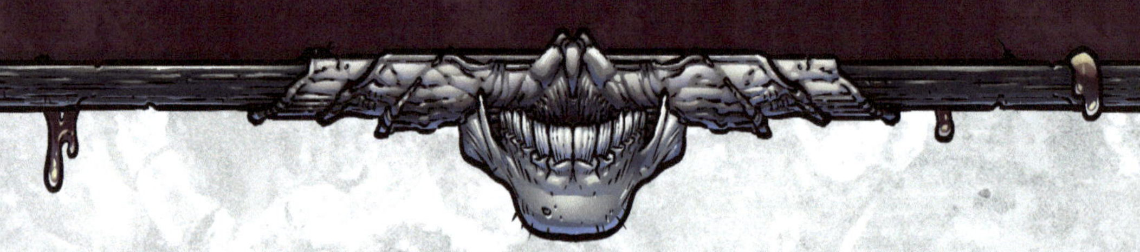

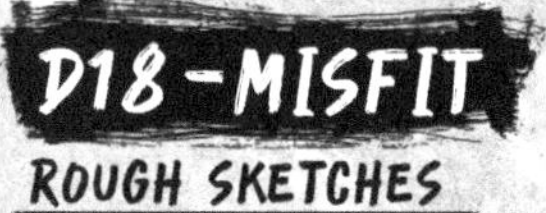
D18 - MISFIT
ROUGH SKETCHES

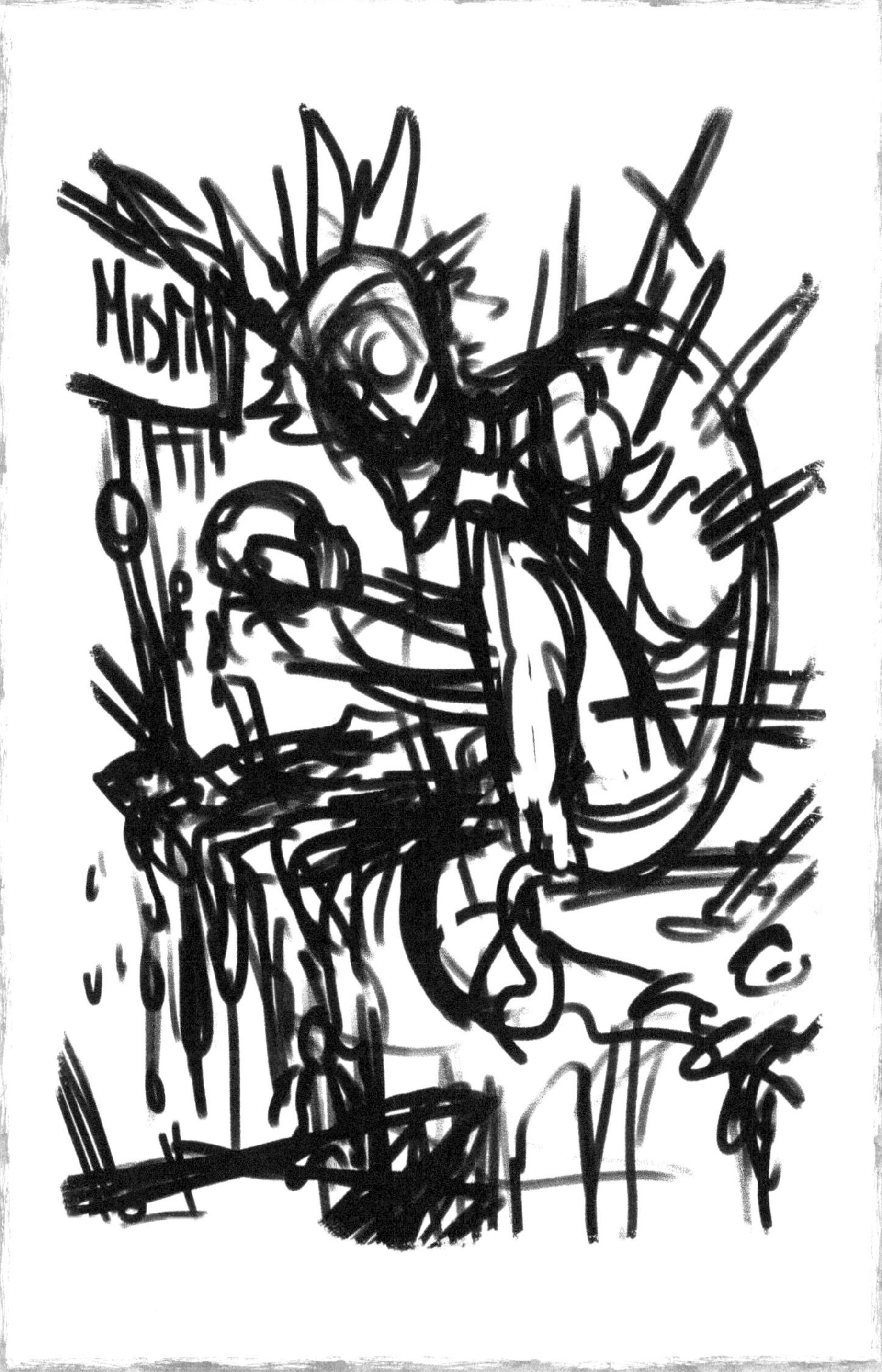

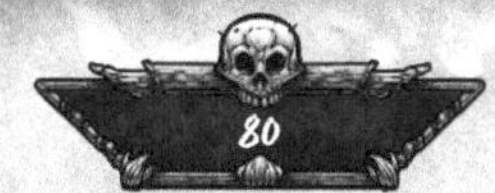

D18 - MISFIT

FINAL LINE ART

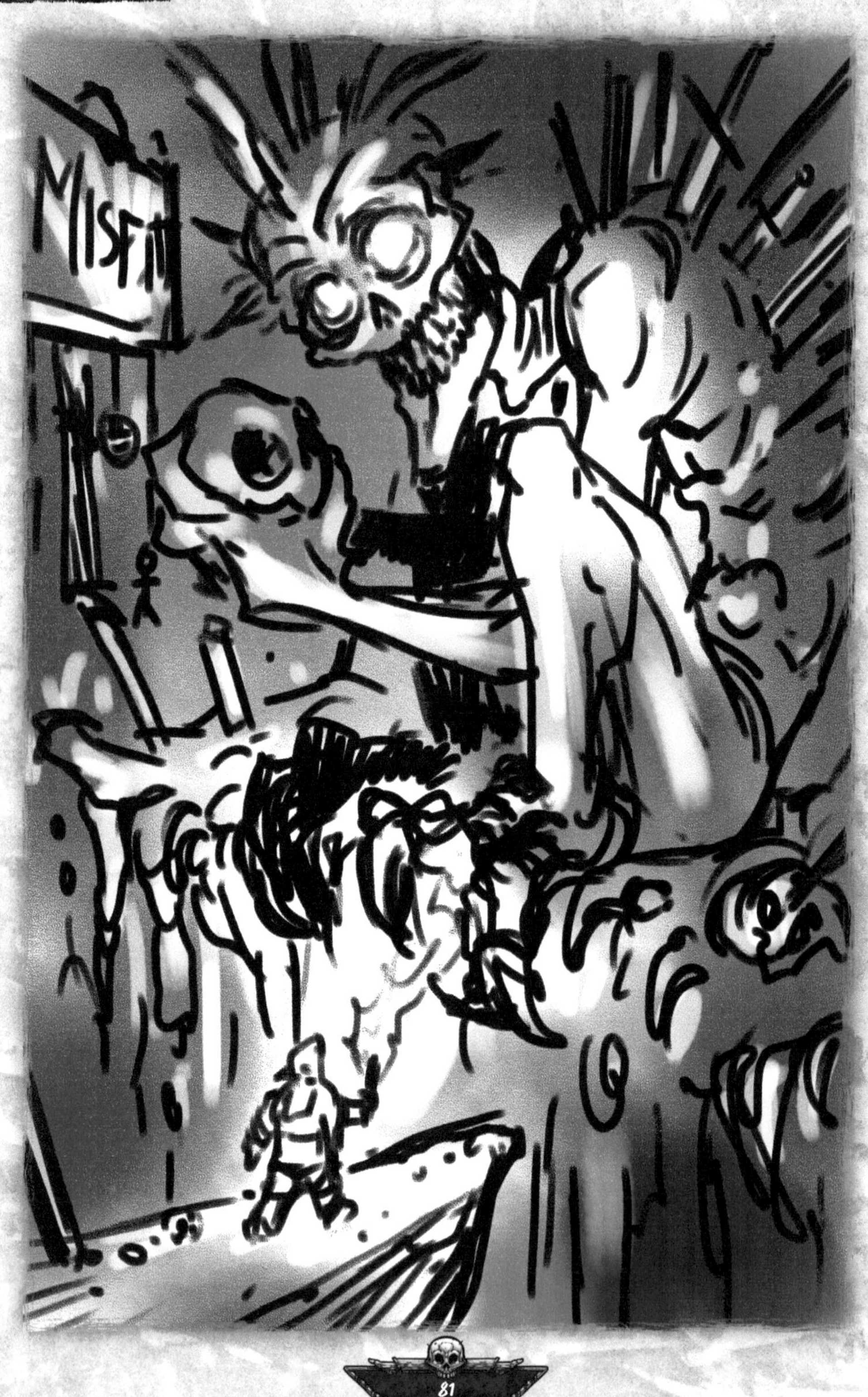

D18 - MISFIT

FINAL ILLUSTRATION

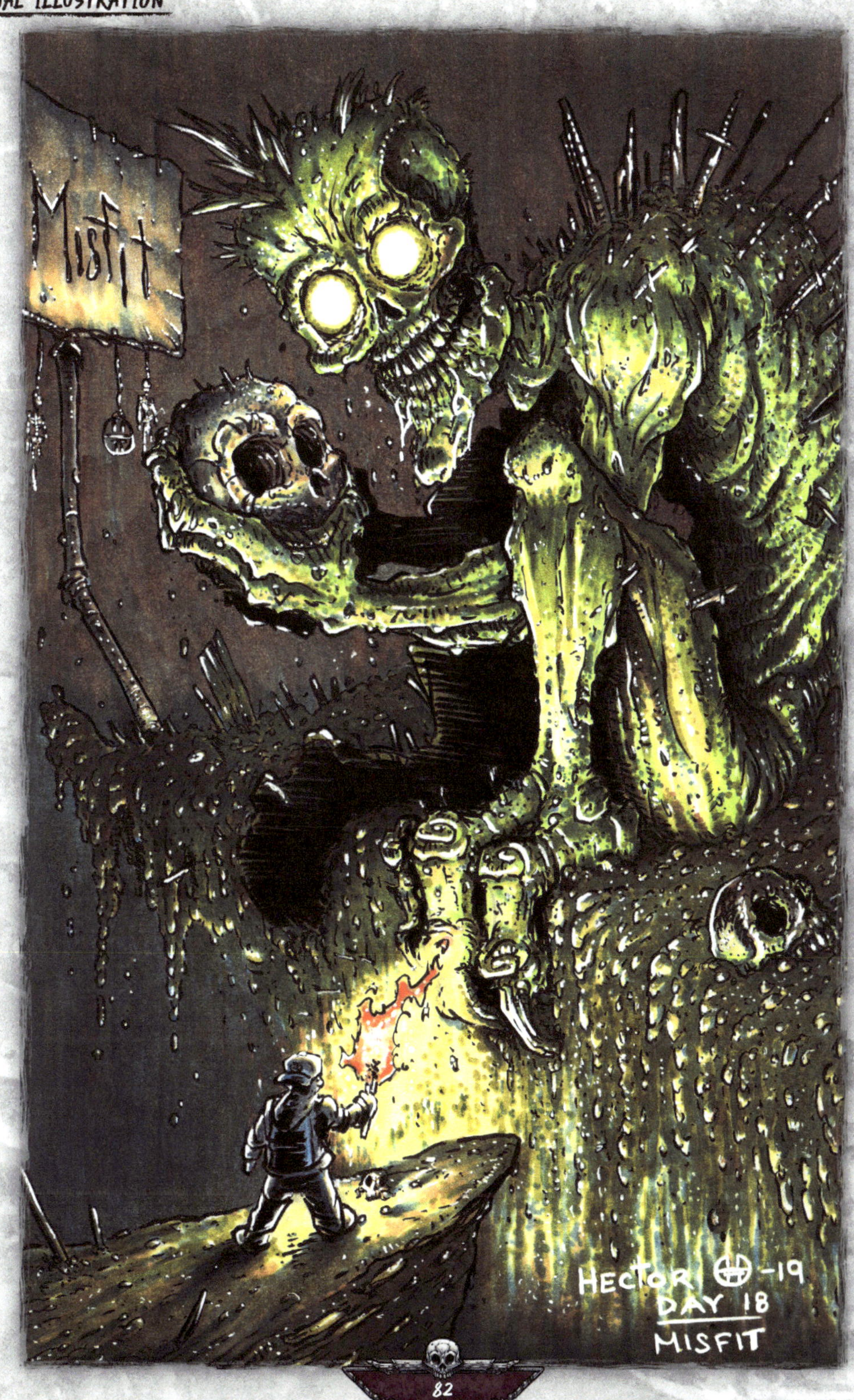

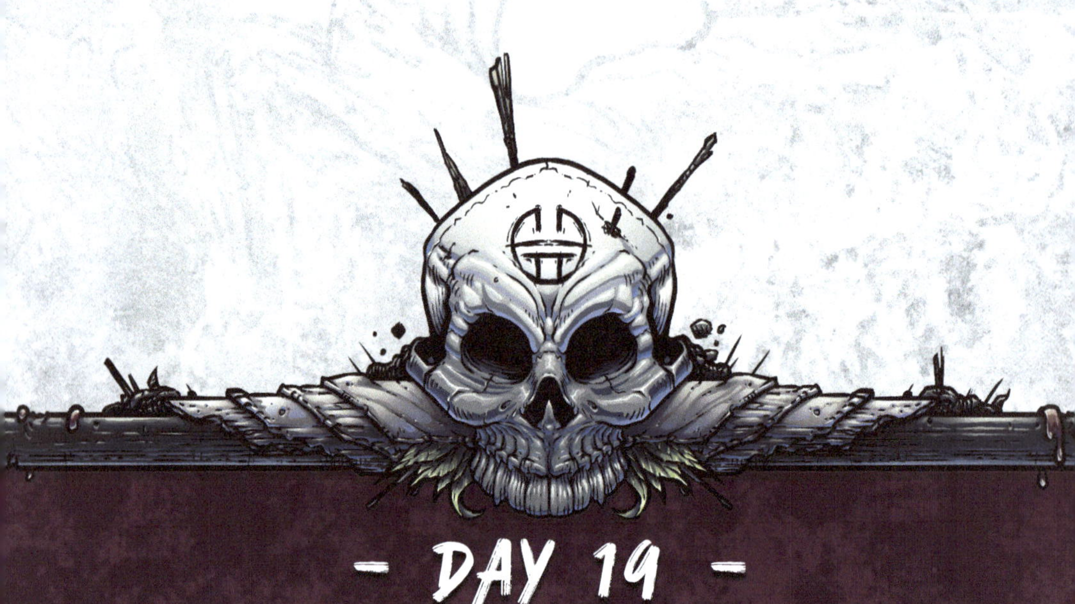

- DAY 19 -

SLING

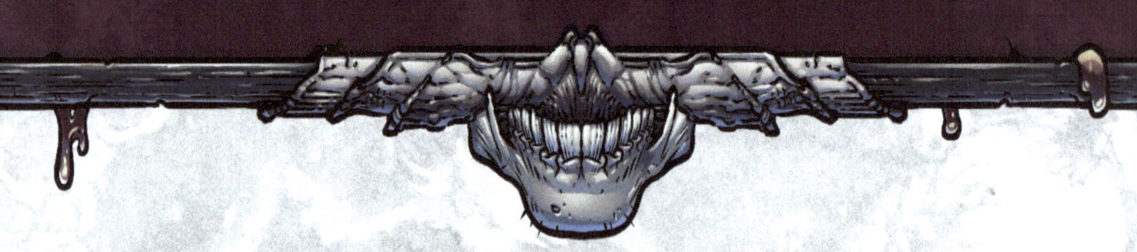

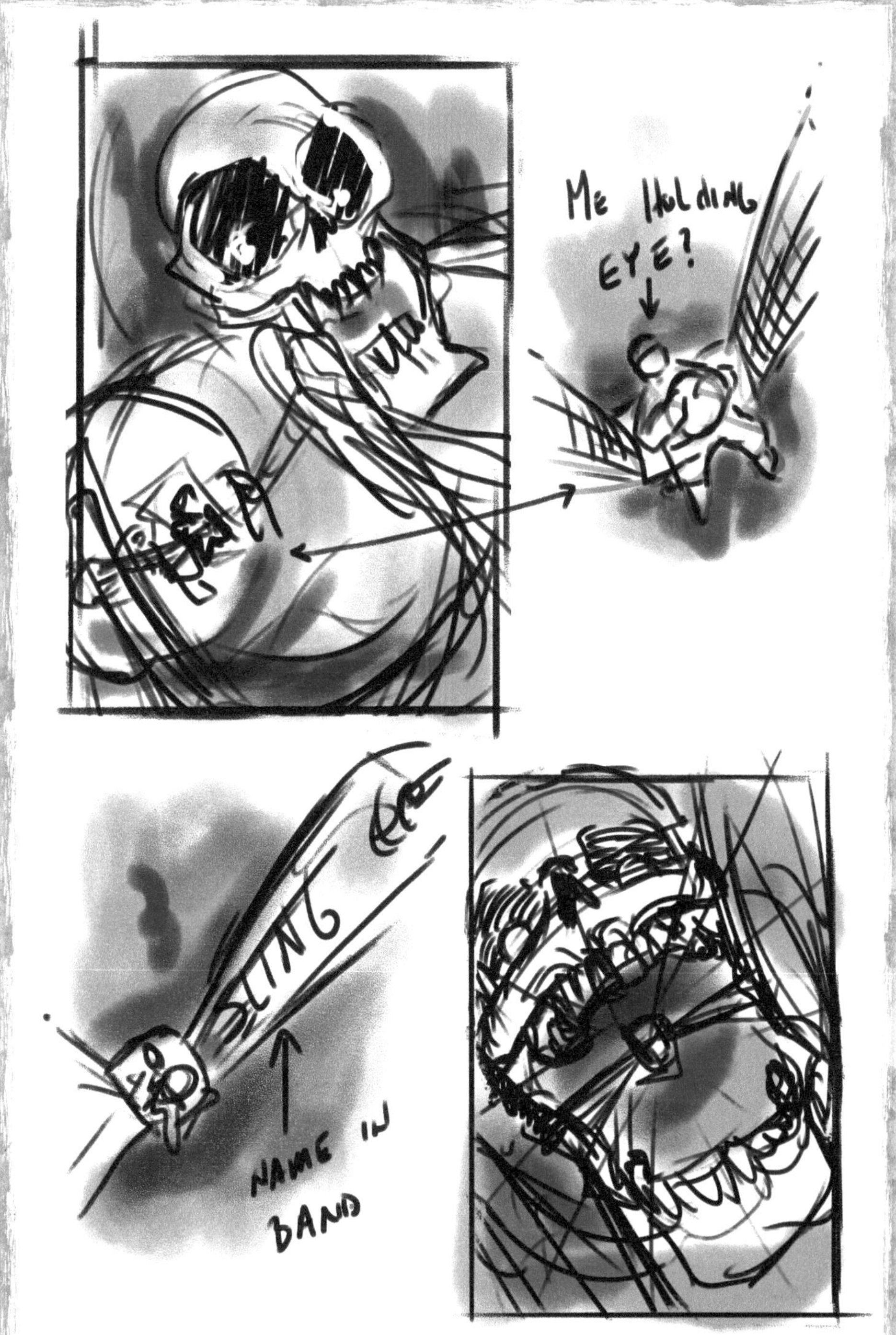

D19 - SLING

ROUGH SKETCHES

Me Holding EYE?

SLING

NAME IN BAND

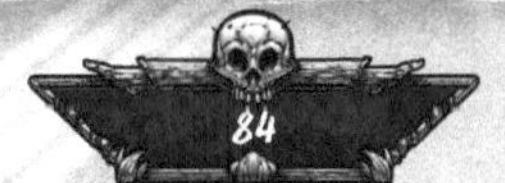

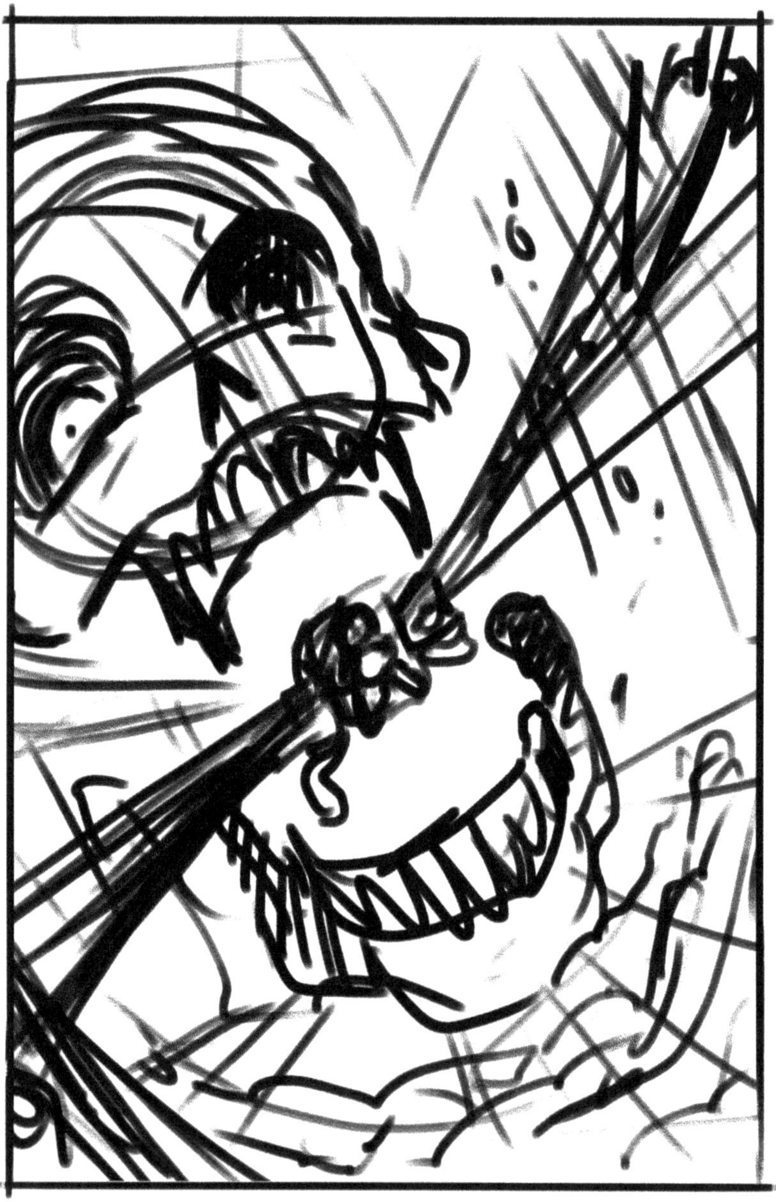

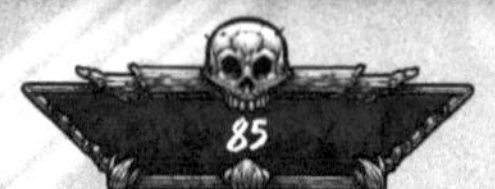

D19 - SLING

FINAL LINE ART

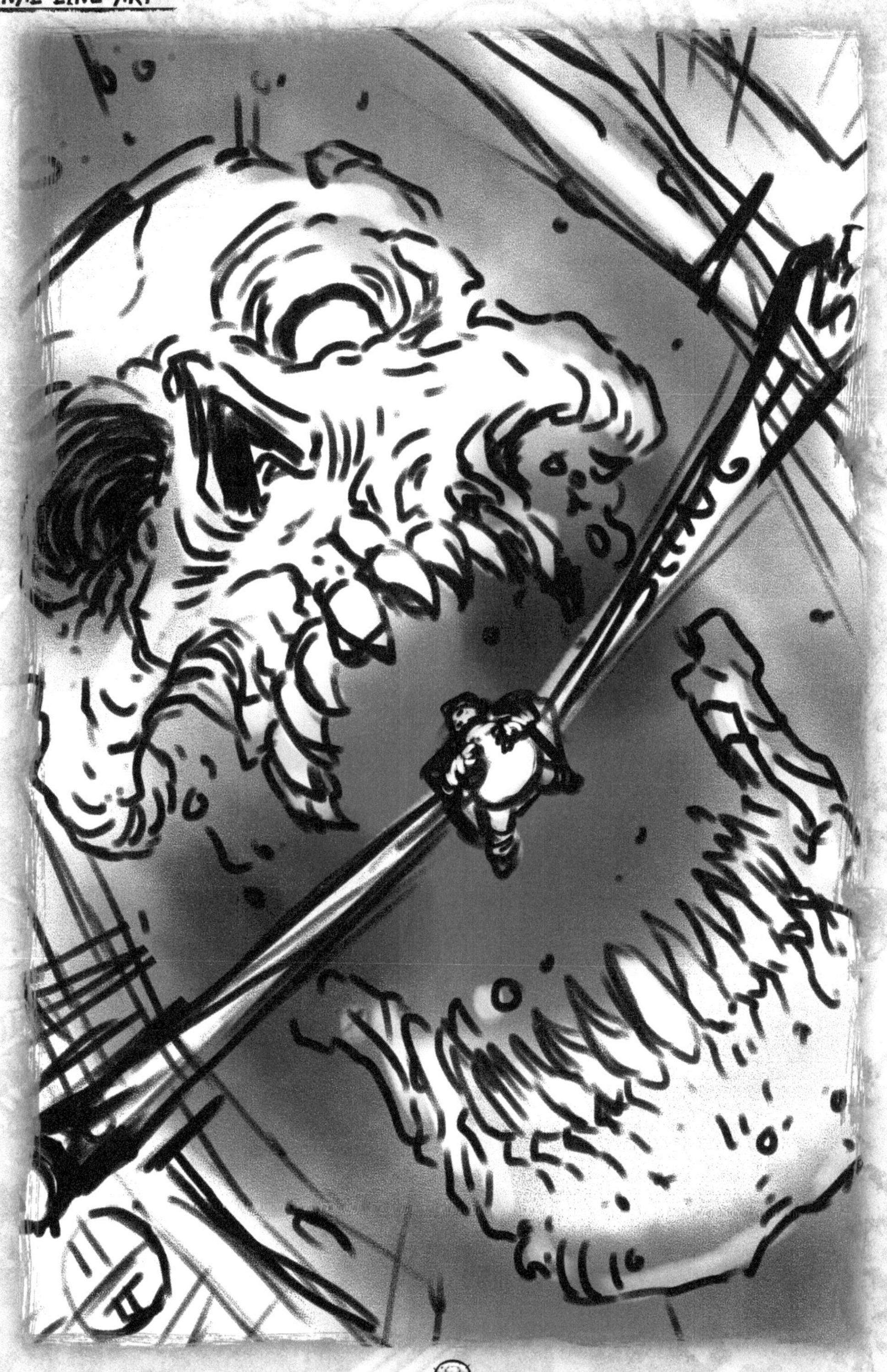

D19 - SLING

FINAL ILLUSTRATION

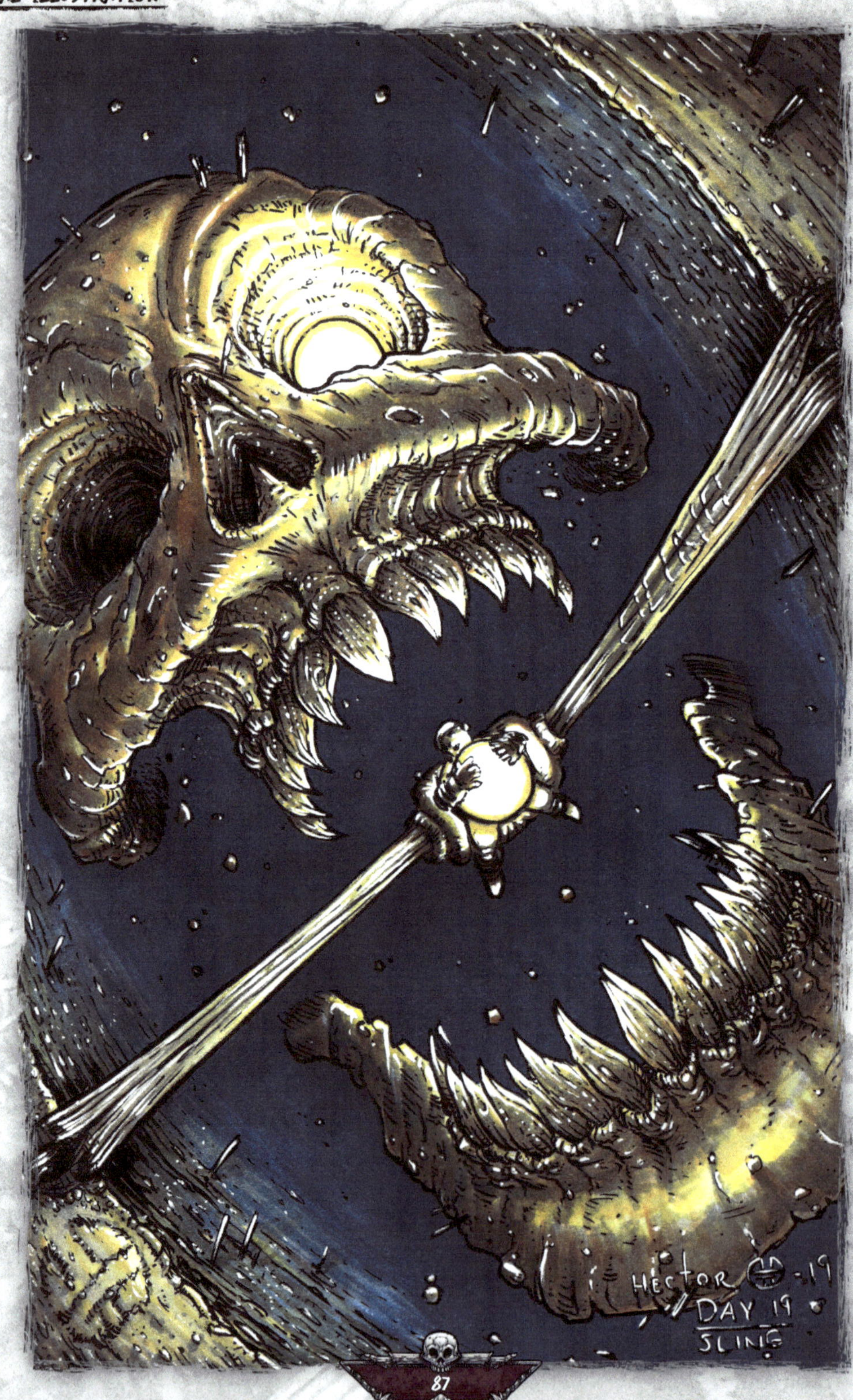

- DAY 20 -

TREAD

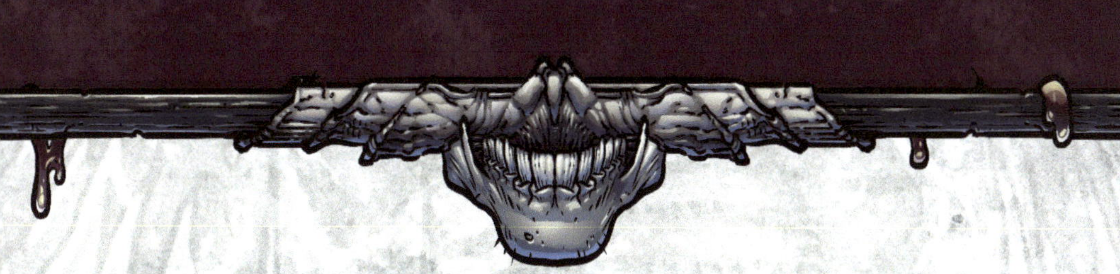

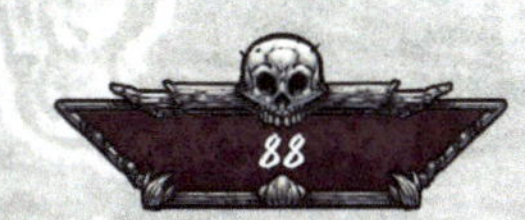

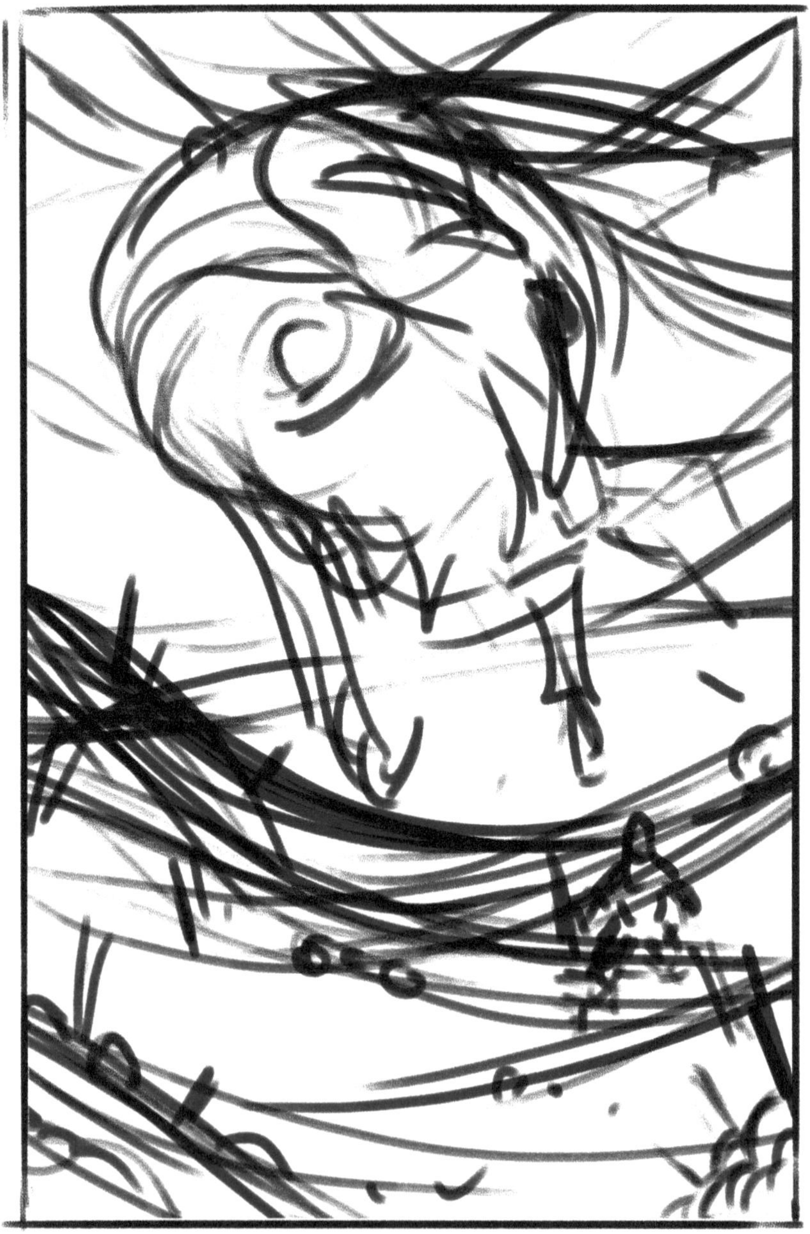

D20-TREAD

FINAL LINE ART

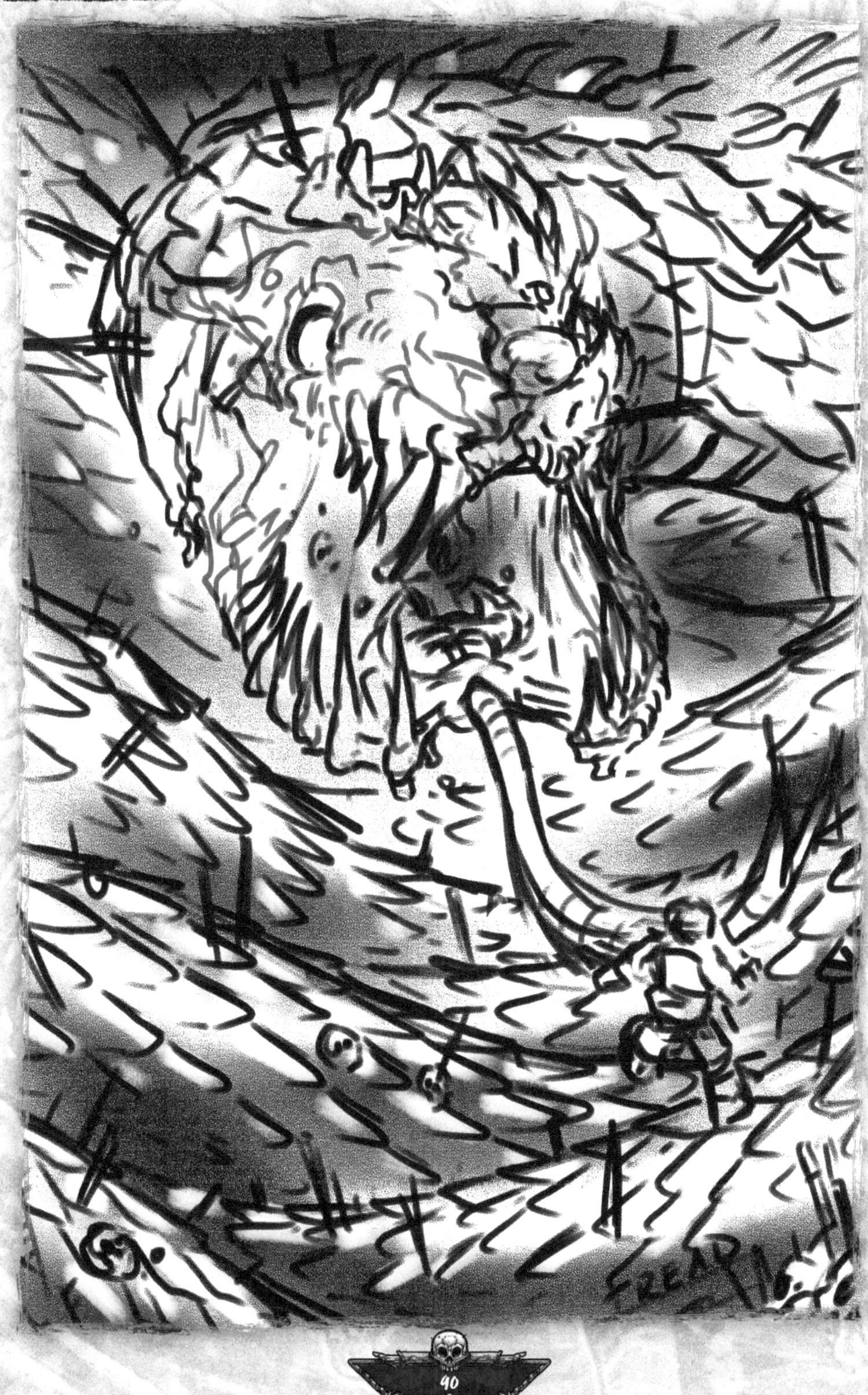

D20 - TREAD

FINAL ILLUSTRATION

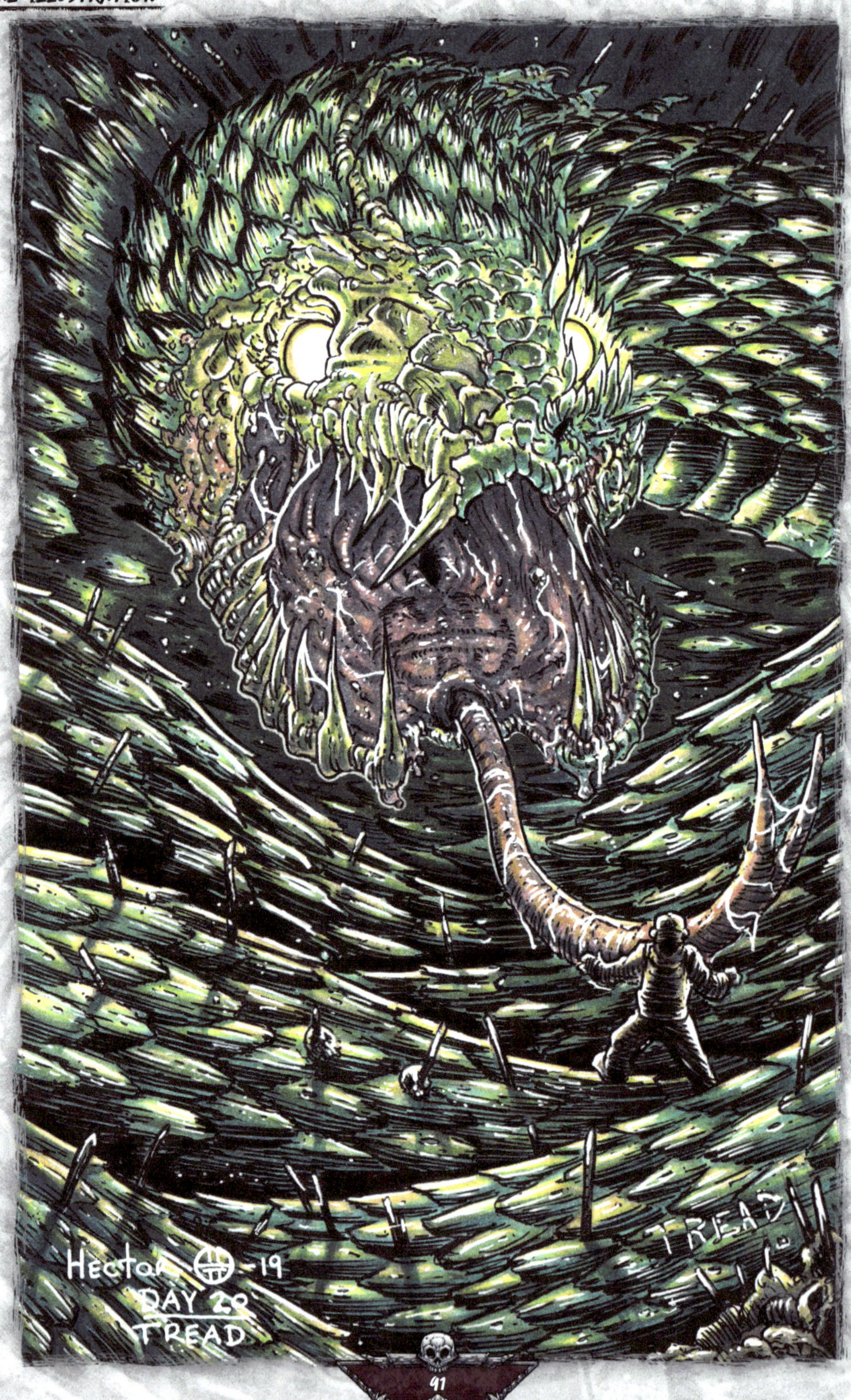

- DAY 21 -

TREASURE

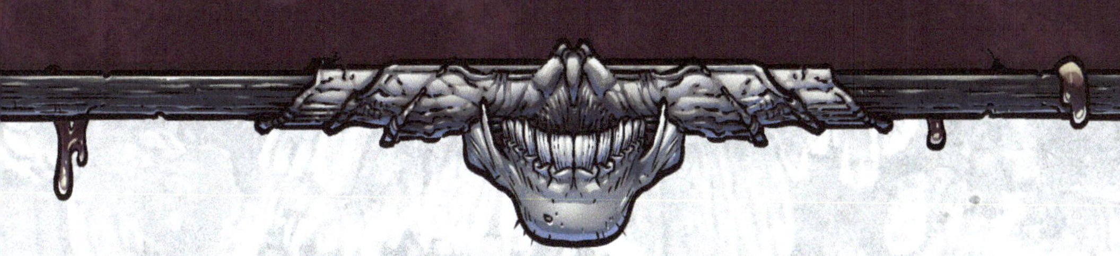

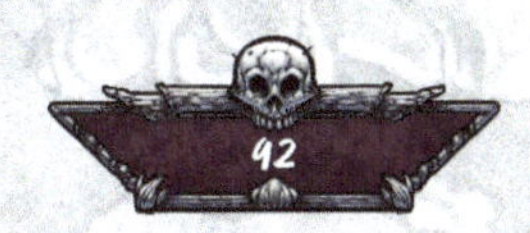

D21 - TREASURE

ROUGH SKETCHES

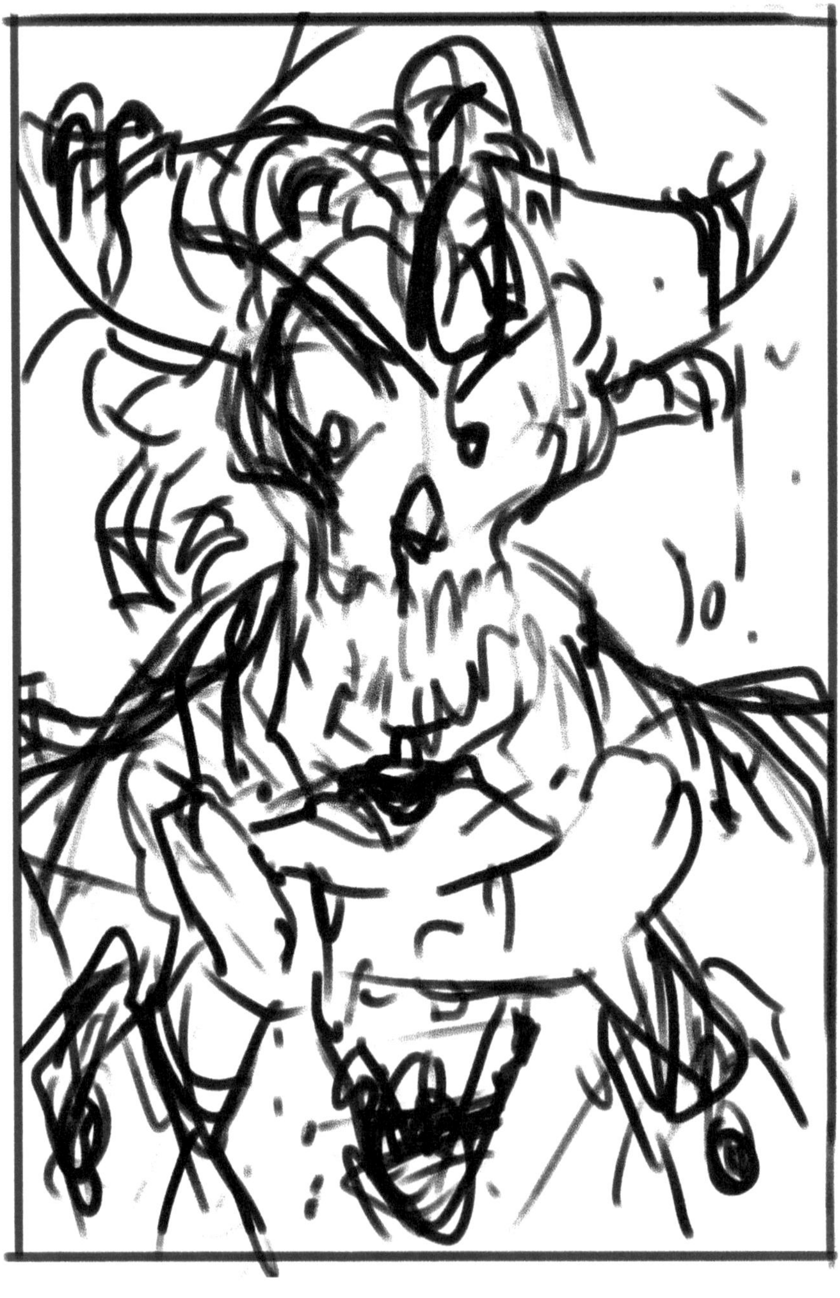

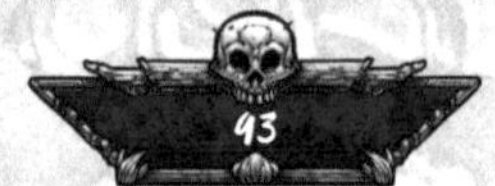

D21-TREASURE

FINAL LINE ART

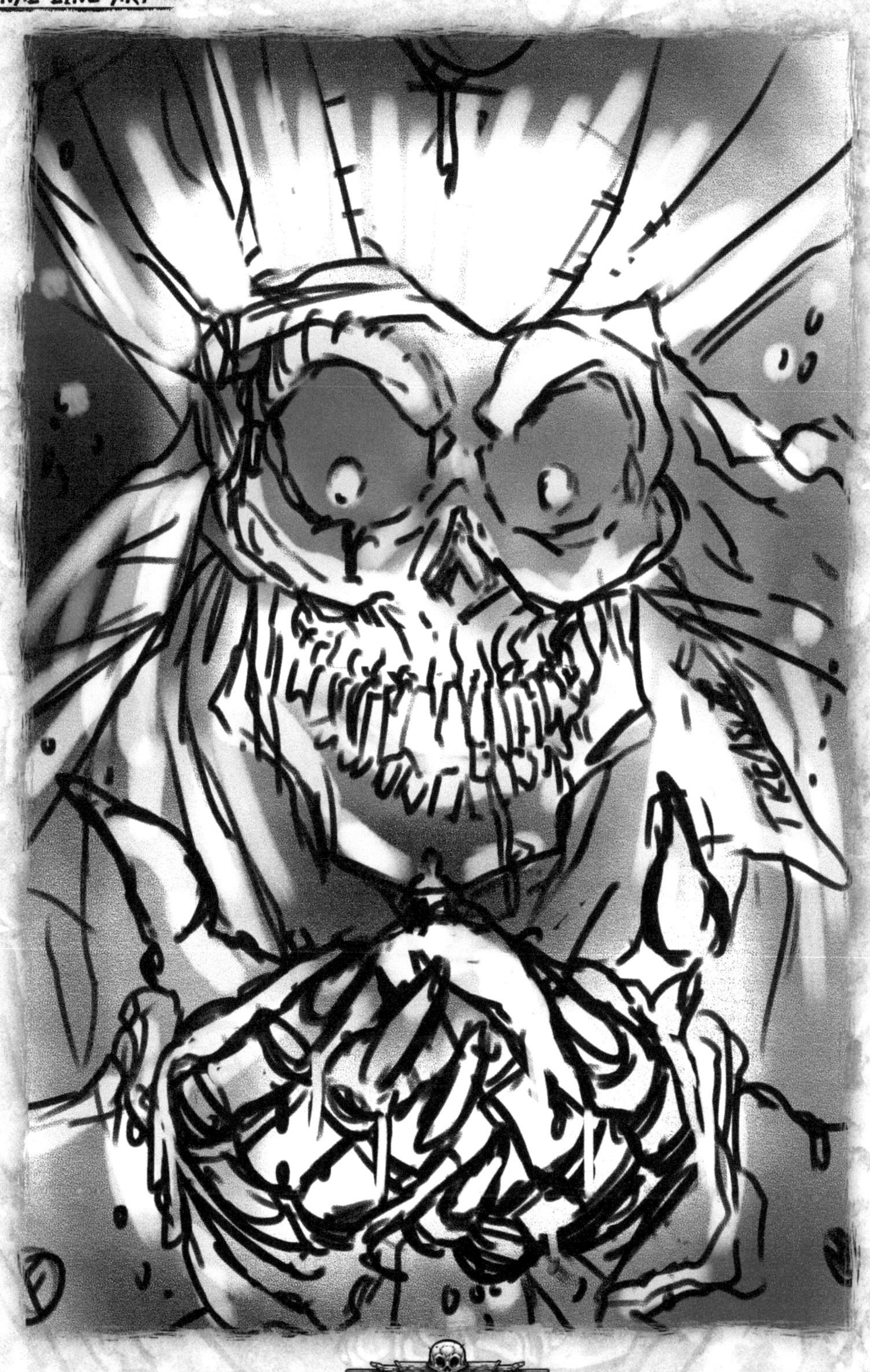

D21 - TREASURE

FINAL ILLUSTRATION

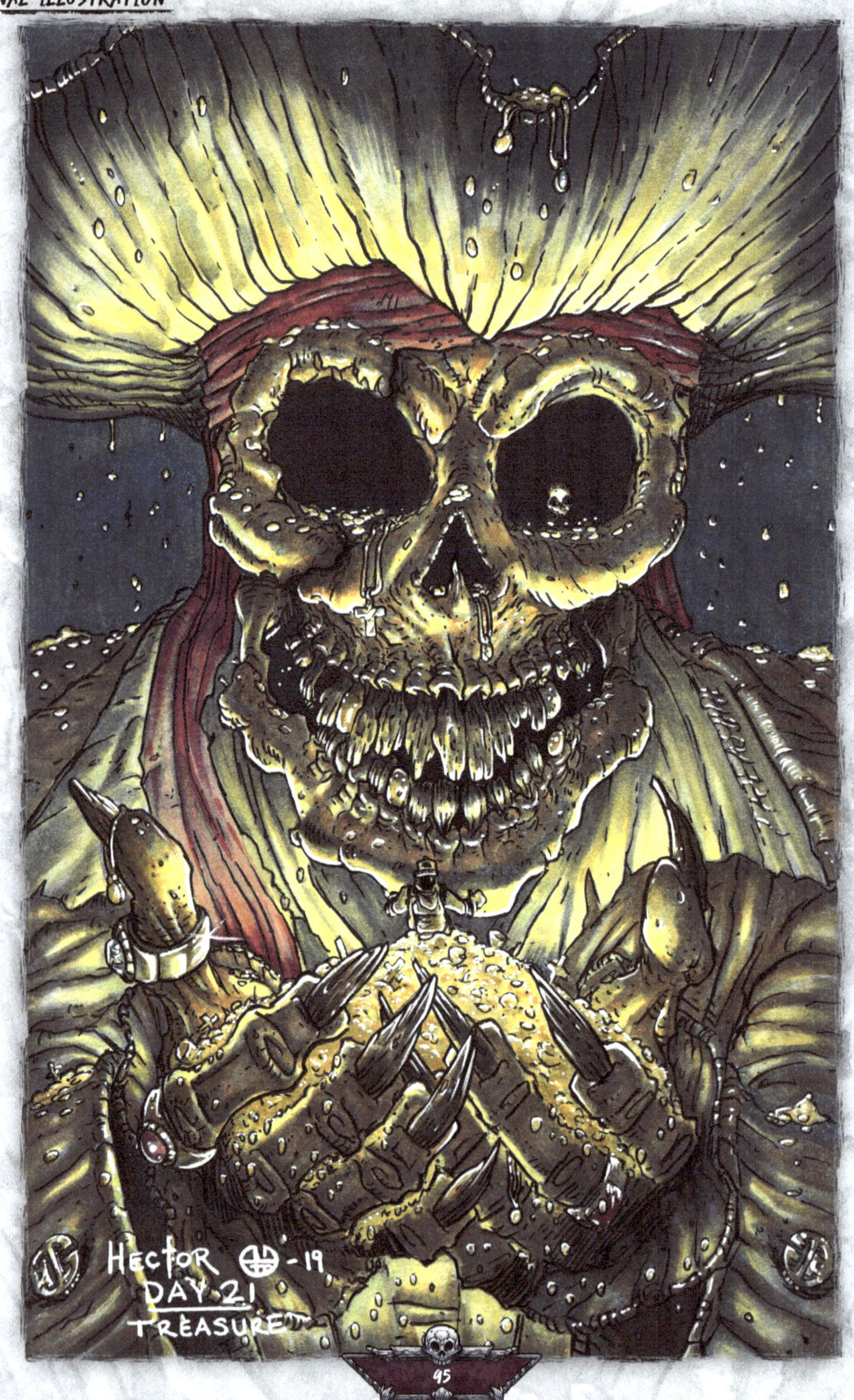

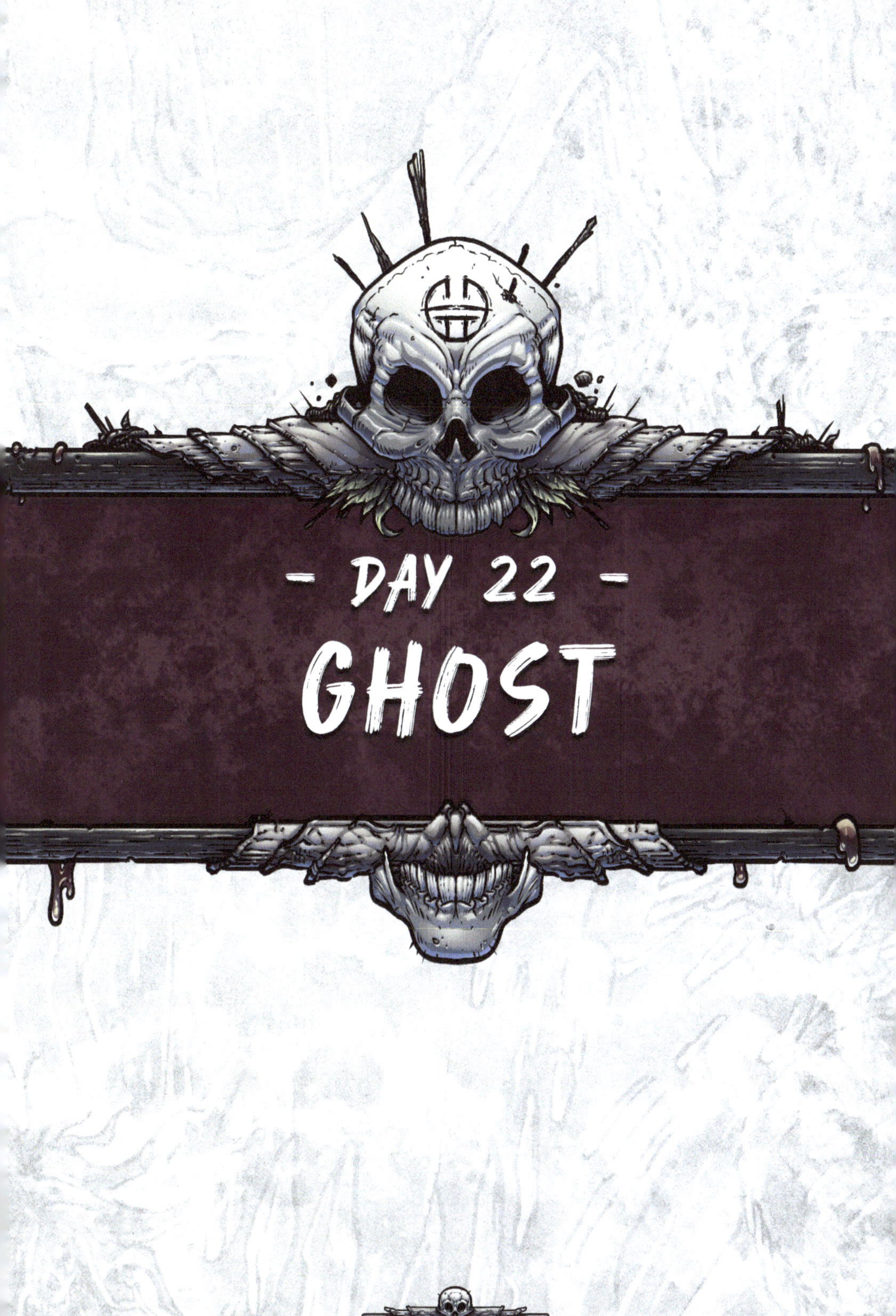

- DAY 22 -
GHOST

D22-GHOST

ROUGH SKETCHES

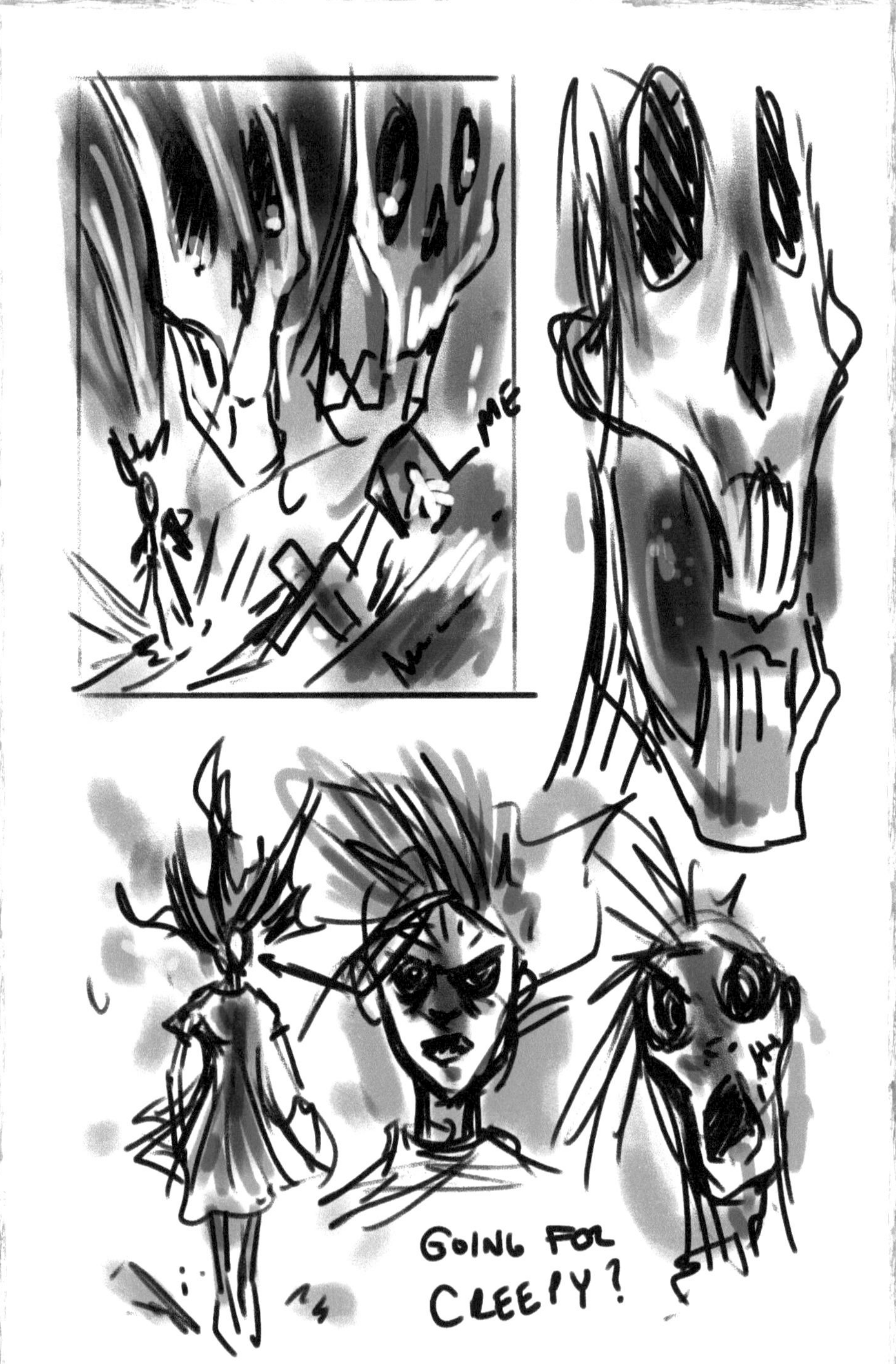

ME

GOING FOR CREEPY?

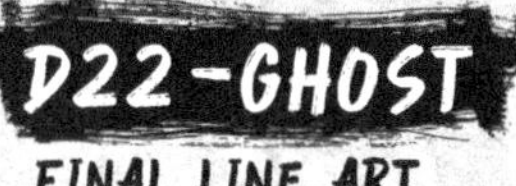
D22-GHOST
FINAL LINE ART

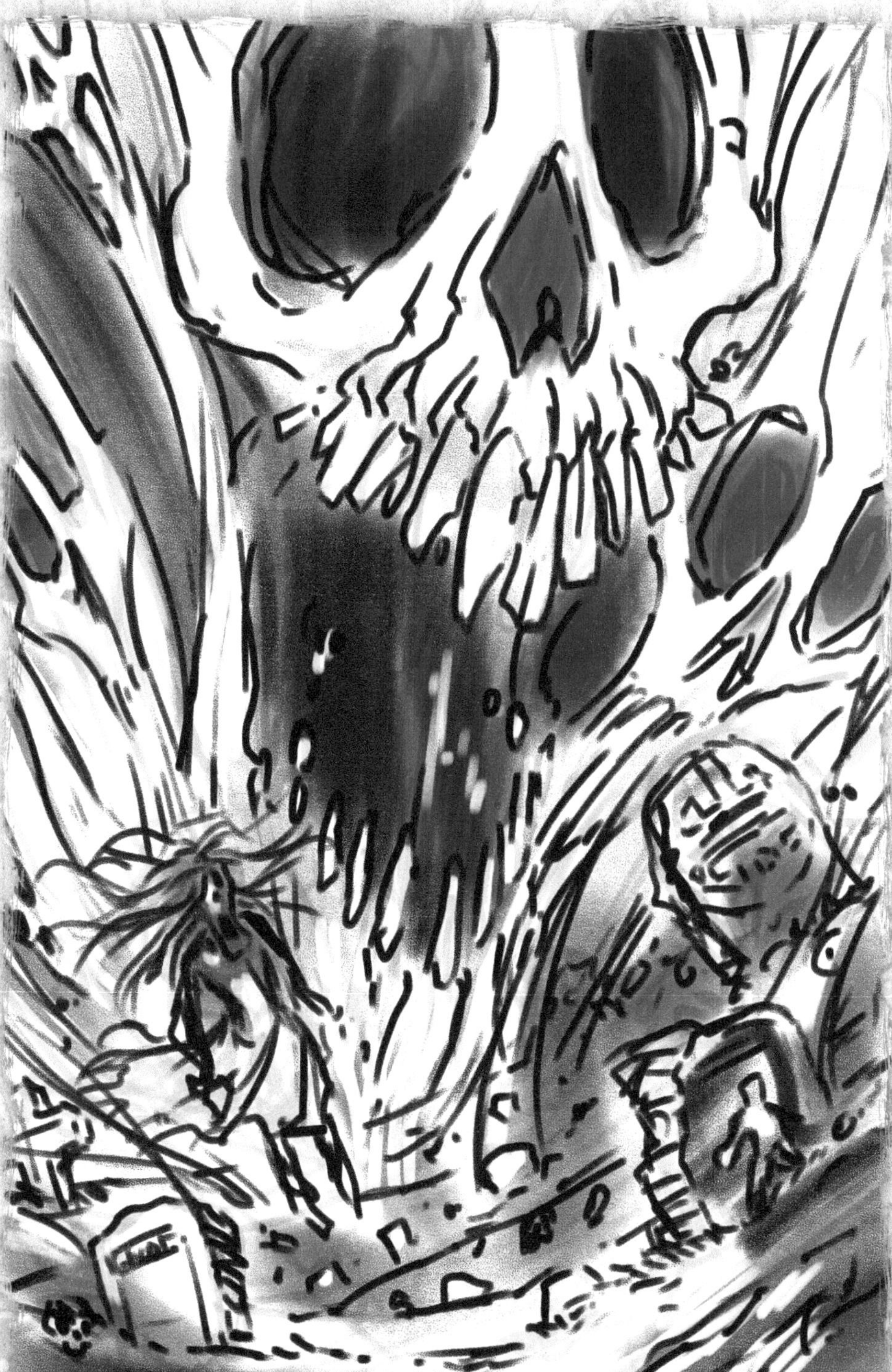

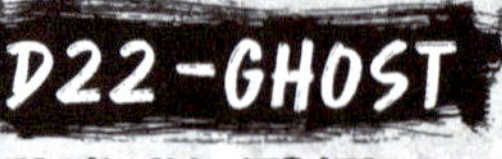

D22-GHOST

FINAL ILLUSTRATION

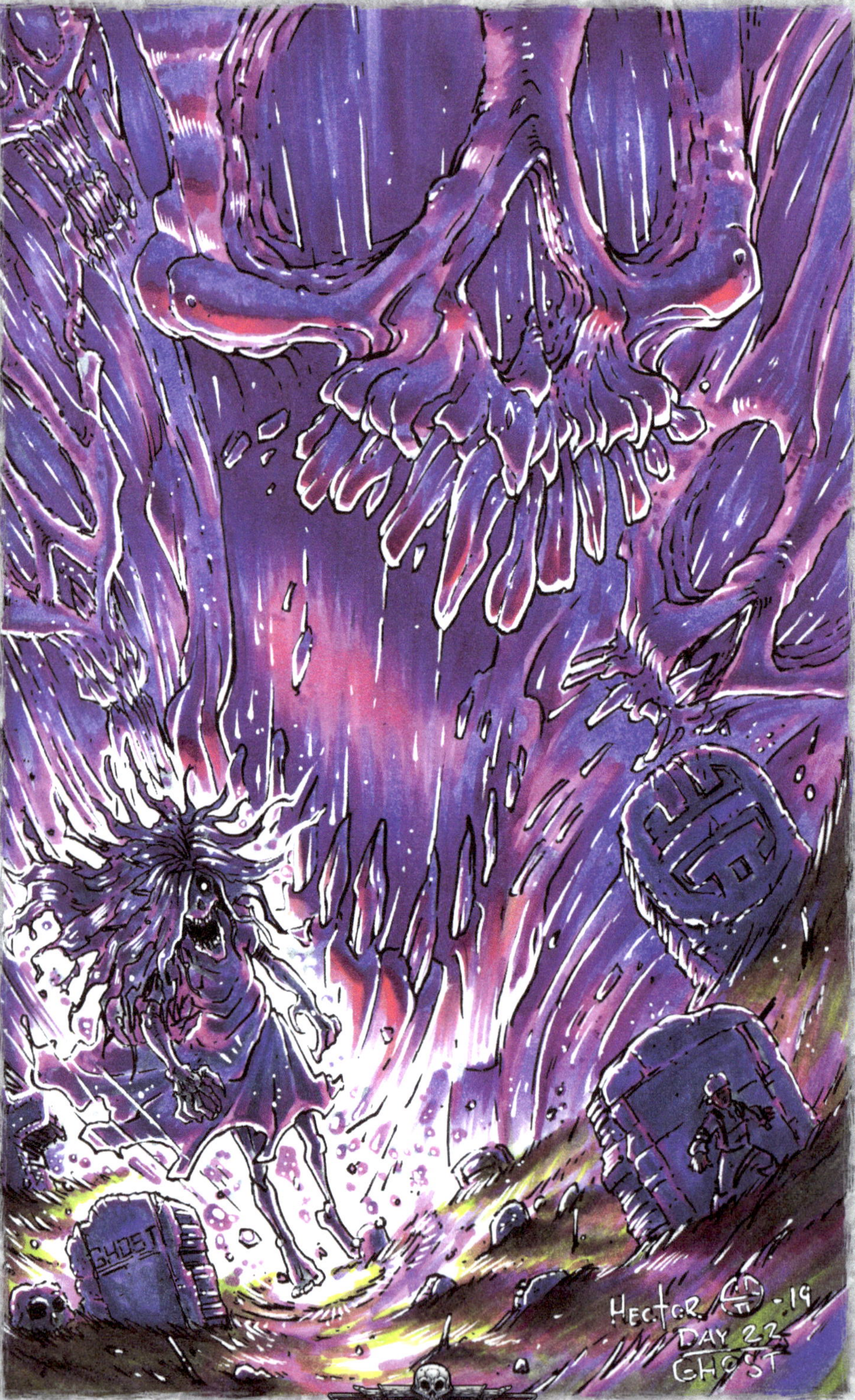

- DAY 23 -

ANCIENT

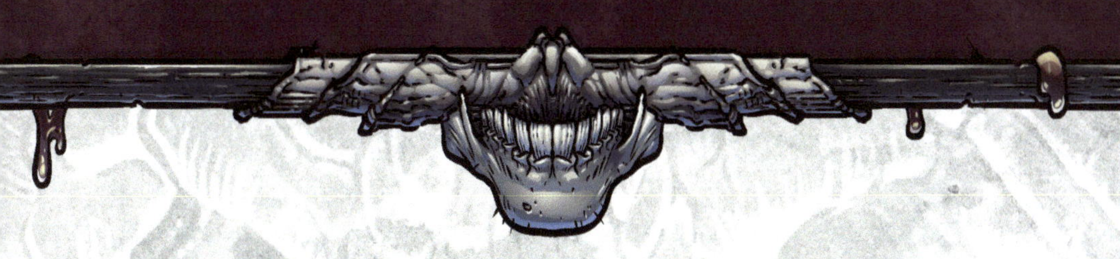

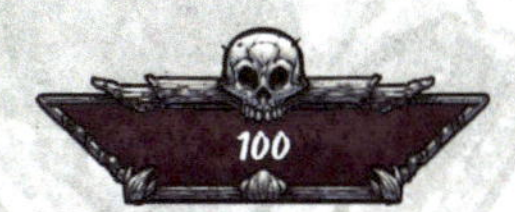

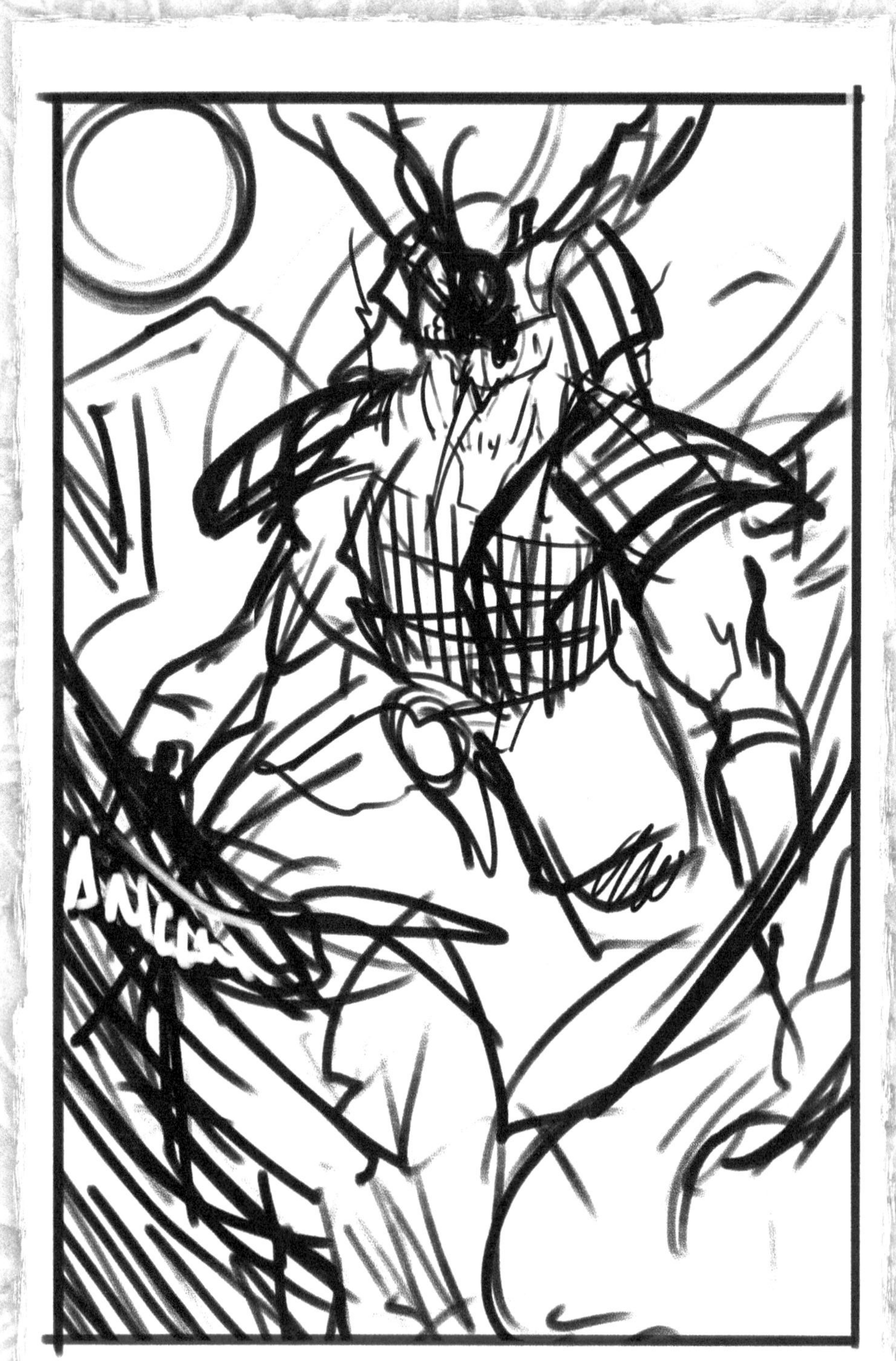

D23–ANCIENT

ROUGH SKETCHES

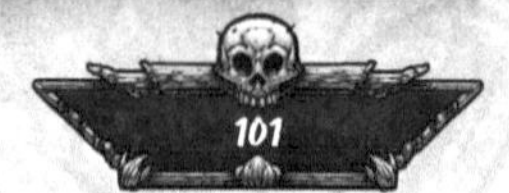

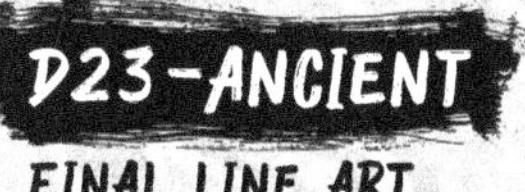

FINAL LINE ART

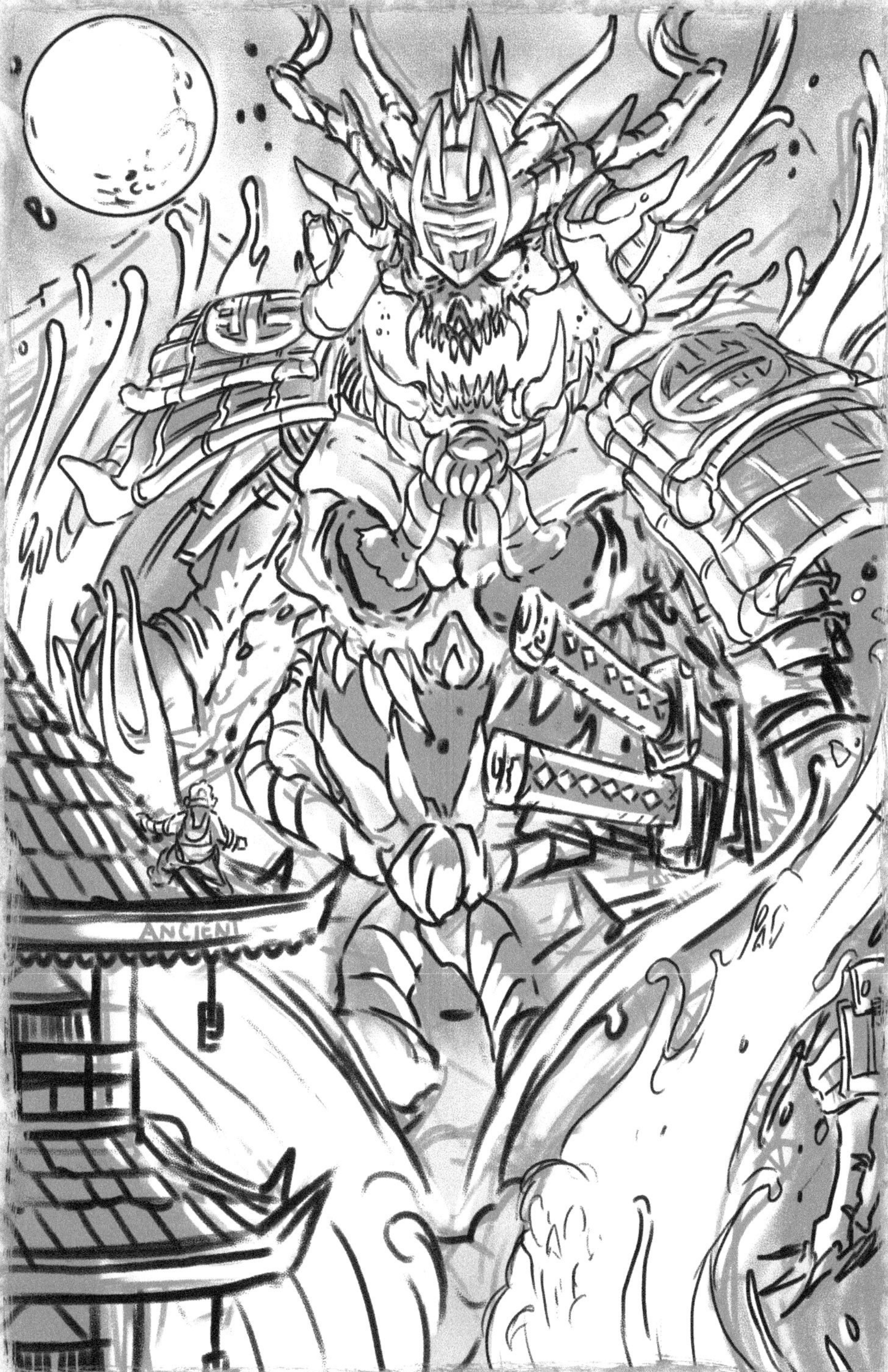

D23 - ANCIENT

FINAL ILLUSTRATION

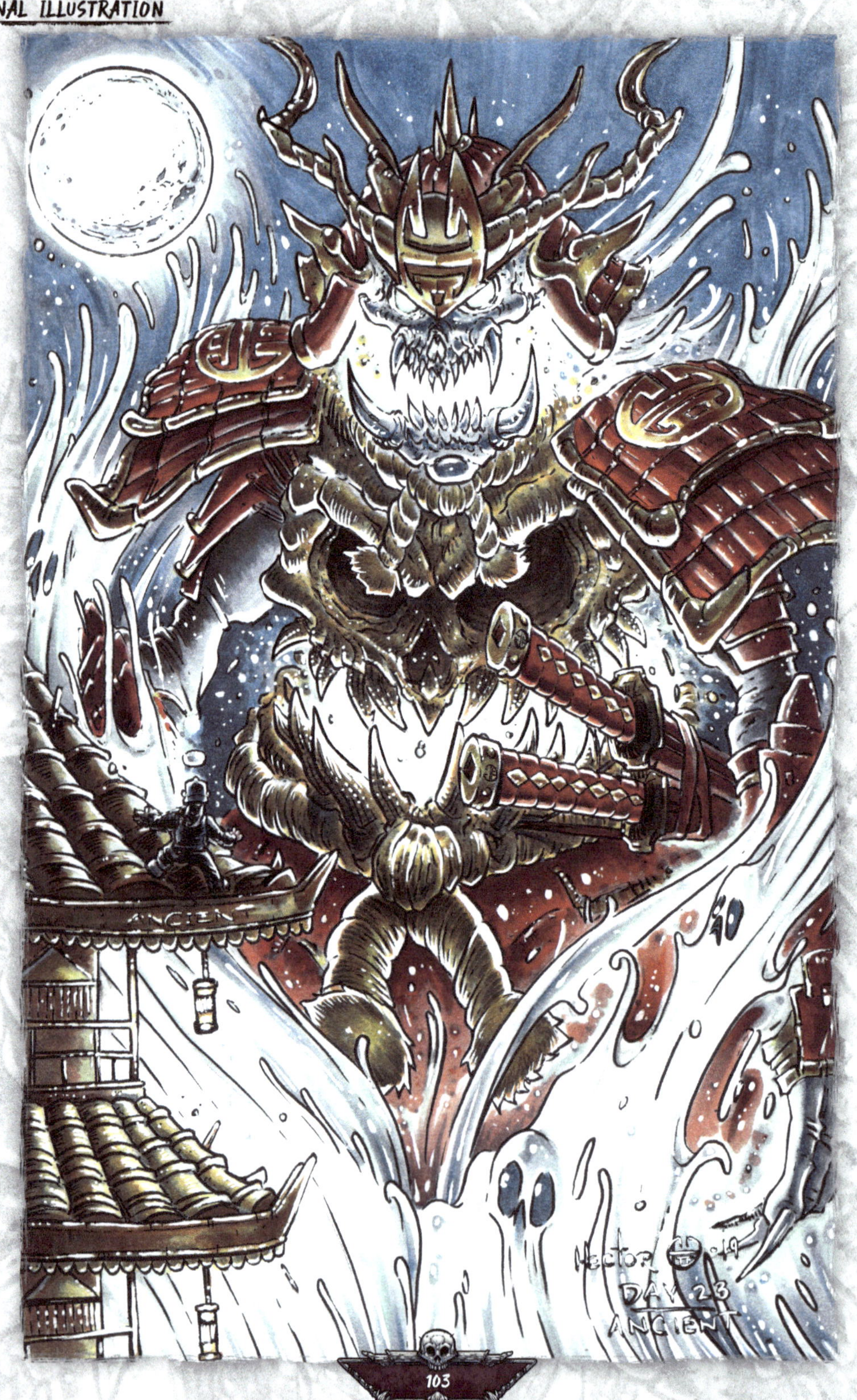

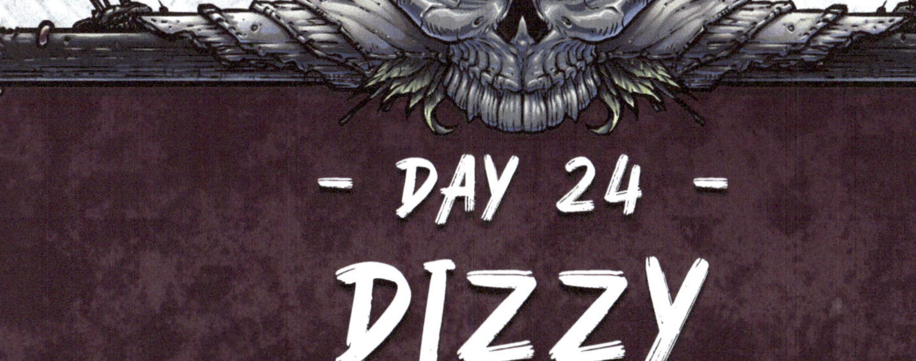

- DAY 24 -

DIZZY

D24 - DIZZY

ROUGH SKETCHES

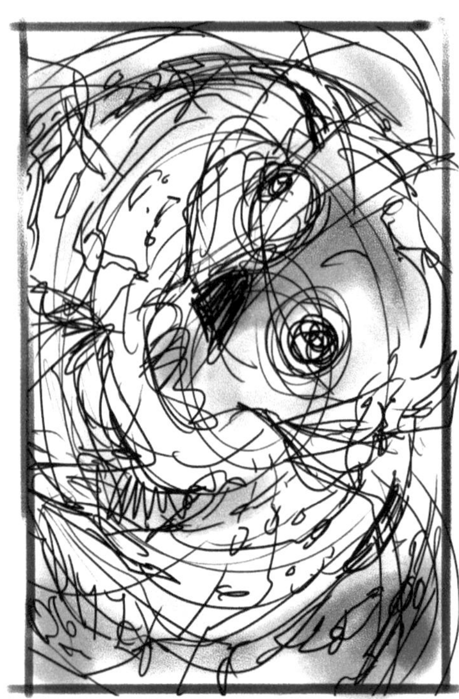

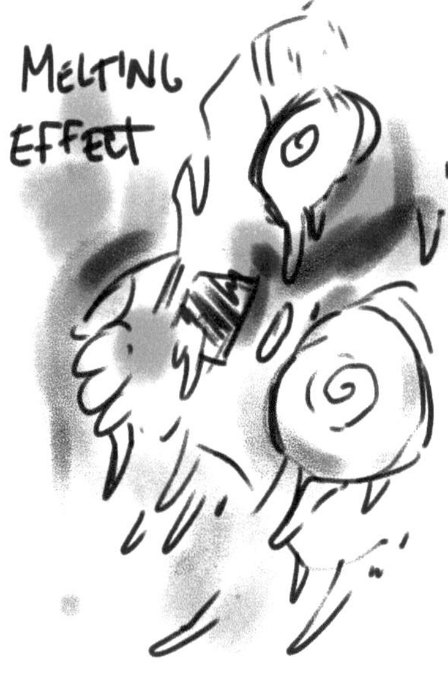

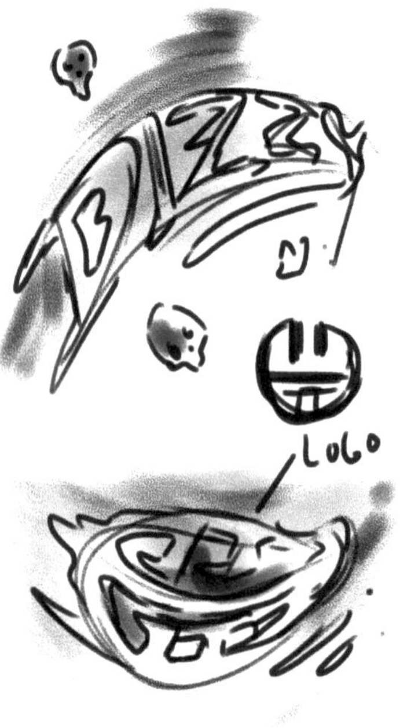

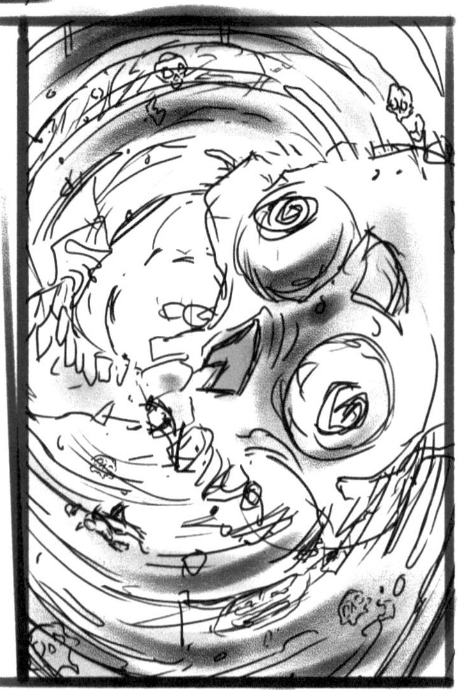

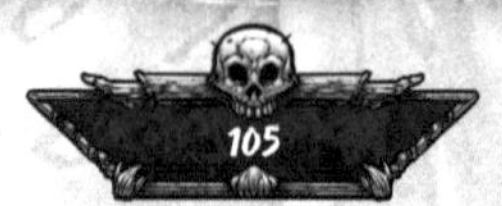

D24 - DIZZY

FINAL LINE ART

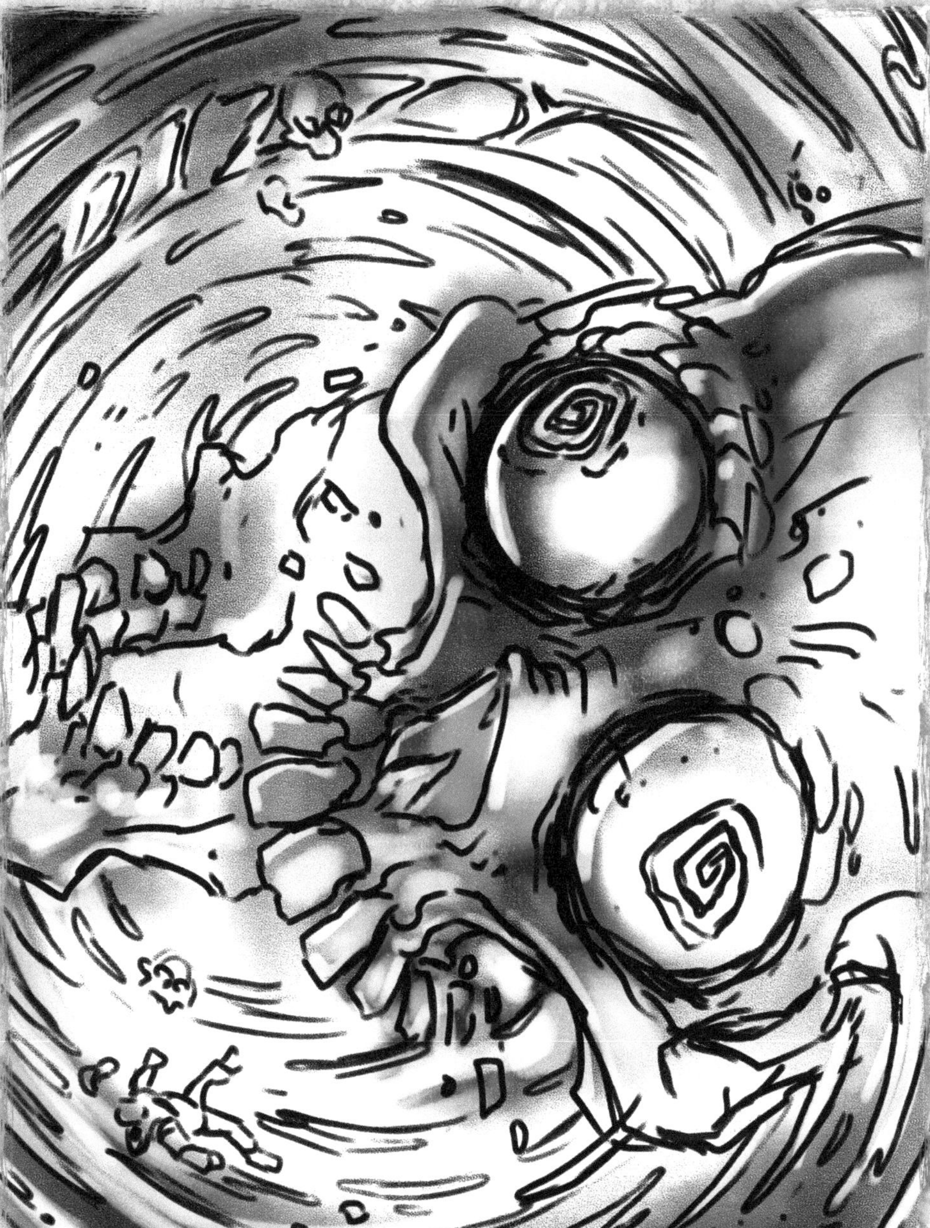

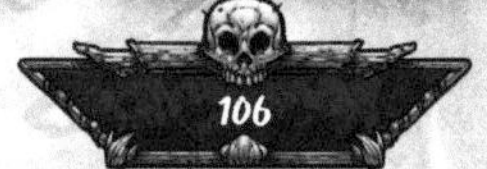

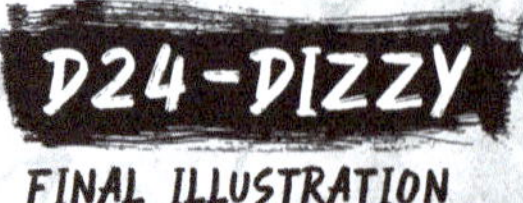
D24-DIZZY
FINAL ILLUSTRATION

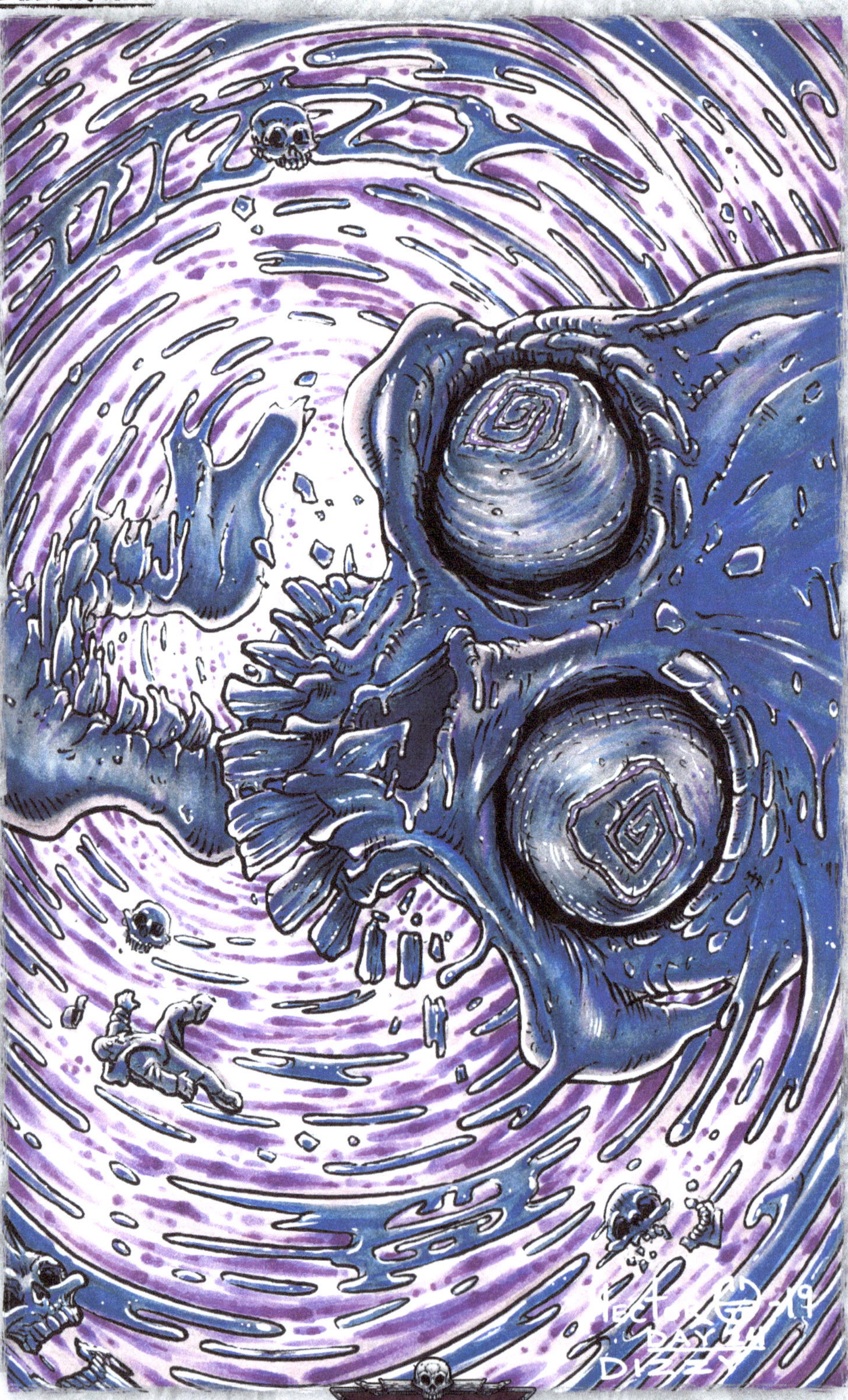

- DAY 25 -

TASTY

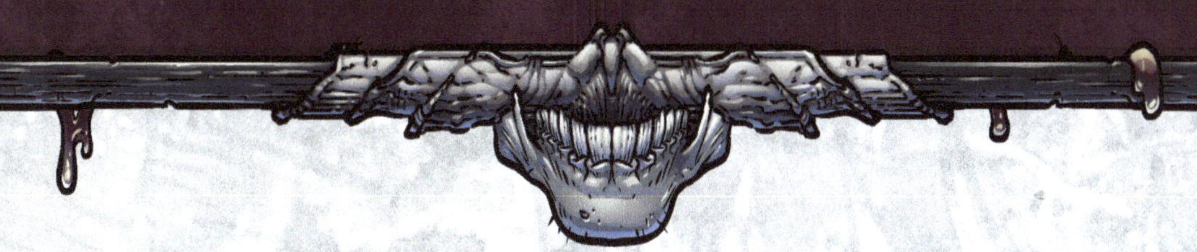

D25 - TASTY

ROUGH SKETCHES

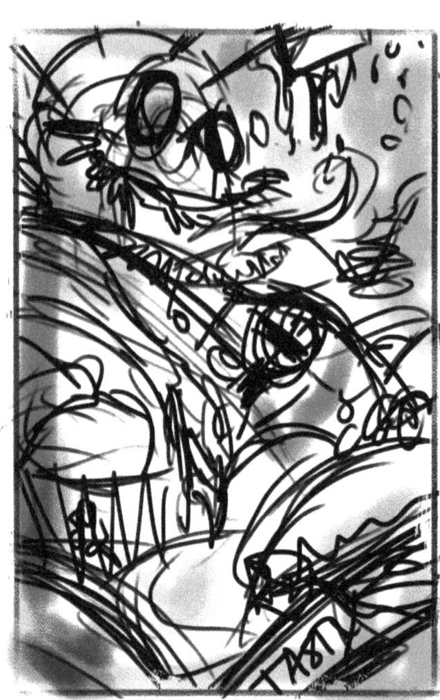

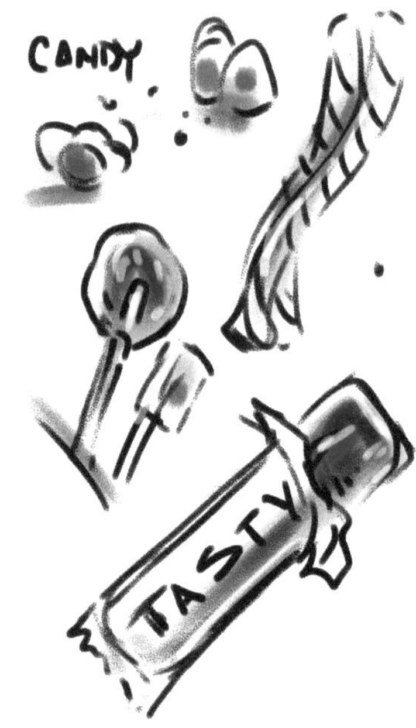

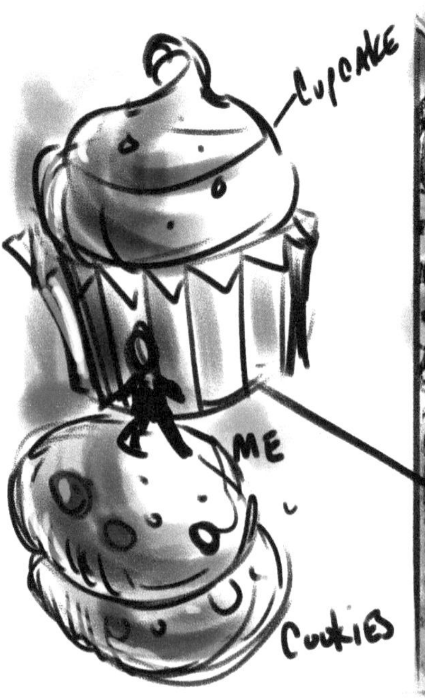

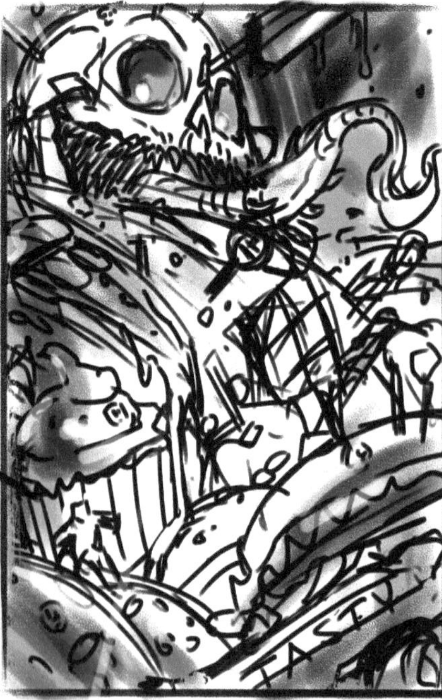

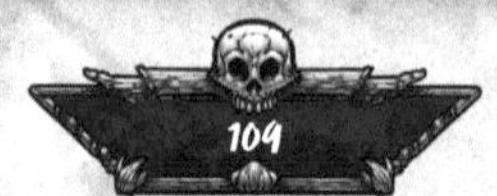

D25 - TASTY

FINAL LINE ART

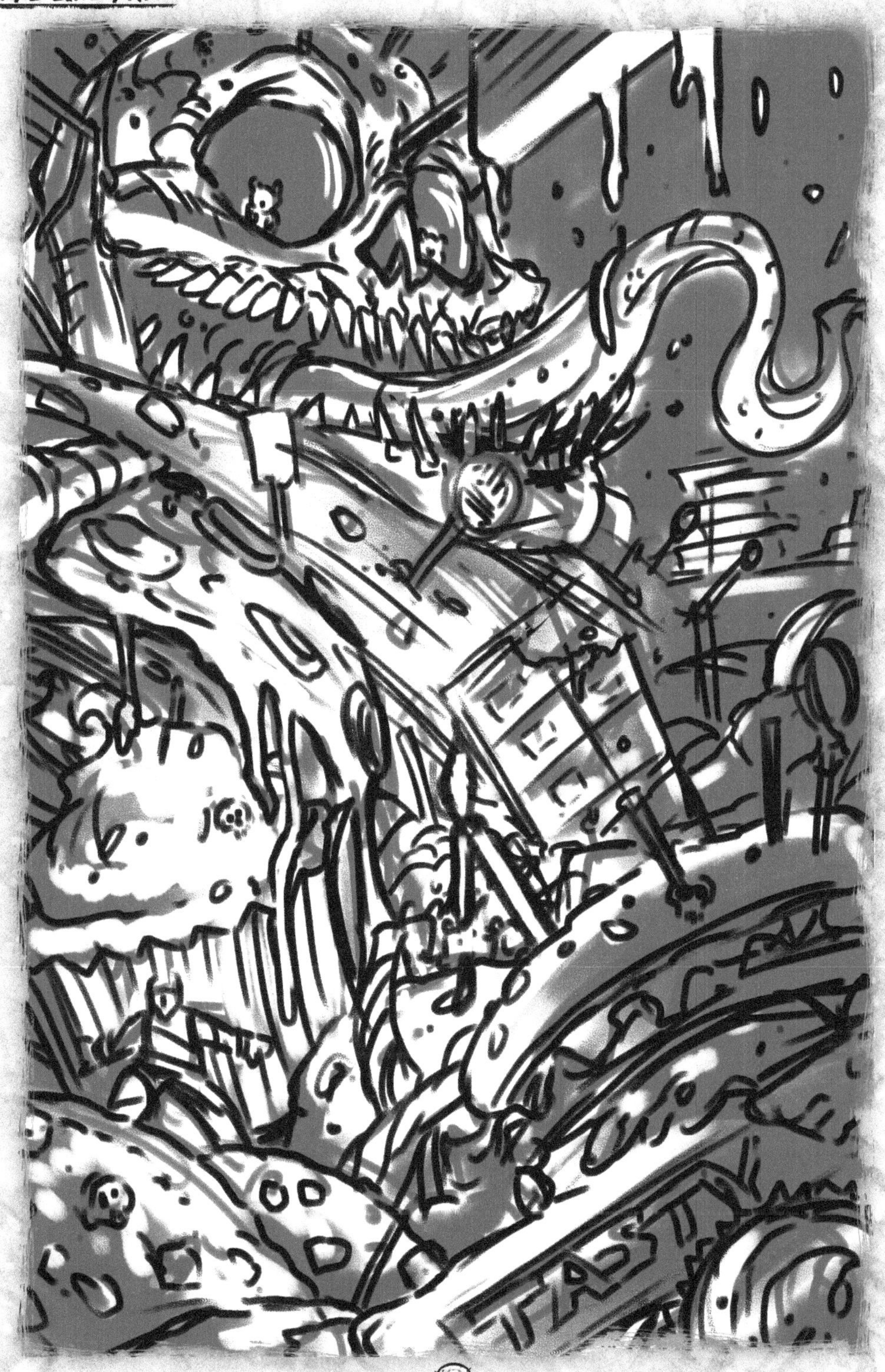

D25 - TASTY

FINAL ILLUSTRATION

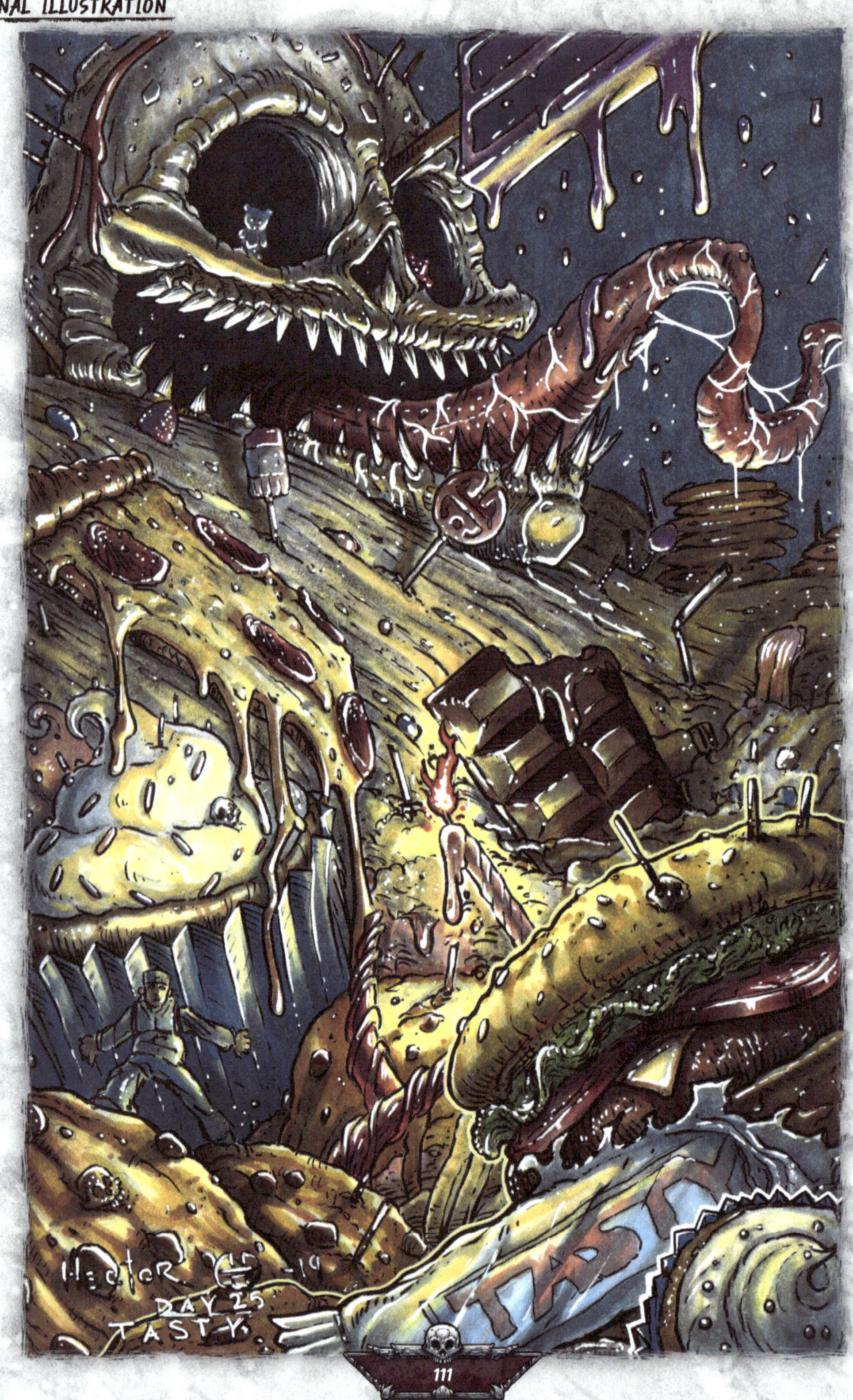

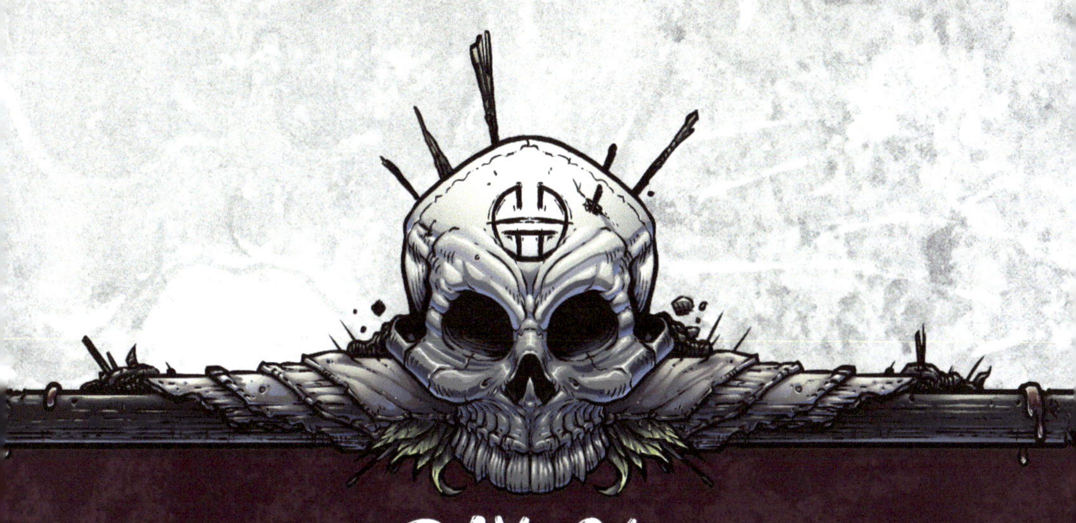

- DAY 26 -

DARK

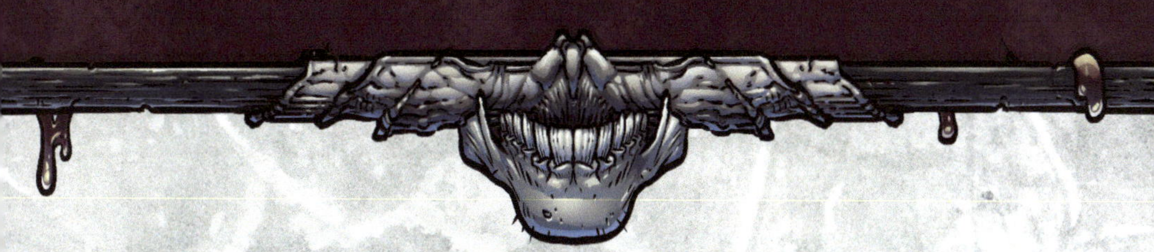

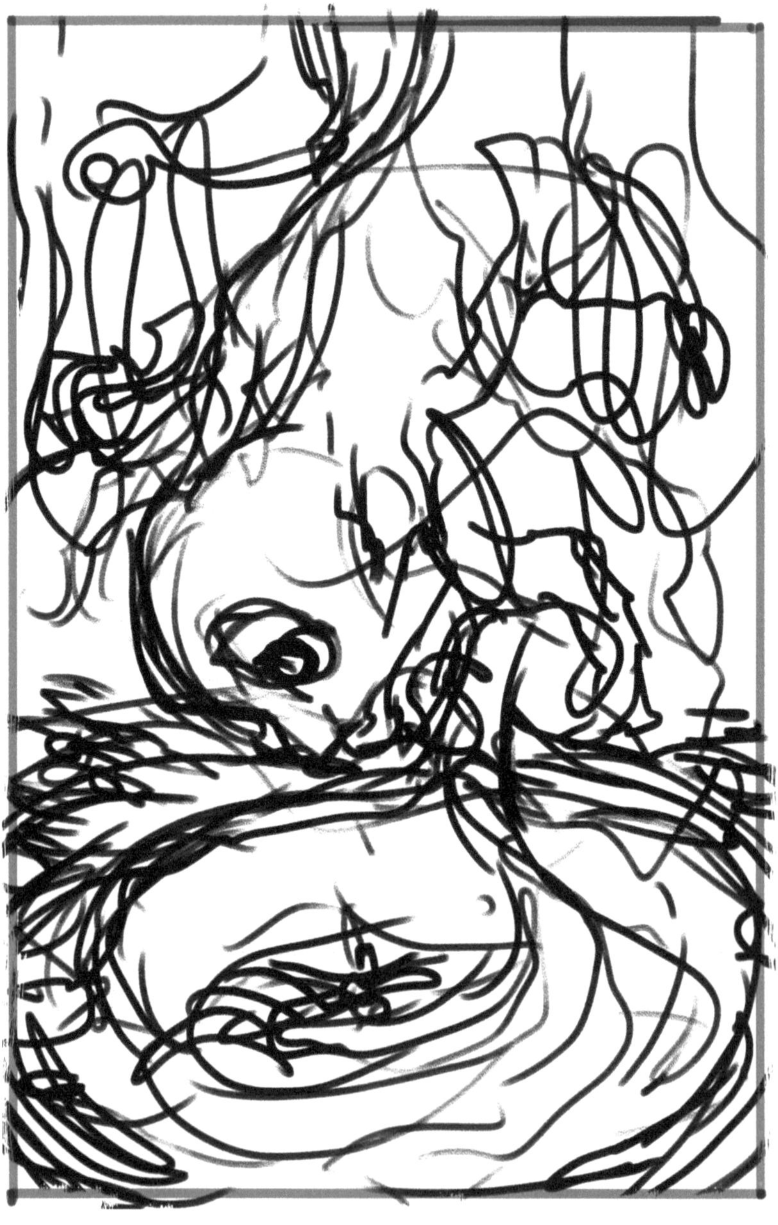

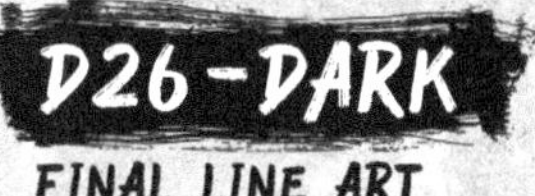

D26 - DARK

FINAL LINE ART

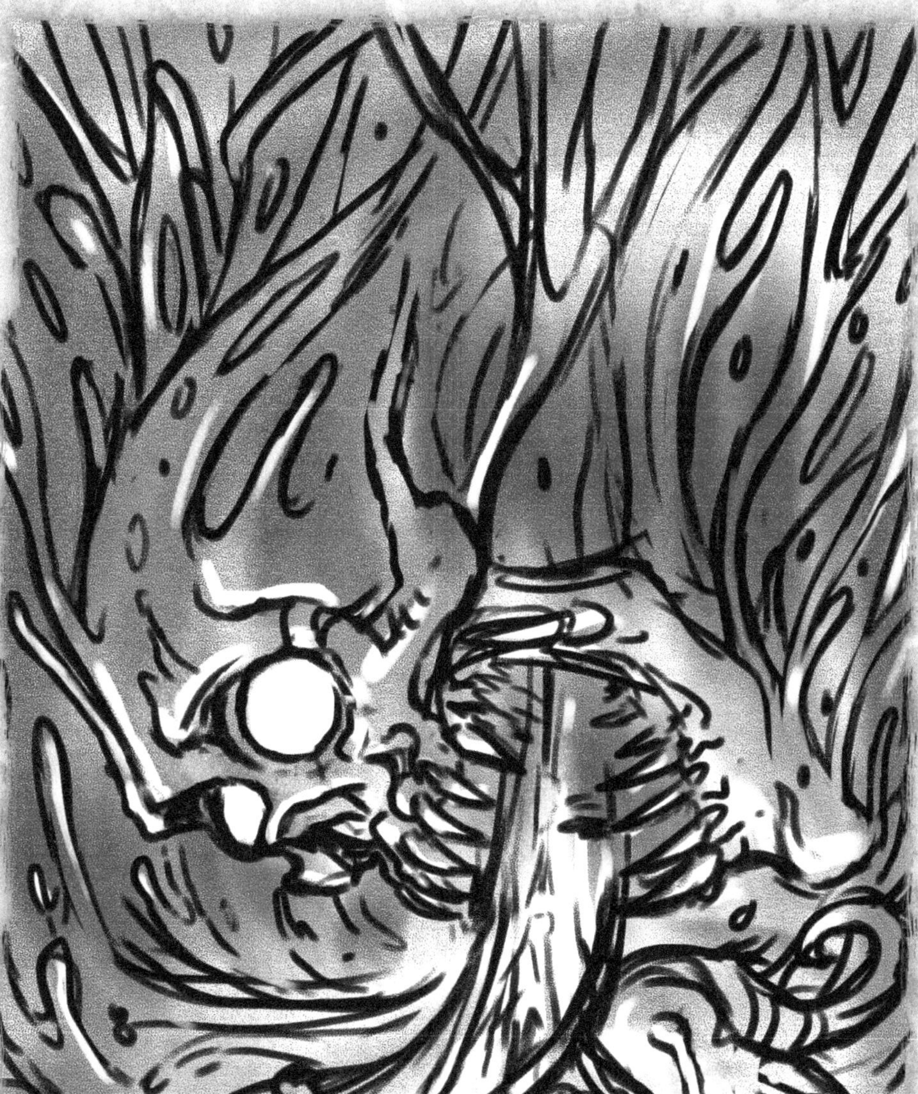

D26-DARK

FINAL ILLUSTRATION

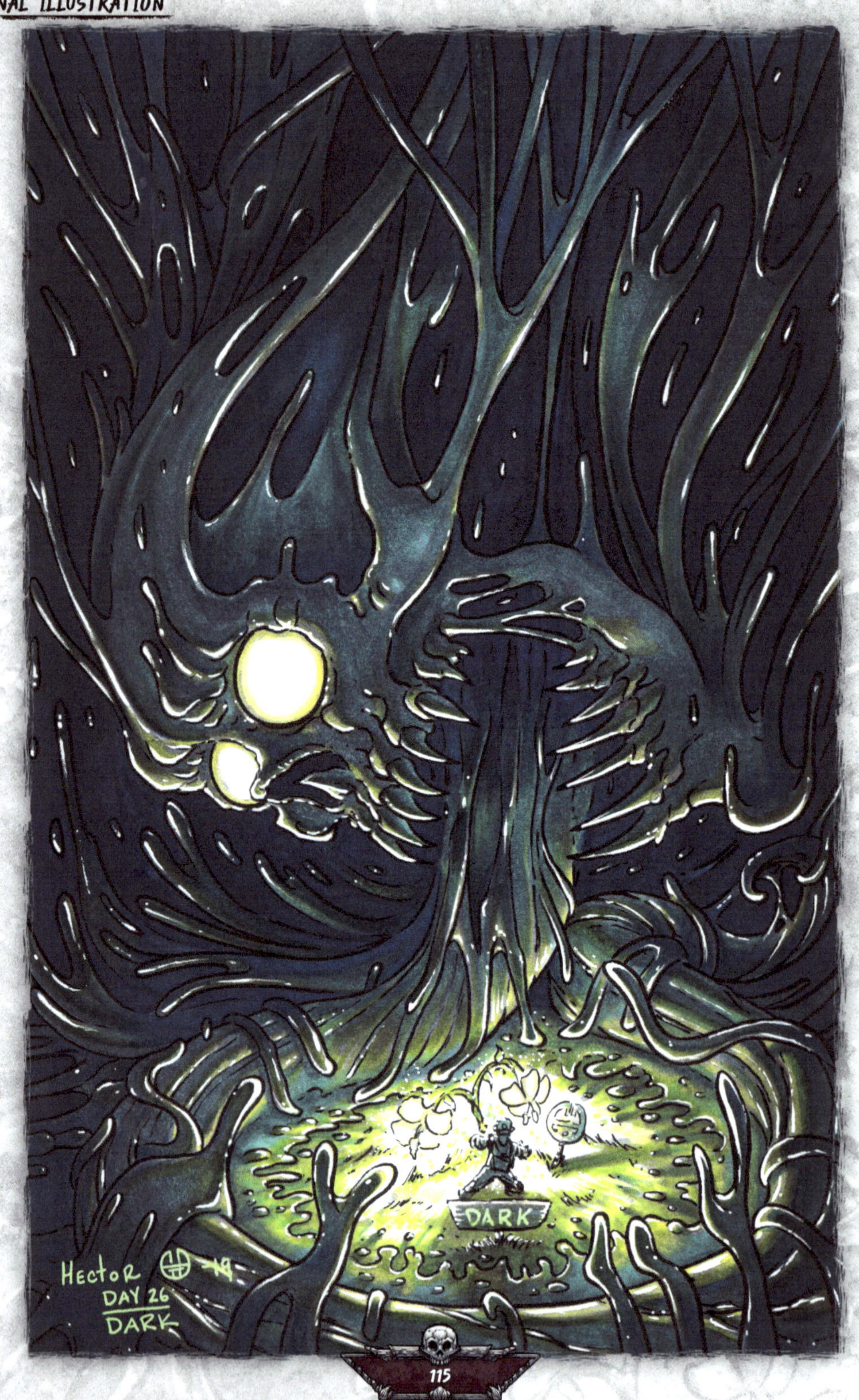

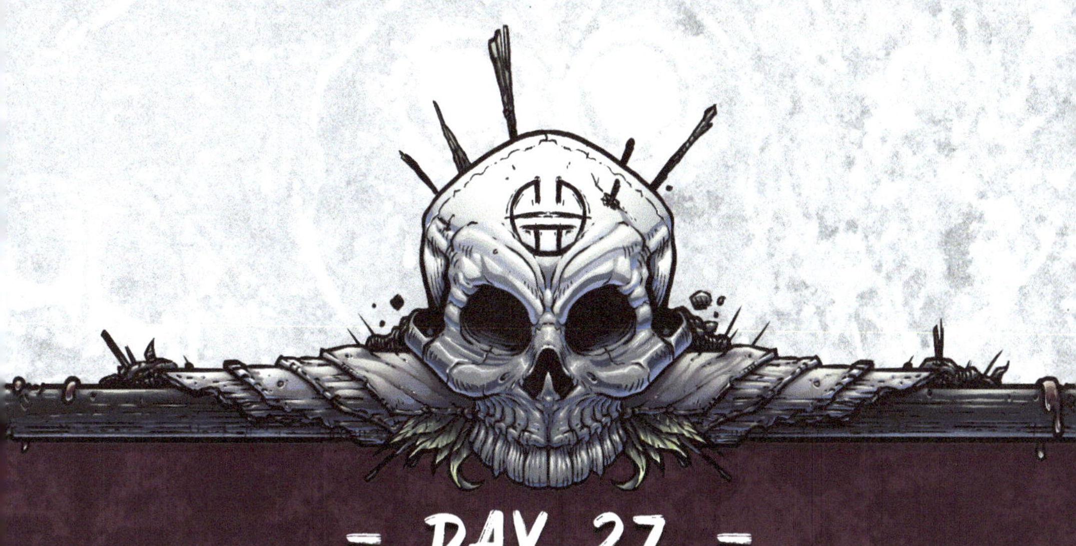

- DAY 27 -

COAT

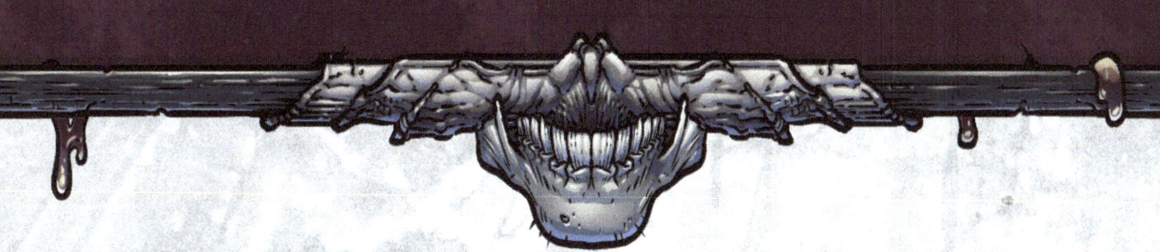

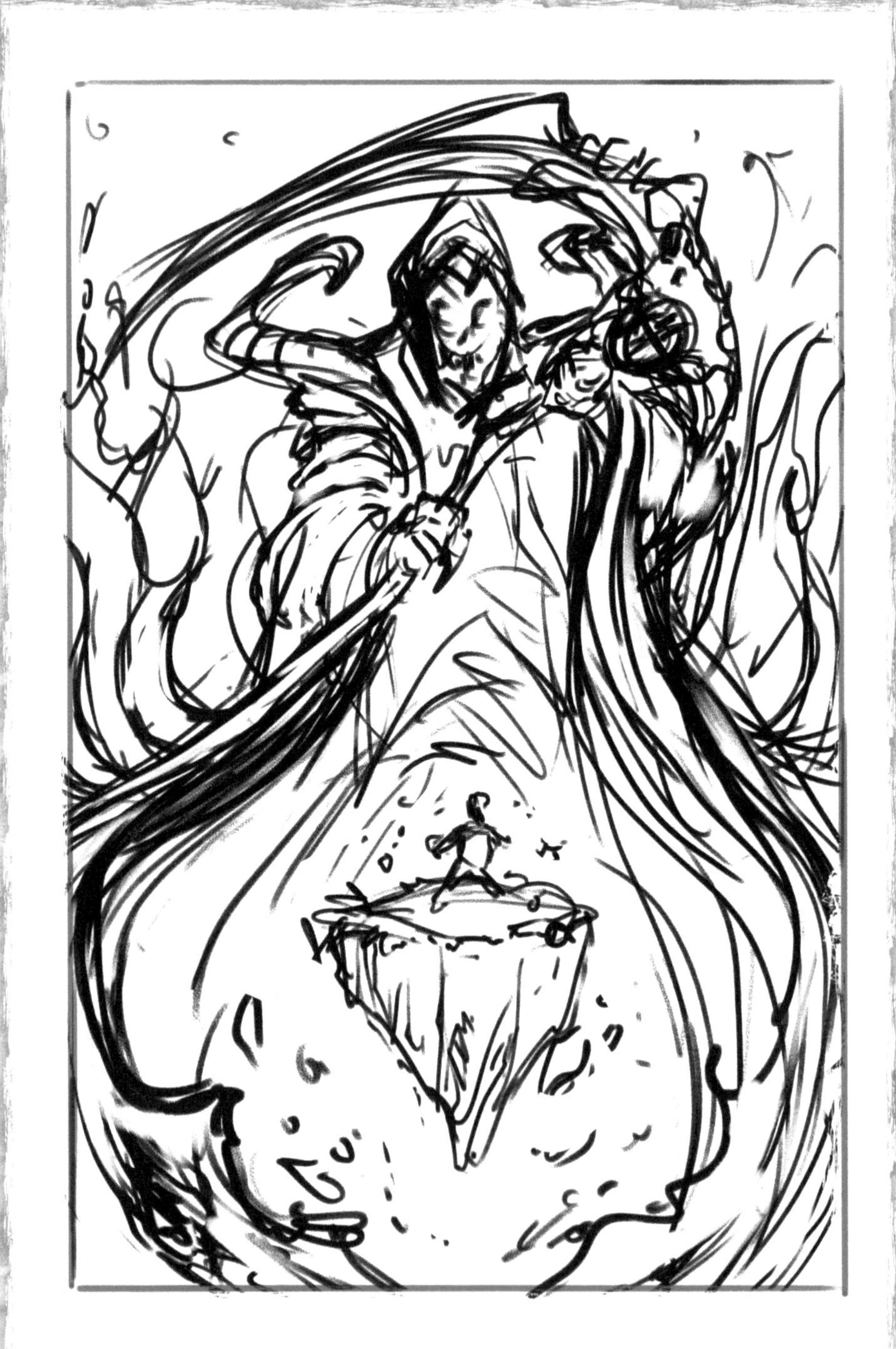

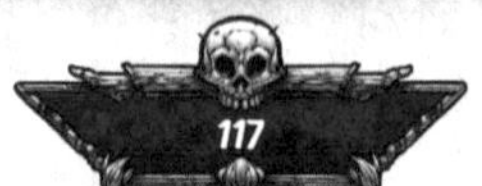

D27 - COAT

FINAL LINE ART

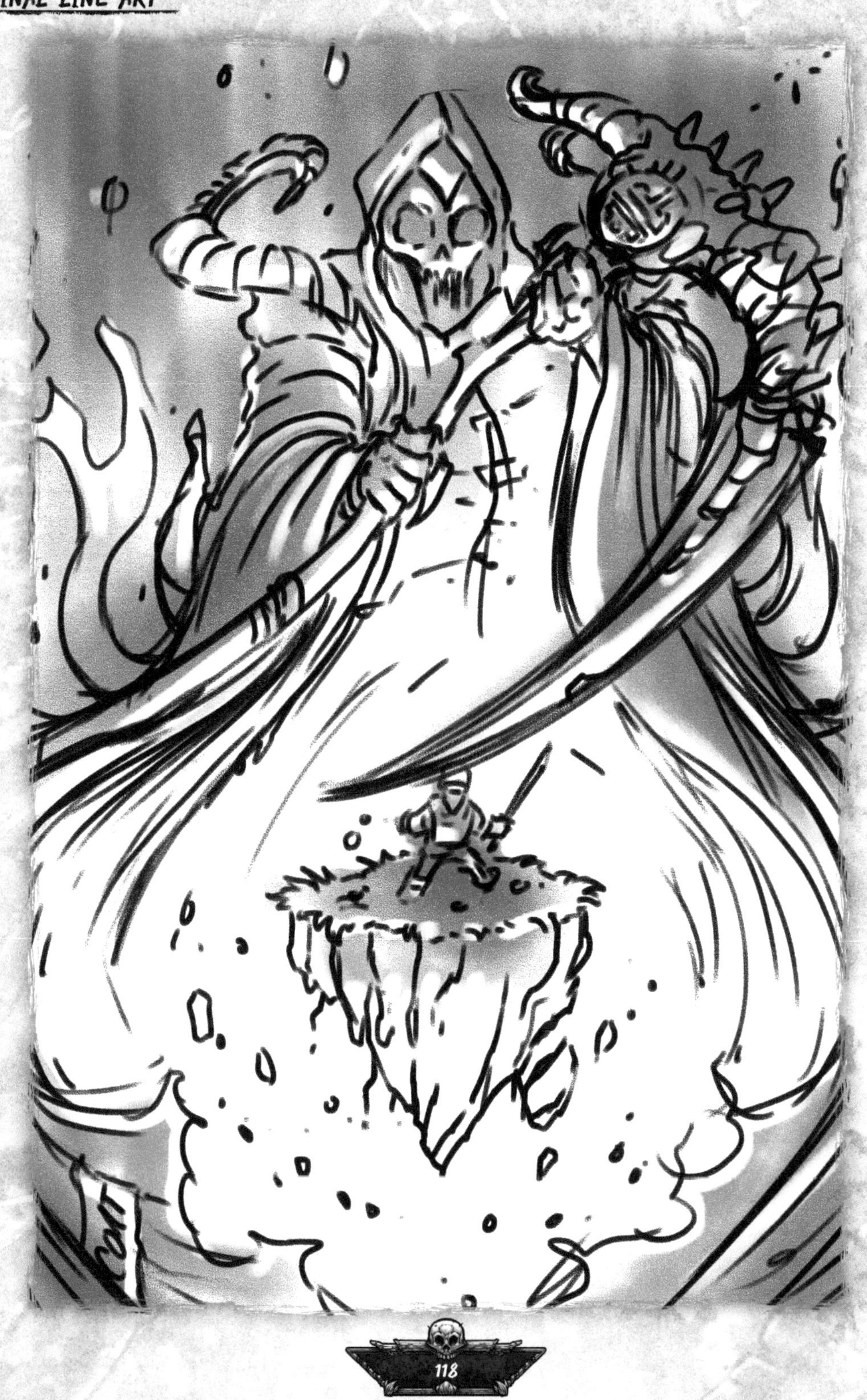

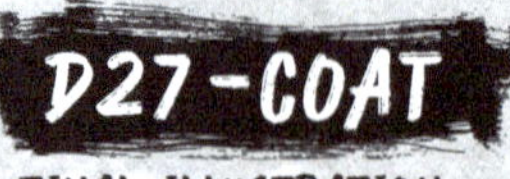

FINAL ILLUSTRATION

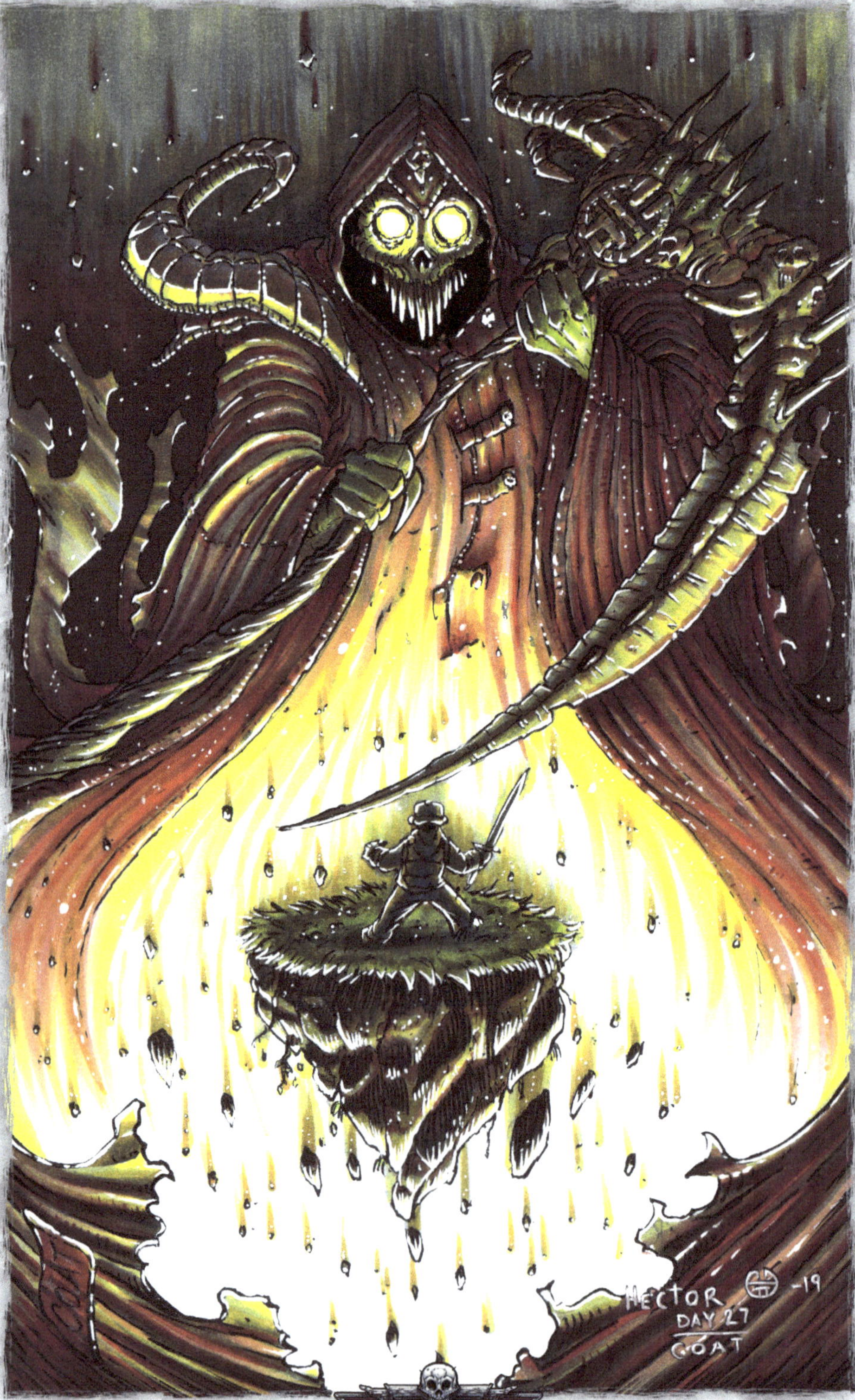

- DAY 28 -

RIDE

D28-RIDE

ROUGH SKETCHES

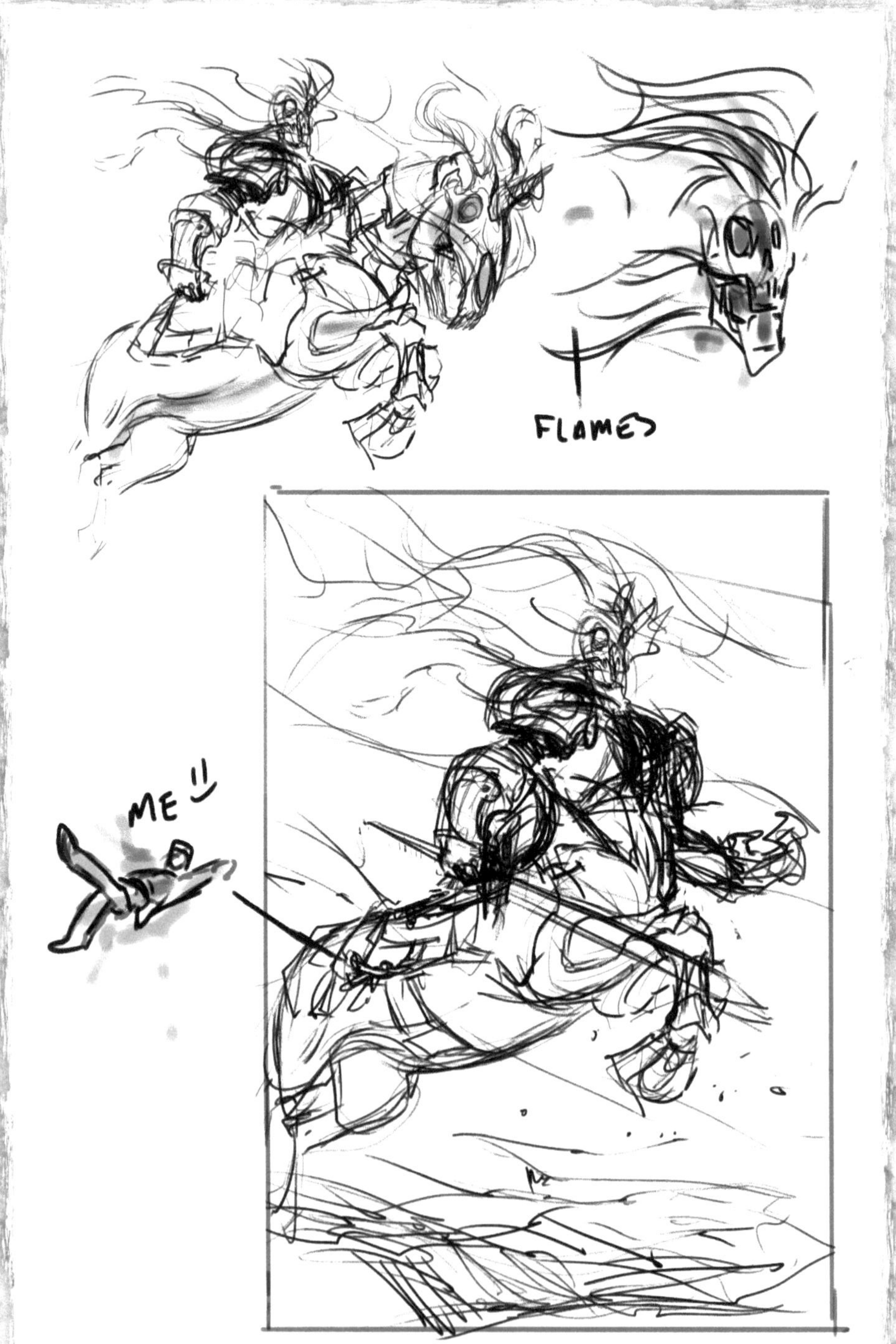

FLAMES

ME !!

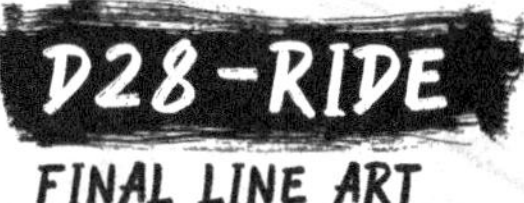

D28-RIDE

FINAL LINE ART

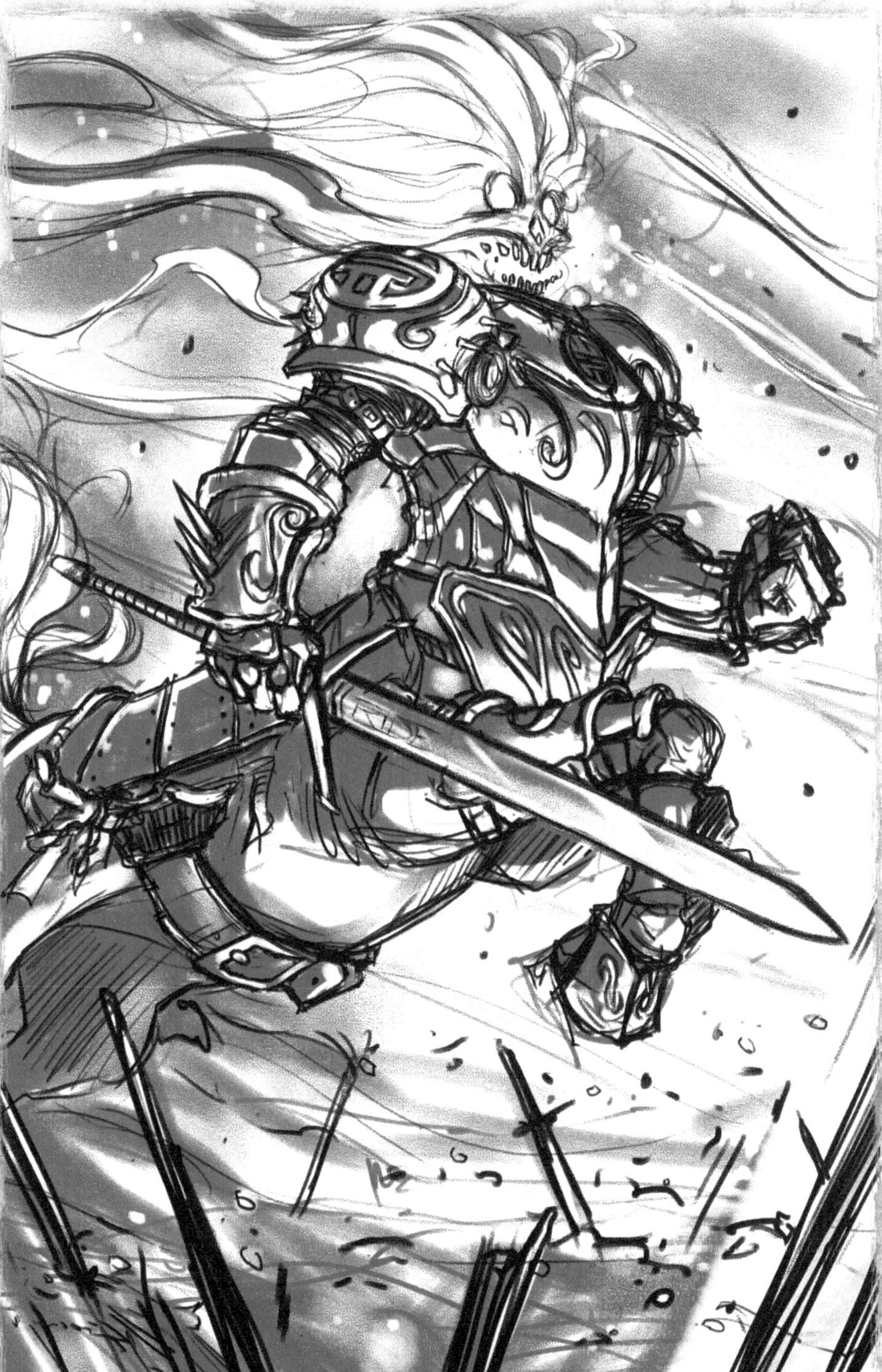

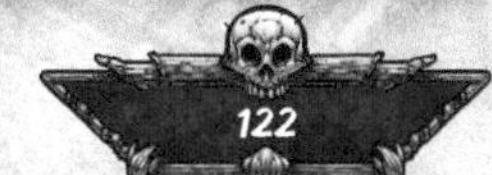

D28-RIDE

FINAL ILLUSTRATION

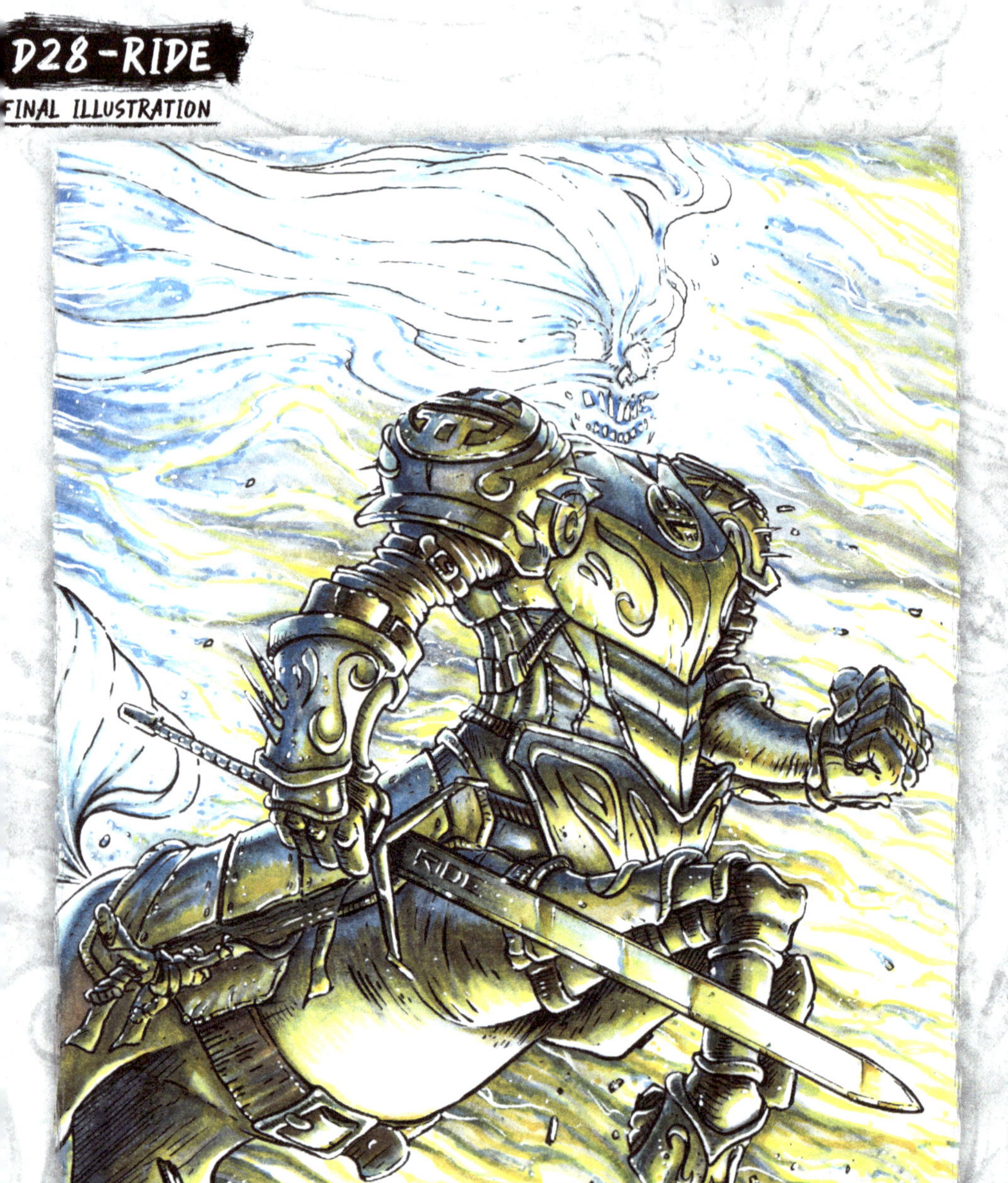

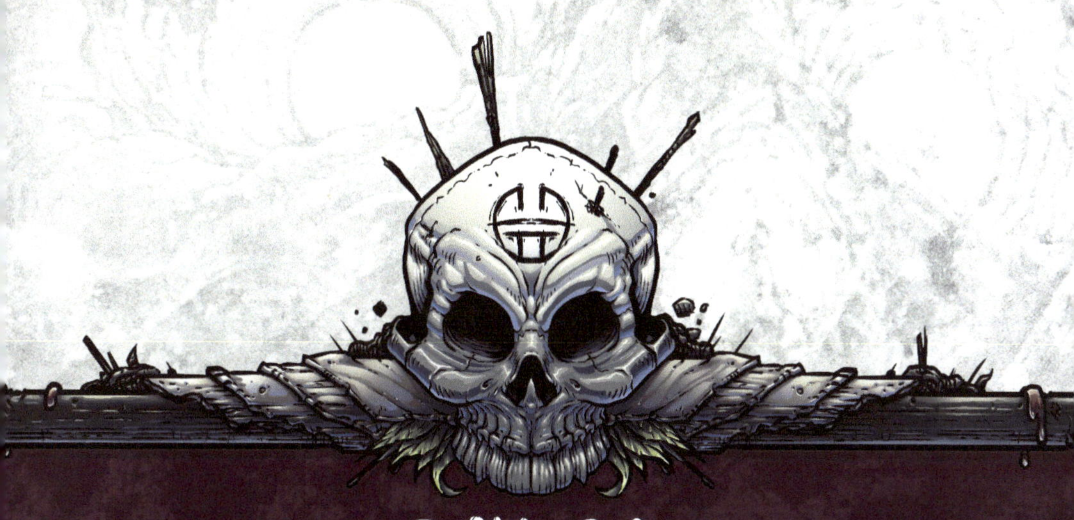

- DAY 29 -

INJURED

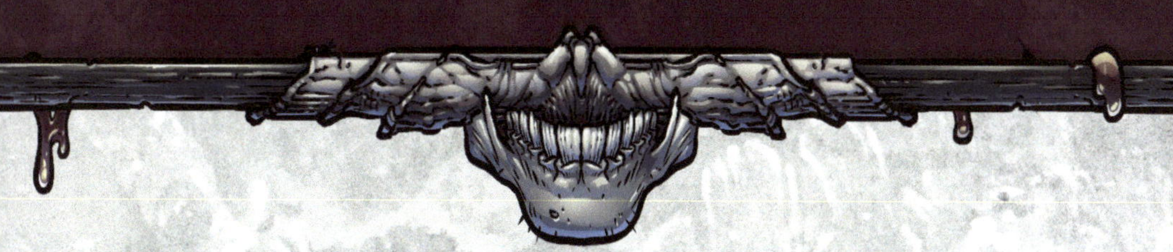

D29 - INJURED

ROUGH SKETCHES

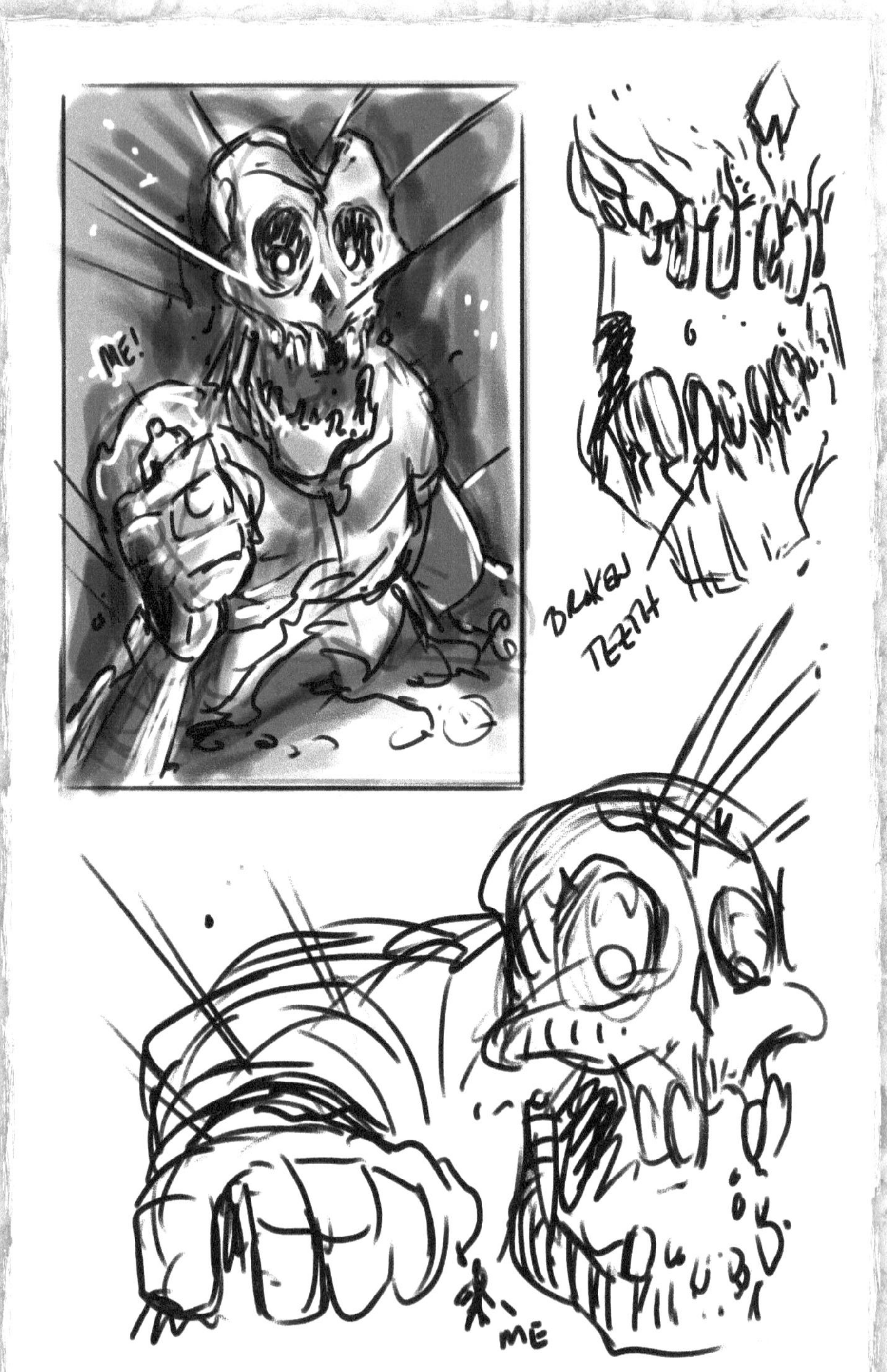

D29 - INJURED

FINAL LINE ART

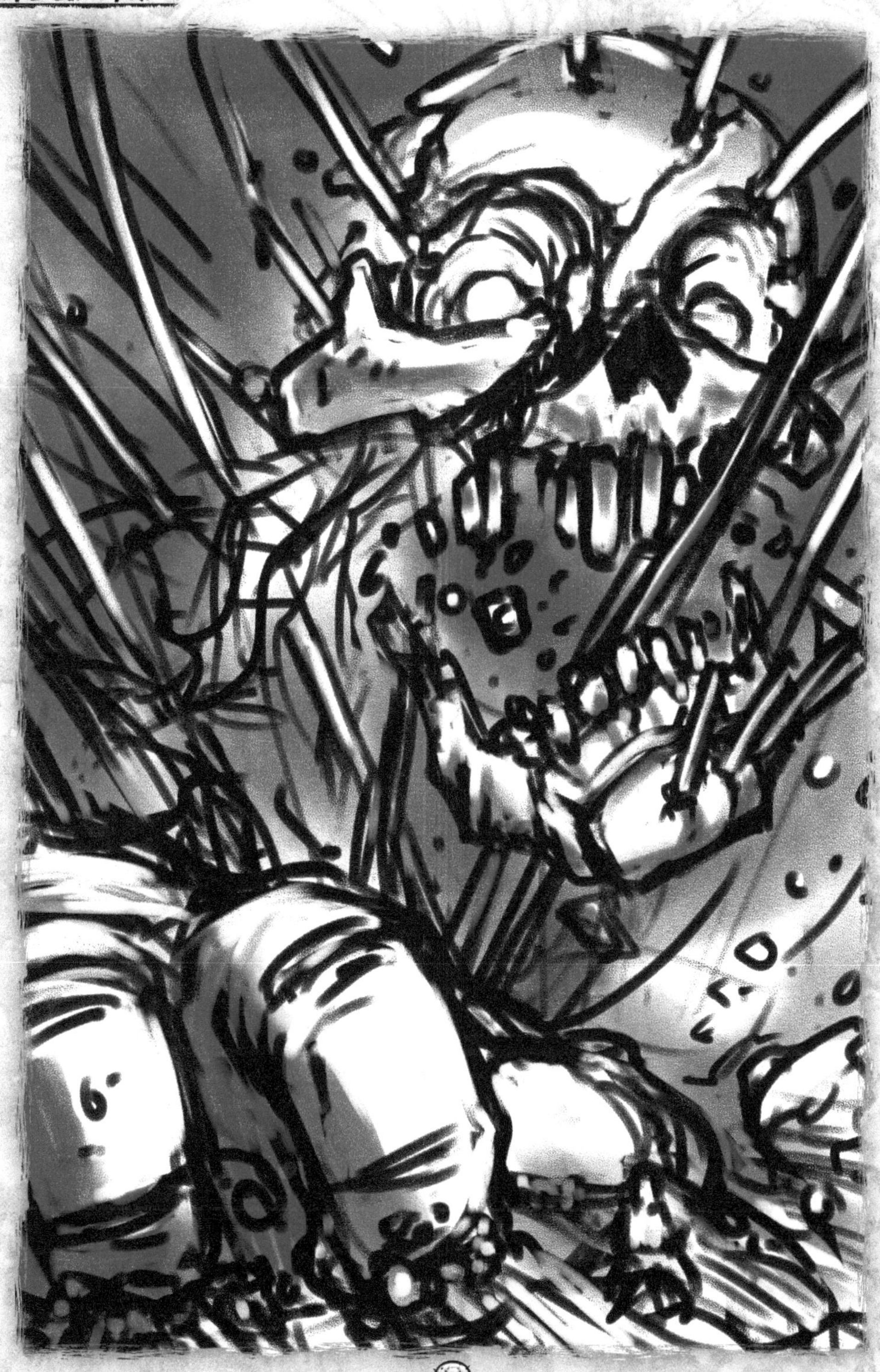

D29 - INJURED

FINAL ILLUSTRATION

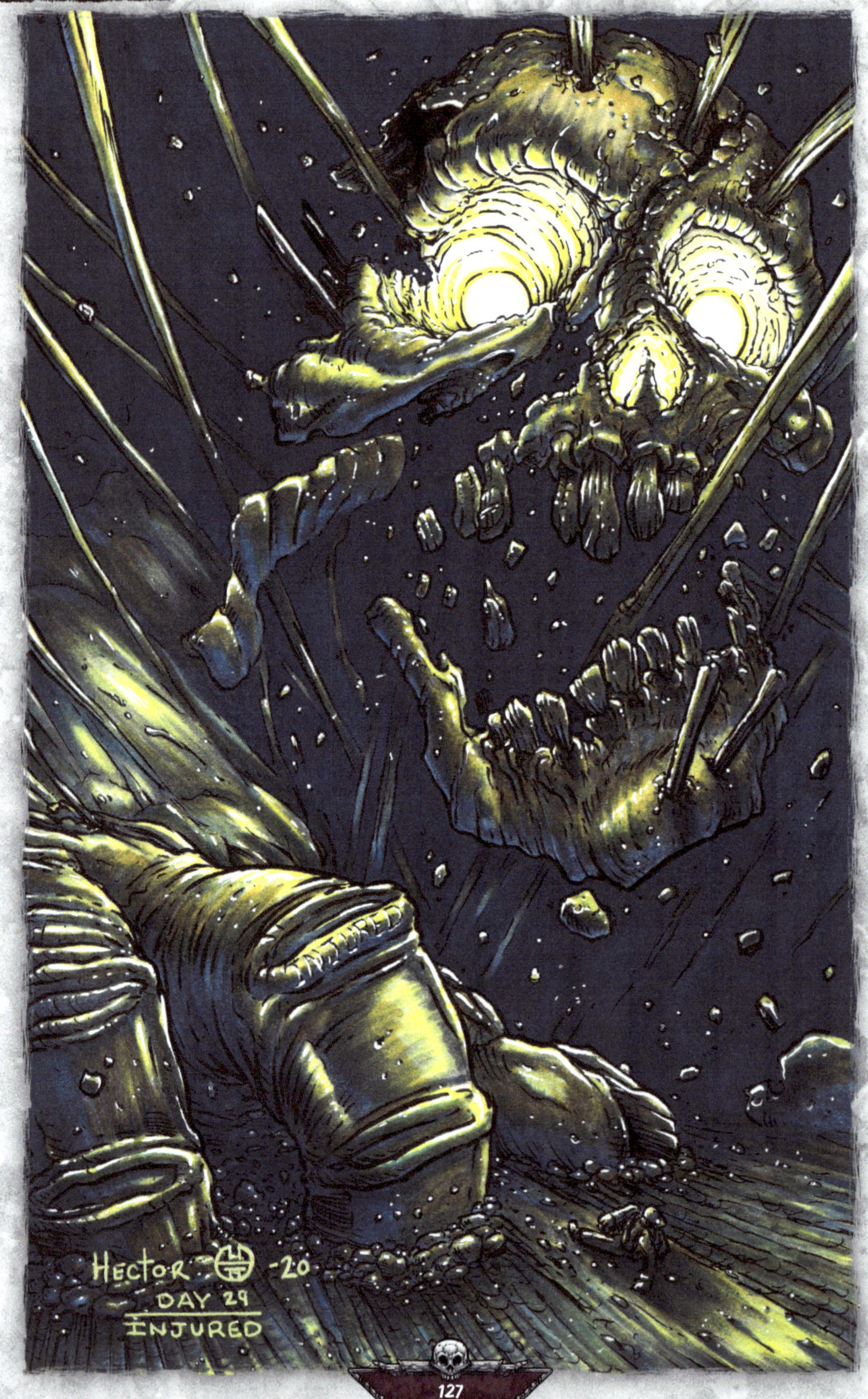

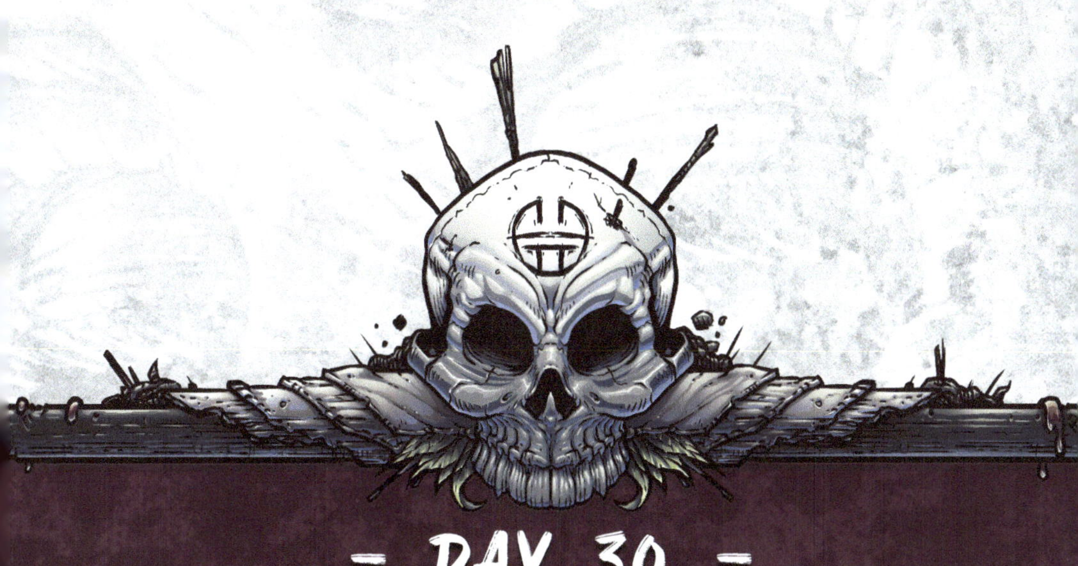

DAY 30
CATCH

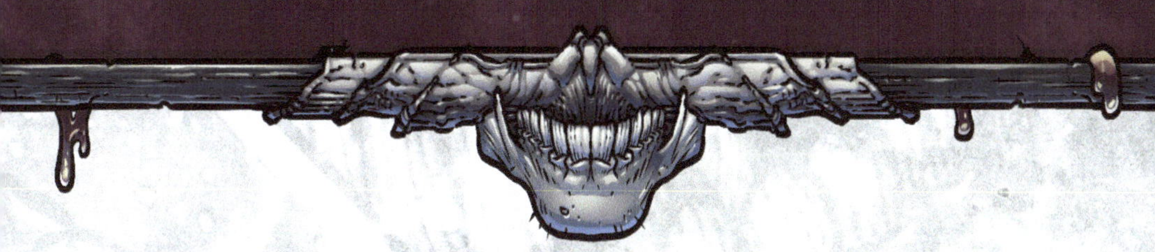

ME!!

CAGE?

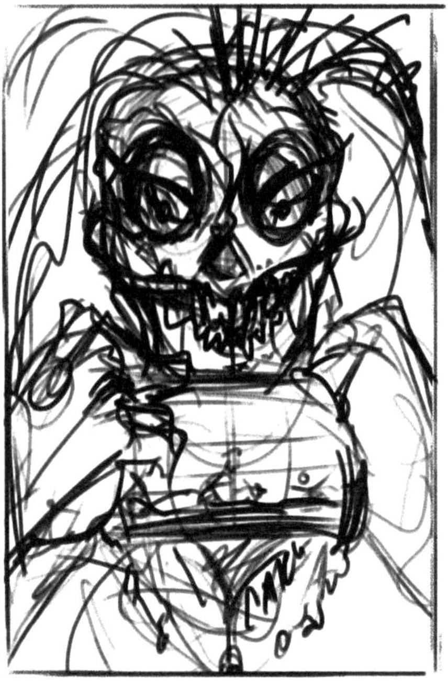

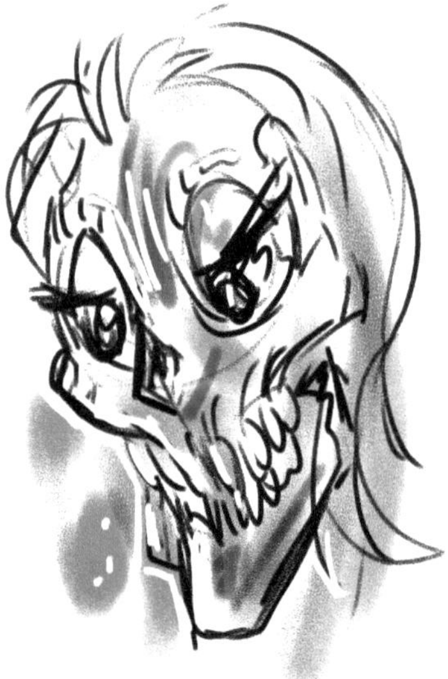

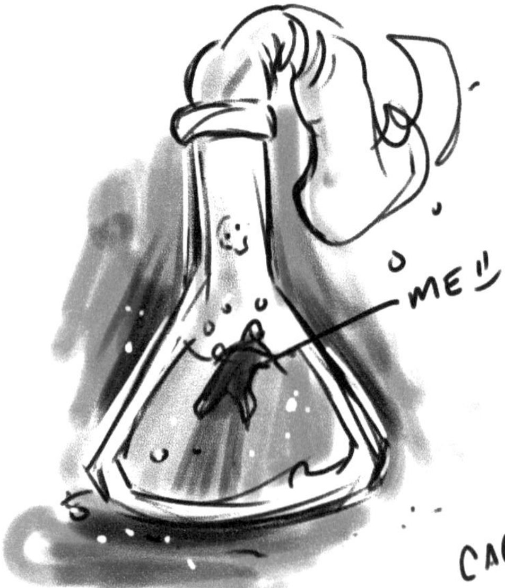

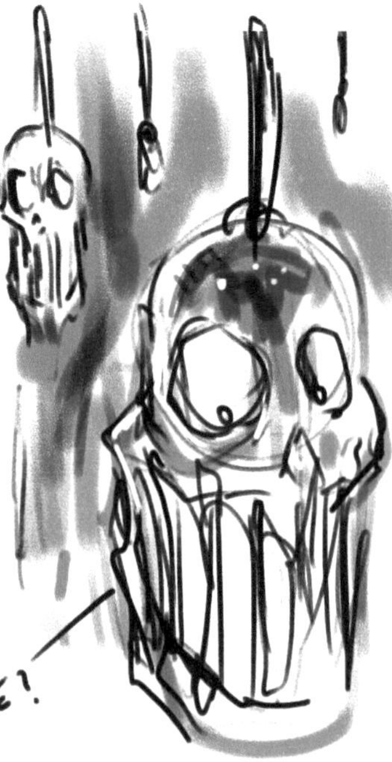

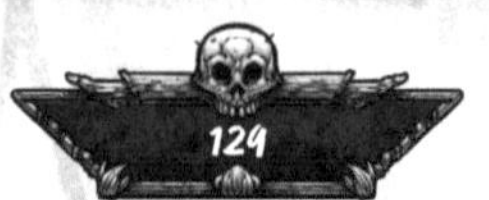

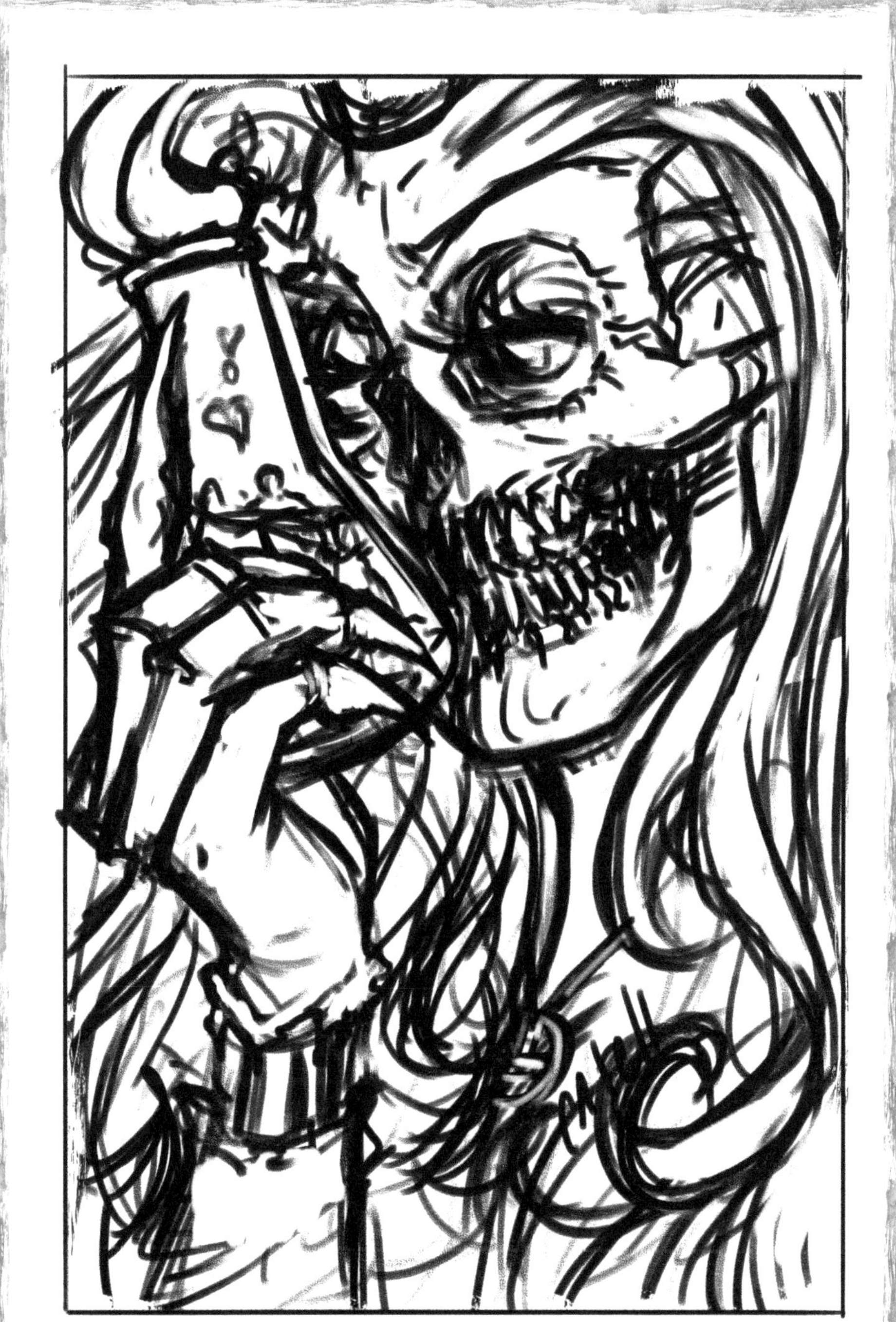

D30 - CATCH

FINAL LINE ART

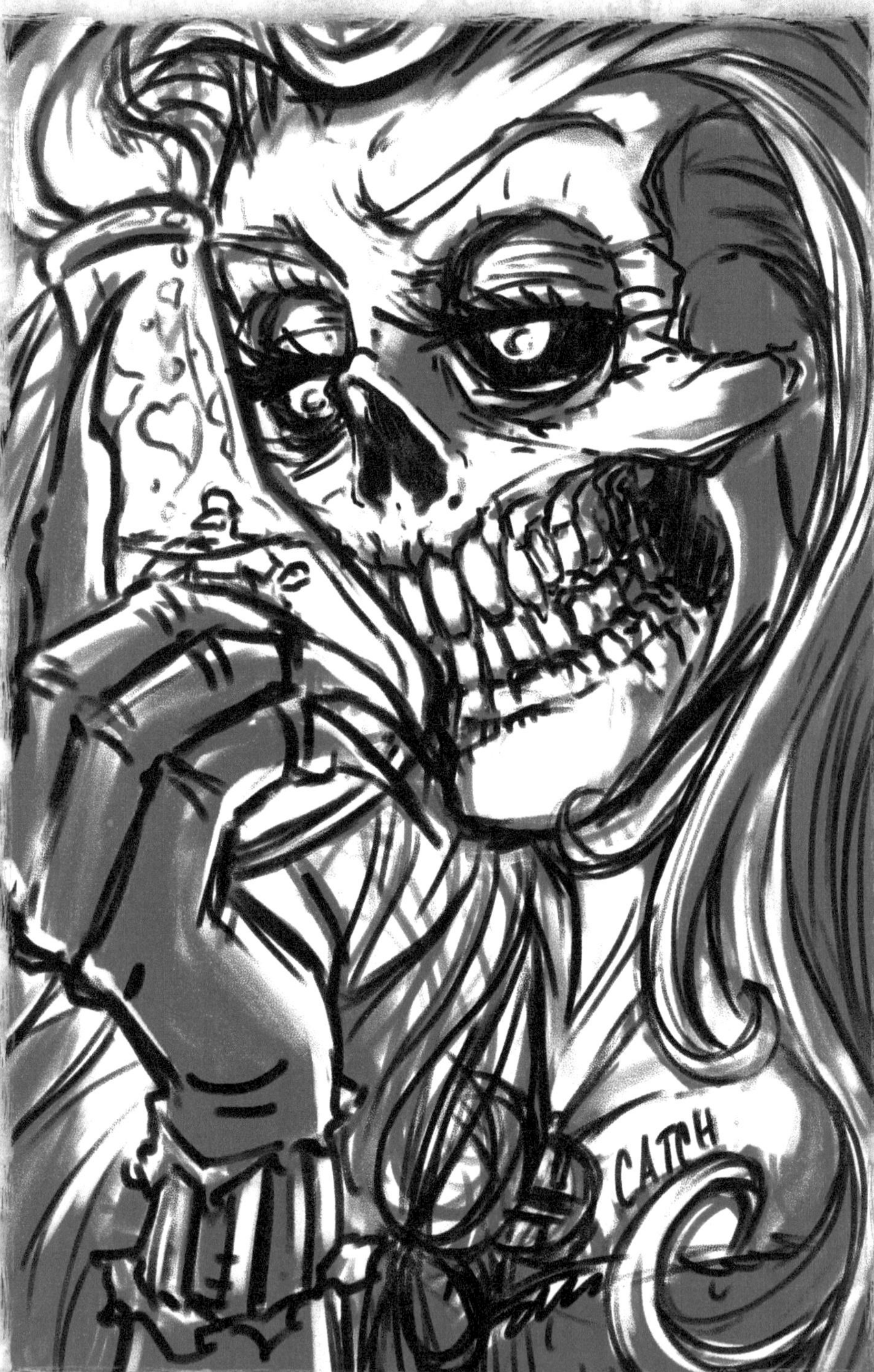

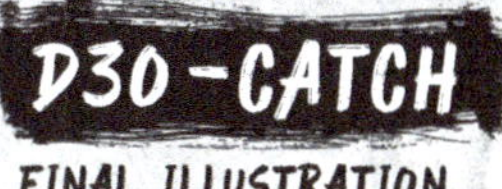

FINAL ILLUSTRATION

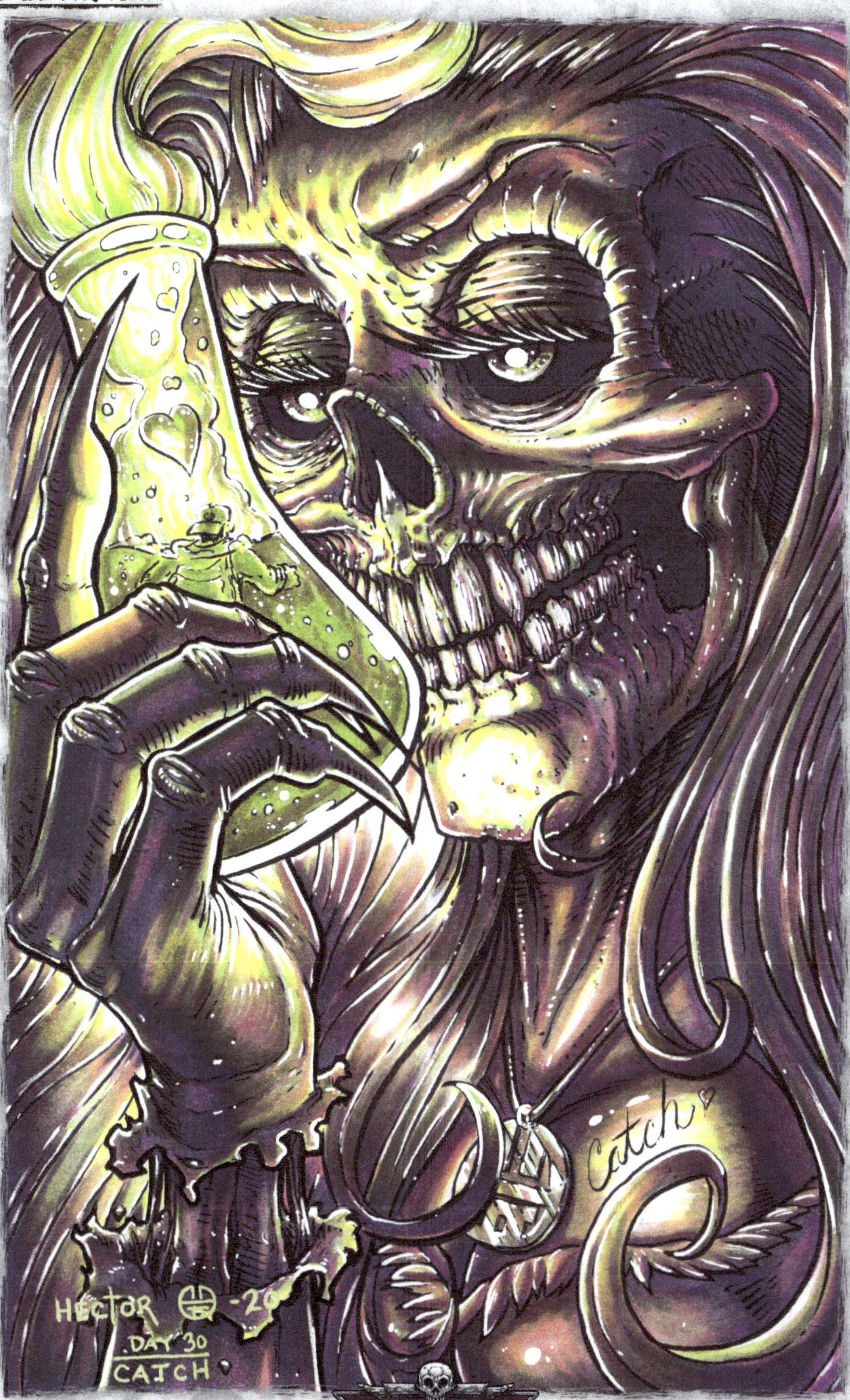

- DAY 31 -

RIPE

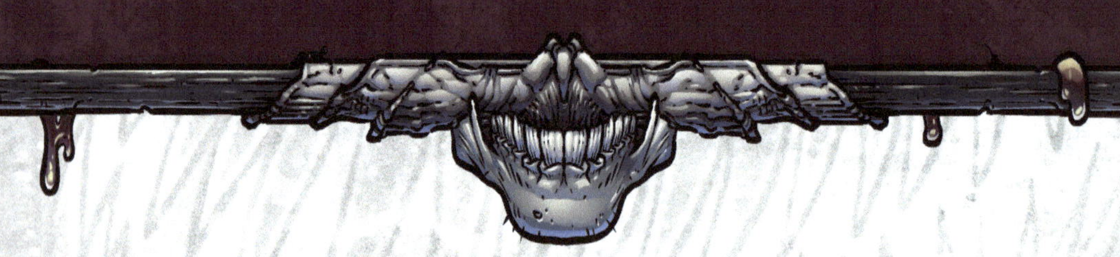

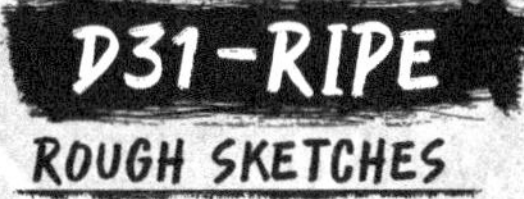

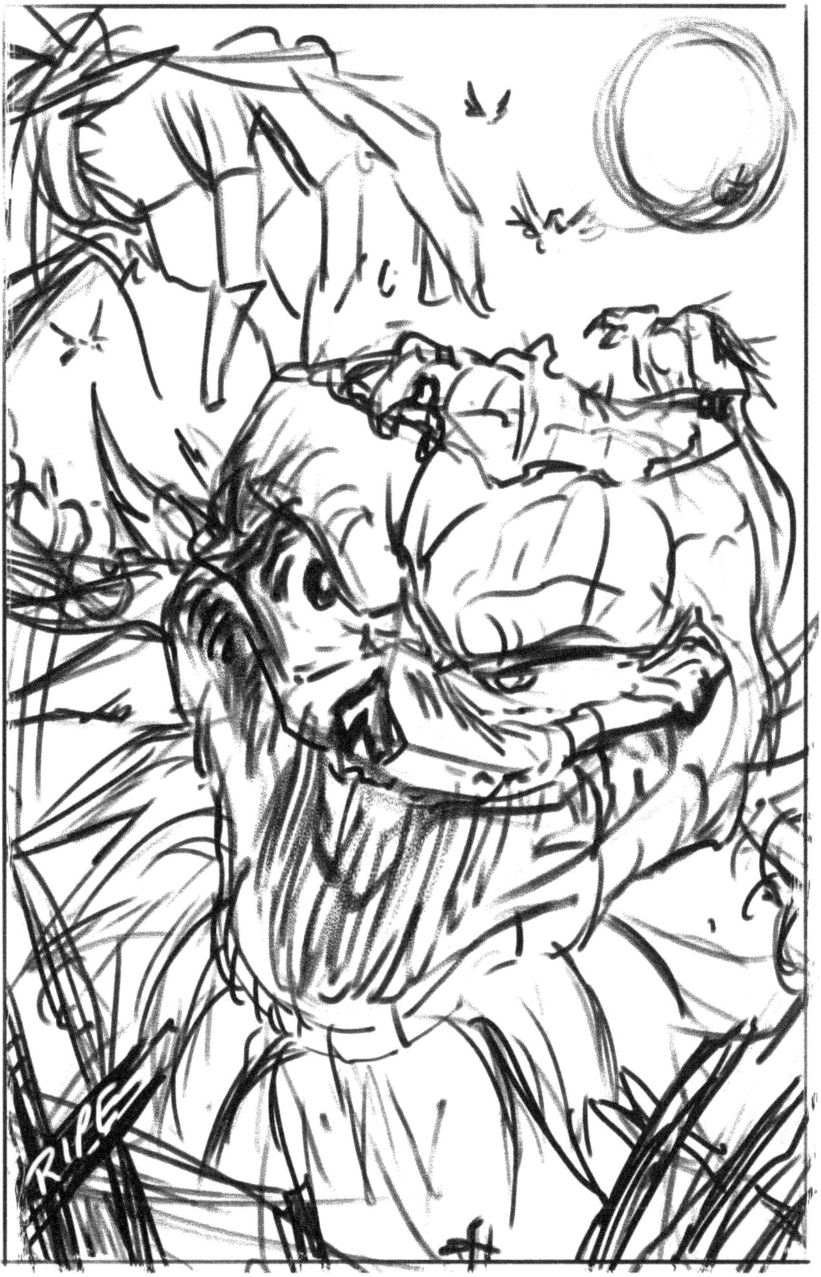

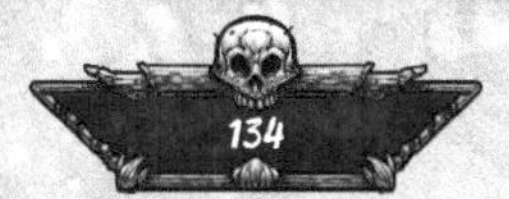

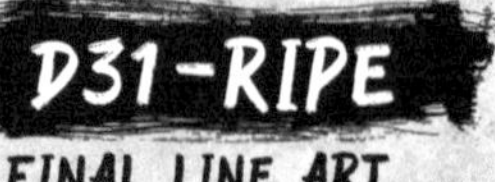

D31-RIPE

FINAL LINE ART

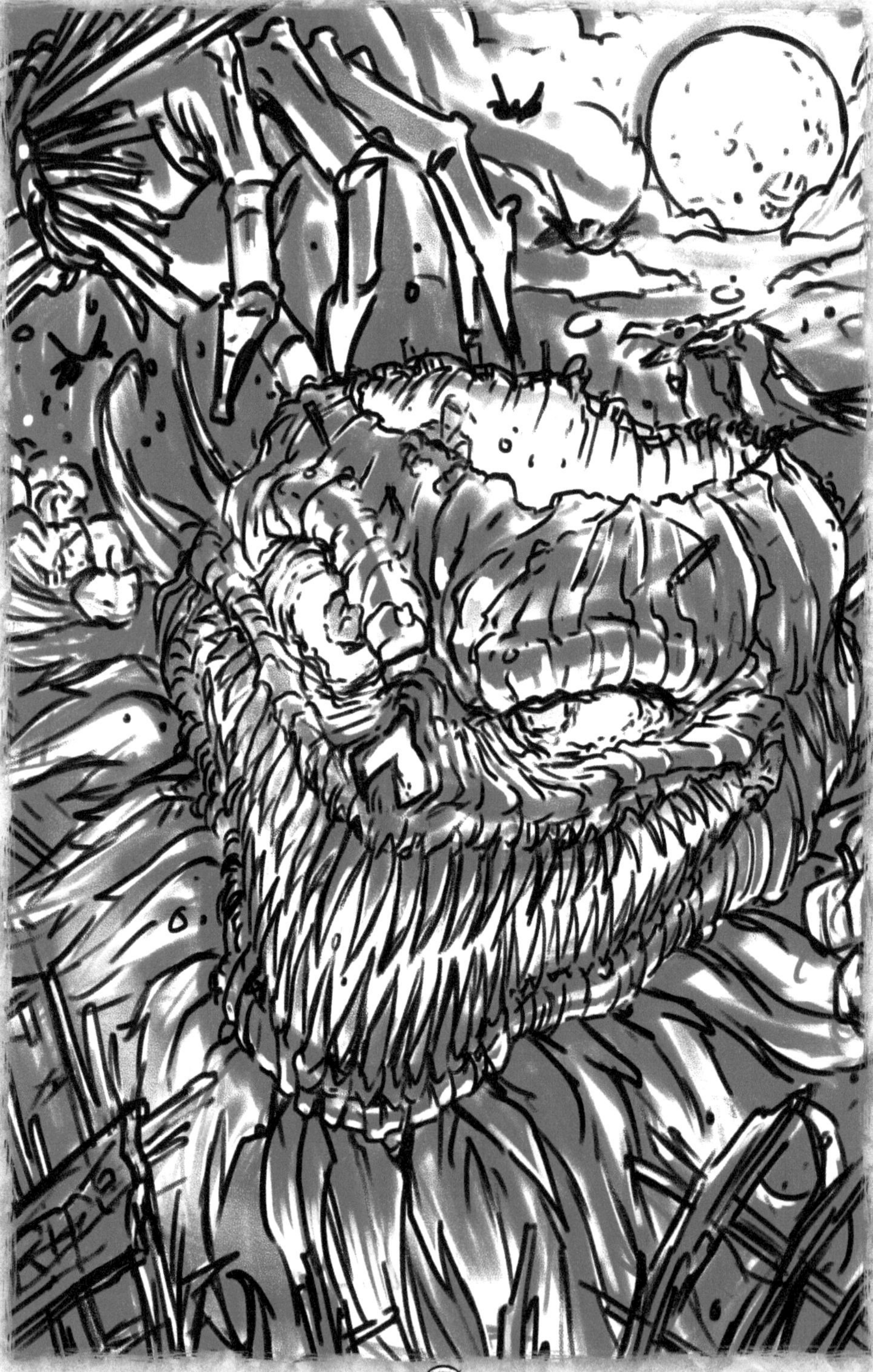

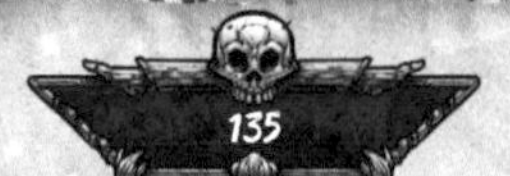

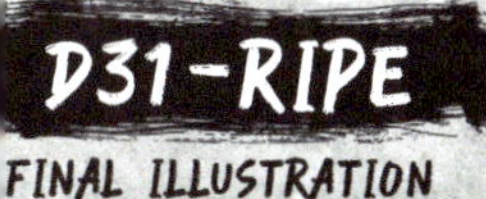

FINAL ILLUSTRATION

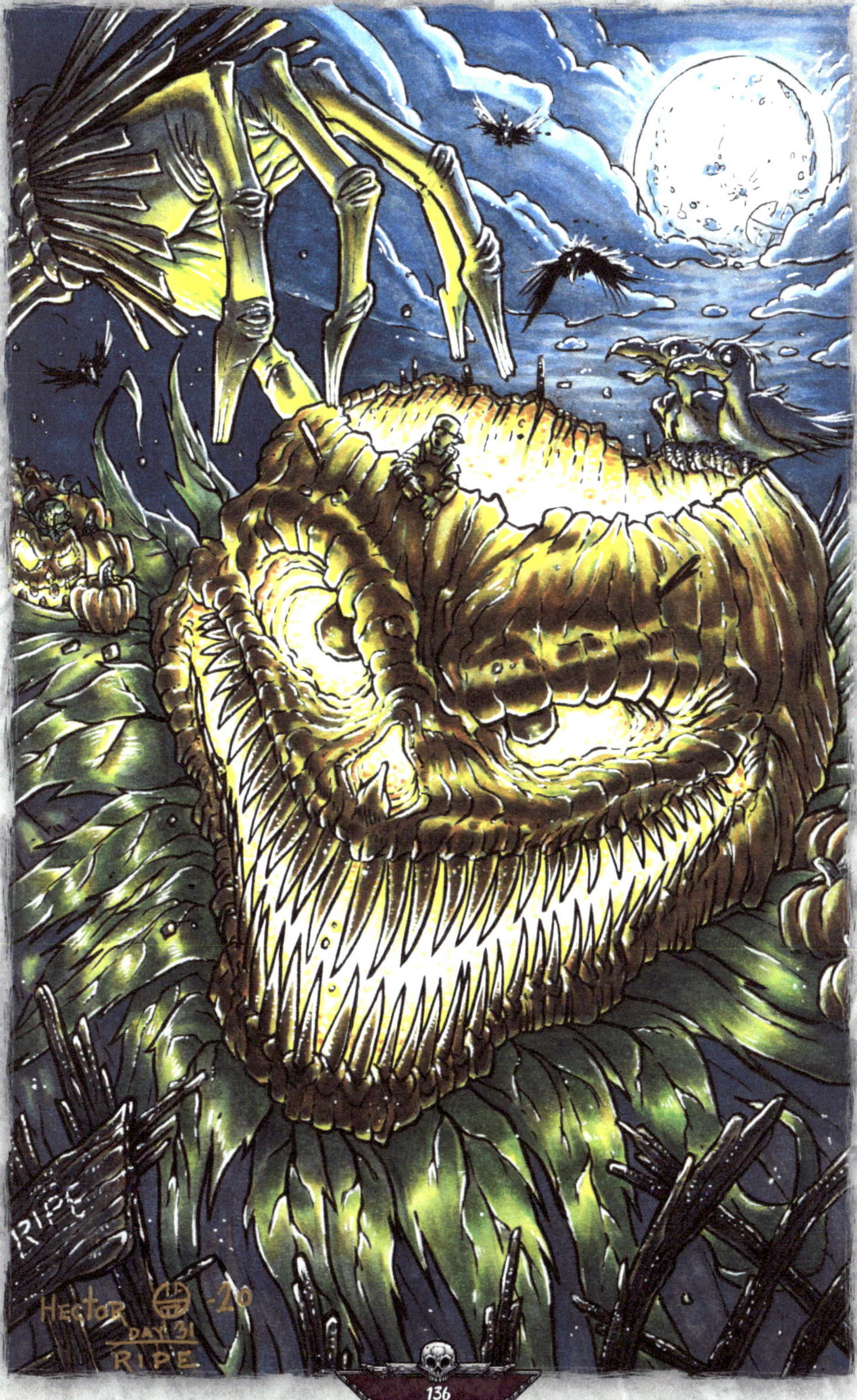

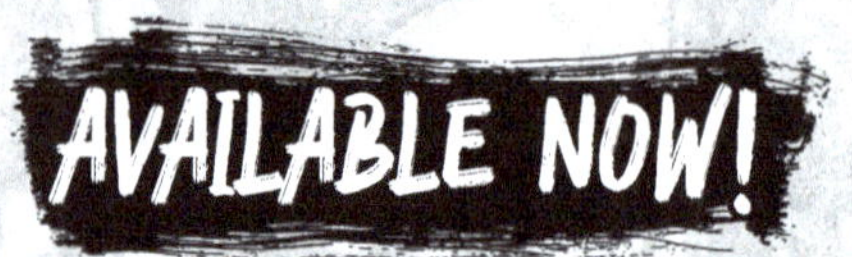

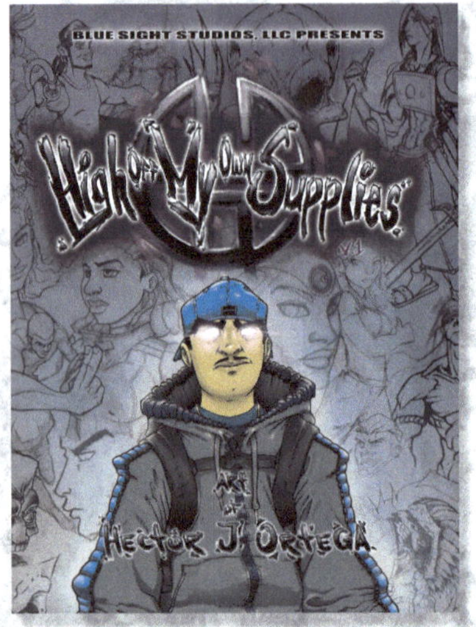

HIGH OFF MY OWN SUPPLIES: ART OF HECTOR J. ORTEGA

ISBN: 978-0-692-13827-4

High Off My Own Supplies is an art book by Hector J. Ortega. This book is filled with some of his best, and not so good sketches and rough drawings. Think of it as having his personal sketch book in your hands. Hector wishes to inspire all artist with a dream, to not be afraid to display their work, no matter how bad they think their work my be and to always push their creativity to the next level.

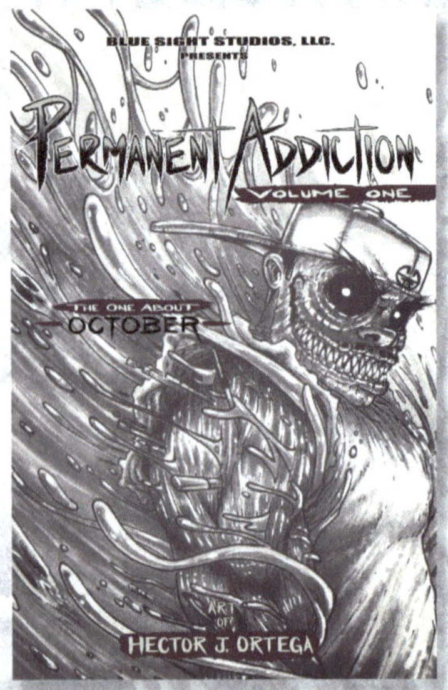

PERMANENT ADDICTION VOLUME ONE: THE ONE ABOUT OCTOBER

ISBN: 978-0-578-44151-1

Hector J. Ortega is back with another collection of his visual greatness. This time he decided to compile all the art he did from the Inktober challenge and make it into a book. Hector shows you how he goes from scribbled doodles to grey tone greatness. 31 days 31 illustrations, are you willing to take the challenge?

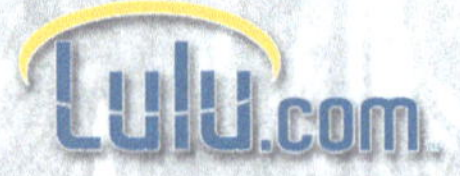

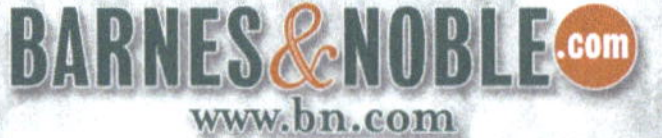

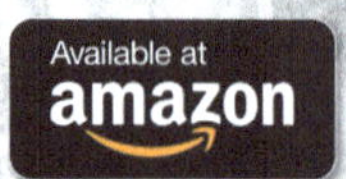

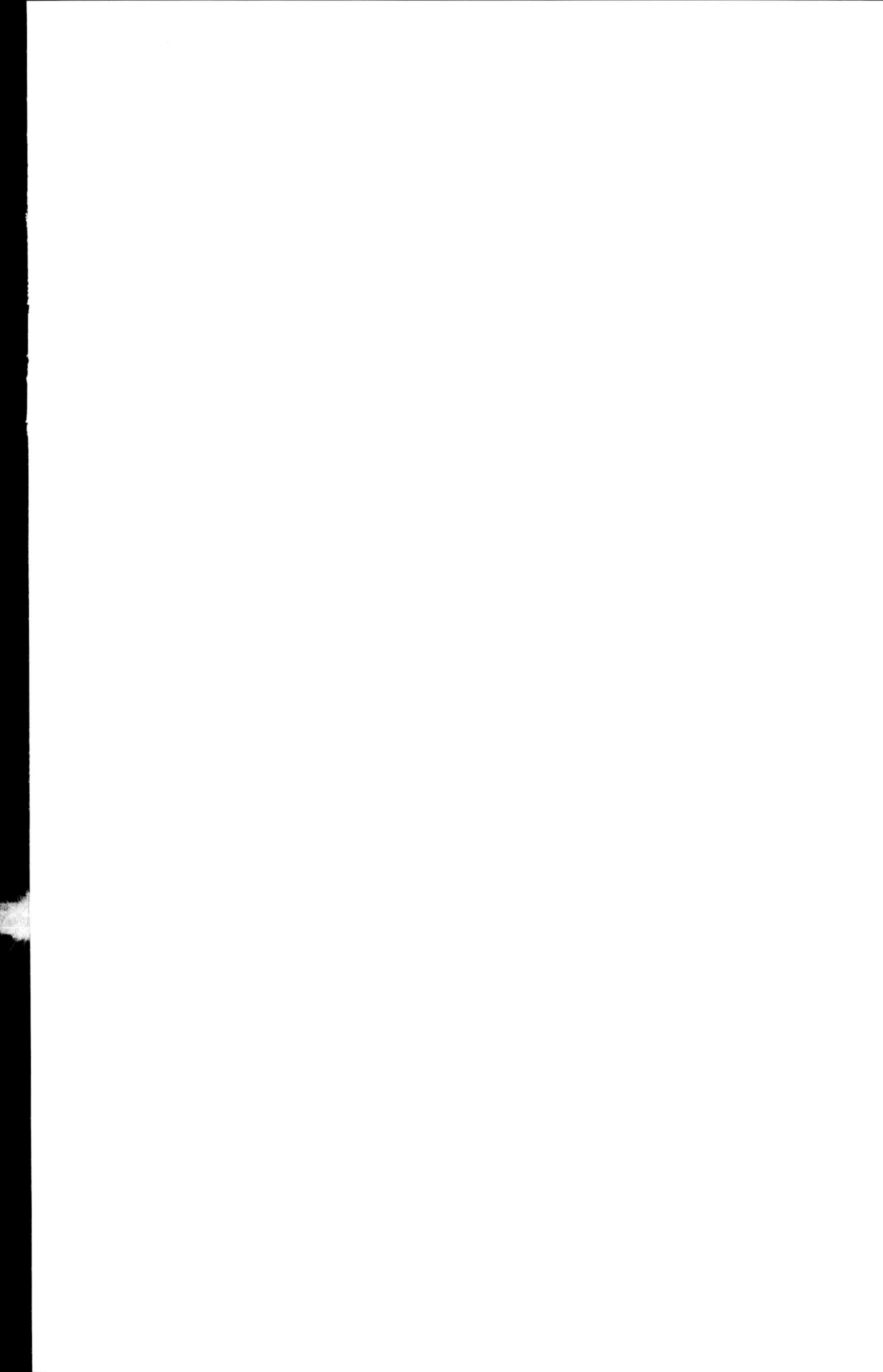

www.ingramcontent.com/pod-product-compliance
Lightning Source LLC
LaVergne TN
LVHW052252100826
845147LV00001B/21